The Transnational Dimension of
Cyber Crime and Terrorism

HOOVER NATIONAL SECURITY FORUM SERIES

The Transnational Dimension of Cyber Crime and Terrorism

EDITORS

Abraham D. Sofaer
Seymour E. Goodman

CONTRIBUTING AUTHORS

Mariano-Florentino Cuéllar
Ekaterina A. Drozdova
David D. Elliott
Seymour E. Goodman
Gregory D. Grove
Stephen J. Lukasik
Tonya L. Putnam
Abraham D. Sofaer
H. H. Whiteman
George D. Wilson

Hoover Institution Press   Stanford University   Stanford, California www.hoover.org

Hoover Institution Press Publication No. 490

Copyright © 2001 by the Board of Trustees of the
Leland Stanford Junior University

First printing 2001

06   05   04   03   02   01   9   8   7   6   5   4   3   2   1

Manufactured in the United States of America

The paper used in this publication meets the minimum requirements
of American National Standard for Information Sciences—Permanence
of Paper for Printed Library Materials, ANSI Z39.48–1984. ⊗

Library of Congress Cataloging-in-Publication Data

The transnational dimension of cyber crime and terrorism /
Abraham D. Sofaer, Seymour E. Goodman [editors] ;
Mariano-Florentino Cuéllar [... et al.].
        p.   cm. — (Hoover national security forum series)
    Includes bibliographical references and index.
    ISBN 0-8179-9982-5 (alk. paper)
    1. Computer crimes—Congresses.   2. Cyberterrorism—
Congresses.   I. Sofaer, Abraham D.   II. Goodman, Seymour E.
III. Cuéllar, Mariano-Florentino.   IV. Series.
HV6773 .T7   2001
364'.47—dc21   2001024693

Contents

Foreword

On December 6 and 7, 1999, the Hoover Institution held a conference on international cooperation to combat cyber crime and terrorism. This conference is part of Hoover's National Security Forum, an ongoing institutional research initiative that involves experts—scholars, practitioners, and government officials—examining and discussing the challenges to international security. This volume summarizes and synthesizes the conference papers and exchanges.

Important to the Hoover Institution's objectives is an increasing awareness of public policy issues, intending to contribute to and to promote meaningful dialogue and possible solutions. In addition to the meetings of experts, the National Security Forum, as a Hoover research initiative, produces books that collect, summarize, and synthesize the views of these experts for wide distribution.

The December 1999 conference followed on the National Security Forum's inaugural event, a November 16–18, 1998, conference that called attention to the serious threat of biological and chemical weapons. The 1998 conference was followed by a substantial volume, *The NEW Terror: Facing the Threat of Biological and Chemical Weapons* (Hoover Institution Press, 1999).

Today's information infrastructure is increasingly under attack by cyber criminals and terrorists. The number, cost, and sophistication of these attacks are rising at alarming rates, with aggregate annual damage worldwide now measured in billions of dollars. In fact, in the midst of preparing this volume, the archetype I Love You virus attacked millions of computers, causing huge repair costs and lost time. Cyber attacks threaten the substantial and growing reliance of commerce, governments, and the public on the information infrastructure to conduct business, carry messages, and process information.

At the December 1999 conference, organized by Abraham D. Sofaer, Hoover's George P. Shultz Senior Fellow, and Seymour E. Goodman, director of Stanford University's Consortium for Research on Information Security and Policy (CRISP), more than forty participants from government, industry, nongovernmental organizations, and academia from around the world assembled at the Hoover Institution to address the pertinent issues of the nature and threat of cyber crime and how to combat, deter, identify, and control it. Hoover senior fellow and former U.S. secretary of defense William J. Perry delivered the keynote address at the conference. (The full conference agenda is included as an appendix to this book.)

During the conference, a clear consensus of the conference participants emerged: greater international cooperation is required, and a multilateral treaty focused on criminal penalties for the abuse of cyber systems would help build the necessary cooperative framework. This volume includes a proposed convention, "International Convention to Enhance Security from Cyber Crime and Terrorism," that emerged from the conference.

The success of the December 1999 conference and the publication of this book owe much to the persistent, hard work of many people at Hoover, CRISP, and Stanford's Center for International Security and Cooperation (CISAC). Abe Sofaer has responsibility for the National Security Forum and deserves special thanks. He has been aided effectively in these activities by Research Fellow George D. Wilson.

CRISP director Seymour Goodman and CRISP members Ekaterina A. Drozdova, David D. Elliott, Gregory D. Grove, and Stephen J. Lukasik, all highly experienced in the cyber arena, along with Stanford doctoral students Mariano-Florentino Cuéllar and Tonya L. Putnam, were tireless in their efforts throughout the conference as well as in the organization, writing, and editing of the book. In addition, the conference and book benefited from the efforts of a number of Stanford students, including Catalin Cosovanu, Joanne Rosario, Miles D. Townes, and Xiaogang Wang.

CISAC codirector Michael M. May is also acknowledged for his support of the conference. The active role of the many conference participants, in particular Drew C. Arena, Jack L. Goldsmith, Raisuke Miyawaki, Dietrich Neumann, Donn B. Parker, and H. H. Whiteman, is recognized.

Substantial credit is also due to Hoover associate director Richard Sousa for his management of the conference and the book production process, as well as to many dedicated Hoover staff members, including David Arizaga, Frank Coronado, Kelly Hauge Doran, Patricia D. Herrmann, Jonathan L. Hopwood, Teresa Terry Judd, and Craig Snarr. In addition, as always, Patricia A. Baker, Marshall Blanchard, and E. Ann Wood, all of the Hoover Institution Press, expertly edited and produced the book.

The Hoover Institution and all of us personally are grateful to Mary V. Mochary, a member of the Hoover Institution Board of Overseers, who provided generous financial support for this volume.

John Raisian
Director
Hoover Institution

Contributing Authors/Editors

ABRAHAM D. SOFAER   George P. Shultz Senior Fellow, Hoover Institution; Professor of Law, by Courtesy, Stanford Law School. He served as Legal Adviser to the U.S. Department of State from 1985 to 1990, negotiating several treaties, including extradition and mutual legal assistance agreements, and led the U.S. delegation in negotiations on the International Maritime Organization Convention for the Suppression of Unlawful Acts against the Safety of Maritime Navigation (the "Maritime Terrorism Convention"). He was a federal district judge in New York City from 1979 to 1985, a Professor of Law at Columbia University School of Law from 1969 to 1979, and a federal prosecutor from 1967 to 1969. He has written extensively on international legal subjects, and currently teaches a course on Transnational Law and Institutions at Stanford Law School.

SEYMOUR E. GOODMAN   Professor of International Affairs and Computing, Georgia Institute of Technology, Atlanta; Director, Consortium for Research on Information Security and Policy (CRISP), Stanford University; Visiting Professor, Institute for International Studies (IIS), Stanford University. Professor Goodman studies international developments in the information technologies and related public policy issues. In this capacity, he has served on many government and industry advisory study committees. He has been the International Perspectives Contributing Editor for the Communications of the ACM for the past ten years. He earned his Ph.D. from the California Institute of Technology.

MARIANO-FLORENTINO CUÉLLAR   Law Clerk to the Honorable Judge Mary M. Schroeder, U.S. Court of Appeals for the Ninth Circuit. A member of the Bar of the State of California, from 1997 to 1999 he served as Senior Adviser to the Under Secretary for Enforcement, U.S. Department of the Treasury. While in Washington, D.C., he cochaired the Initiatives Subcommittee of the Attorney General's Council on White Collar Crime. He has also worked at the President's Council of Economic Advisers and the American Bar Foundation. He holds a Ph.D. in political science from Stanford University and a J.D. from Yale Law School.

EKATERINA A. DROZDOVA   Doctoral Candidate, Department of Information Systems, Stern School of Business, New York University; former Researcher, Consortium for Research on Information Security and Policy (CRISP), Stanford University; Center for International Security and Cooperation (CISAC), Stanford University. She holds a master's degree in international policy studies from Stanford and has experience in information-technology consulting in the Silicon Valley. She has conducted an in-depth survey and analysis of national laws in fifty countries to determine the extent of international consensus against cyber crime, and has published on the impact of the Internet on human rights.

DAVID D. ELLIOTT   Member, Executive Committee, Consortium for Research on Information Security and Policy (CRISP), Stanford University; Consulting Professor, Center for International Security and Cooperation (CISAC), Stanford University; former senior staff member, U.S. National Security Council. A physicist, he has served in senior positions in government and the defense industry, including supervising the SRI International's Strategic Study Center and, as Senior Vice President, overseeing strategic planning at Science Applications International Corporation (SAIC). He has a Ph.D. in high-energy physics from the California Institute of Technology.

GREGORY D. GROVE   Visiting Scholar, Consortium for Research on Information Security and Policy (CRISP), Stanford University; Visiting Scholar, Center for International Security and Cooperation (CISAC), Stanford University. A member of the Bar of the State of California, he has served as a criminal prosecutor, studied military law, and has practiced intellectual property and high-technology venture-capital law. His recent publications include a study of legal restrictions upon, and resulting discretion in, the use of military personnel to protect critical infrastructures and an analysis of international legal implications of active defense responses to computer attack. Mr. Grove received an S.B. in electrical engineering from the Massachusetts Institute of Technology and a J.D. from Harvard Law School.

STEPHEN J. LUKASIK   Visiting Scholar, Consortium for Research on Information Security and Policy (CRISP), Stanford University; Visiting Professor, Georgia Institute of Technology; Director Emeritus, Advanced Research Projects Agency (ARPA, now Defense Advanced Research Projects Agency [DARPA]); former chief scientist, Federal Communications Commission (FCC). In addition to long government service involving various leadership and advisory roles with the National Research Council (NRC) and Office of Technology Assessment (OTA), among others, he has held senior positions in industry, including vice president of TRW, Inc., the Xerox Corp., the Northrop Corp., and RAND Corporation. He has lectured at Pepperdine University, and has served on the Board of Trustees of Stevens Institute of Technology and Harvey Mudd College, and on the Engineering Advisory Council for the University of California, Berkeley.

TONYA L. PUTNAM   Doctoral Candidate, Department of Political Science, Stanford University; J.D. Candidate, Harvard Law School. From 1998 to 1999 she served as a member of counsel on the international legal team of the Republic of Namibia in litigation before the

International Court of Justice. Her primary research concerns the extraterritorial jurisdictional reach of U.S. federal courts and its implications for the development of de facto international regulatory frameworks.

H. H. WHITEMAN Director General, Security and Emergency Preparedness, Transport Canada, Ottawa, Canada. In federal government service with Transport Canada since joining the Canadian Coast Guard in 1973, he has held a number of increasingly senior positions, including Director of Security Policy Planning and Legislative Programs, responsible for the development of security policies, regulations, and measures for air, marine, and rail transportation. In August 1995 he assumed, as Acting Director General, Security and Emergency Planning, responsibility for all aspects of departmental and transportation security and emergency preparedness, and in August 1997 he was appointed Director General. He has overseen a major revision of civil aviation security requirements, managing the transfer of responsibility for aviation security screening equipment from the federal government to the air carrier industry, as well as the implementation of new arrangements for protective policing at airports.

GEORGE D. WILSON Research Fellow, Hoover Institution, Stanford University. Admitted to practice law in California, Colorado, the District of Columbia, and Maryland, as well as various federal courts, he was in private practice in Washington, D.C., and San Francisco from 1987 to 1993, working in the areas of domestic transactional business, legislative, and regulatory law. In 1994 he joined the Hoover Institution as a research assistant, and in 1998 he was appointed a research fellow. At Hoover he focuses on research and writing related to diplomacy, national security, terrorism, and transnational law.

Website Notice

Most of the papers and presentations, along with other information, from the December 6–7, 1999, Hoover Institution National Security Forum Conference "International Cooperation to Combat Cyber Crime and Terrorism" are available for review at:

http://www.oas.org/juridico/english/stanford.htm

The Hoover Institution gratefully acknowledges the very generous support in this website posting of the Department of Legal Cooperation and Information, General Secretariat, Organization of American States (OAS), under the leadership of Dr. Jorge Garcia-Gonzalez, director, and with the assistance of Mr. John M. Izzo, Ms. Magaly McLean, and Mr. Savio d'Souza.

Abbreviations

ACLU	American Civil Liberties Union
AGB	Alliance for Global Business
AIIP	Agency for Information Infrastructure Protection
AOL	America Online
ARPANET	Advanced Research Projects Agency (subsequently Defense Advanced Research Projects Agency, U.S. Department of Defense) Net
ASEAN	Association of Southeast Asian Nations
ATM	Automated Teller Machine
CALEA	Commission on Accreditation for Law Enforcement Agencies
CCIPS	Computer Crime and Intellectual Property Section (U.S. Department of Justice)
CERT	Computer Emergency Response Team
CIDF	Common Intrusion Detection Framework
CISAC	Center for International Security and Cooperation(Stanford University)
CISL	Common Intrusion Specification Language
CITAC	Computer Investigations and Infrastructure Threat Assessment Center (FBI)
CNRI	Corporation for National Research Initiatives (Reston, Va.)
COE	Council of Europe
COTS	Commercial Off-the-Shelf
CRISP	Consortium for Research on Information Security and Policy(Stanford University)
CSD	Computer-Stored Data

CSI	Computer Security Institute (San Francisco)
DARPA	Defense Advanced Research Projects Agency (U.S. Department of Defense)
DOD	Department of Defense (U.S.)
DOJ	Department of Justice (U.S.)
EC	European Community (formerly European Economic Community)
ECSC	European Coal and Steel Community
EPIC	Electronic Privacy Information Center
Euratom	European Atomic Energy Commission
EU	European Union
FAA	Federal Aviation Administration (U.S.)
FATF	Financial Action Task Force (OECD)
FBI	Federal Bureau of Investigation (U.S. Department of Justice)
FIPR	Foundation for Information Policy Research (London)
FIRST	Forum of Incident Response and Security Teams
FSB	Federal Security Bureau (Russia)
FTC	Federal Trade Commission (U.S.)
FTP	File Transfer Protocol
G-8	Group of Eight
GAO	General Accounting Office (U.S.)
GILC	Global Internet Liberty Campaign
I-4	International Information Integrity Institute (SRI)
IAB	Internet Architecture Board
ICAN	International Commission for Air Navigation
ICAO	International Civil Aviation Organization
ICC	International Chamber of Commerce
ICJ	International Court of Justice
IDIP	Intruder Detection and Isolation Protocol
IESG	Internet Engineering Steering Group
IETF	Internet Engineering Task Force
IMO	International Maritime Organization
IO	Information Operations
IP	Internet Protocol

IPv6	Internet Protocol version 6
ISO	International Organization for Standardization
ISP	Internet Service Provider
IT	Information Technology
ITU	International Telecommunication Union
MCCD	Multi-Community Cyber Defense
MLAT	Mutual Legal Assistance Treaty
NASA	National Aeronautics and Space Administration (U.S.)
NATO	North Atlantic Treaty Organization
NII	National Information Infrastructure
NIPC	National Infrastructure Protection Center (FBI)
OAS	Organization of American States
OECD	Organization for Economic Cooperation and Development
PKI	Public Key Infrastructure
PRC	People's Republic of China
PSIRT	Product Security Incident Response Team
RCMP	Royal Canadian Mounted Police
RandD	Research and Development
RFC	Request for Comments
SARPs	Standards and recommended practices
SCADA	Supervisory Control and Data Acquisition
SRI	SRI (formerly Stanford Research Institute, Menlo Park, Calif.)
TCP	Transmission Control Protocol
UN	United Nations
UNDP	United Nations Development Program
U.K.	United Kingdom
U.S.	United States
WIPO	World Intellectual Property Organization
WWW	World Wide Web

CHAPTER I

Cyber Crime and Security

The Transnational Dimension

Abraham D. Sofaer

Seymour E. Goodman

The information infrastructure is increasingly under attack by cyber criminals. The number, cost, and sophistication of attacks are increasing at alarming rates. They threaten the substantial and growing reliance of commerce, governments, and the public upon the information infrastructure to conduct business, carry messages, and process information. Some forms of attack also pose a growing threat to the public, and to critical infrastructures.

Much has been said about the threat posed by cyber crime, including terrorism, but little has been done to protect against what has become the most costly form of such crime: transnational attacks on computers and the information infrastructure. Measures thus far adopted by the private and public sectors fail to provide an adequate level of security against these attacks. The Internet and other aspects of the information infrastructure are inherently transnational. A transnational response sufficient to meet these transnational challenges is an immediate and compelling necessity.

The challenge of controlling transnational cyber crime requires a full range of responses, including both voluntary and legally mandated cooperation. Both the private and public sectors are now actively pursuing transnational initiatives, ranging in form from voluntary, informal exchange of information to a multilateral treaty proposed by the Council of Europe (COE) to establish common crimes and a substantial degree of cooperation in the investigation and prosecution of such crimes.

Public declarations and voluntary international cooperation have no doubt helped in dealing with transnational attacks. Funds are being made available to enhance the technological capacities of national law enforcement personnel engaged in cyber investigations, and through international cooperation, some attacks have been traced, and some perpetrators have been punished. But public pronouncements, educational programs, and voluntary cooperation are not enough. The sources of many transnational attacks have never been determined, and perpetrators of many of the most damaging attacks, even when identified, go unpunished. A great disparity exists, moreover, in the legal and technological capacity of states to meet the challenges of preventing, investigating, and prosecuting cyber crime.

An effective program against transnational cyber crime will require legal cooperation among states that involves the enforcement of agreed standards of conduct. A reasonably broad consensus exists among states concerning many forms of conduct that should be treated as cyber crime within national borders. This consensus must be translated into a legal regime in which all states that are connected to the Internet prohibit forms of conduct widely regarded as destructive or improper. In addition, much remains to be done to encourage and, as soon as practicable, to require states to adopt common positions to facilitate cooperation in investigation, the preservation of evidence, and extradition. States must establish and designate cross-patent agencies to deal with transnational issues, and to cooperate with counterparts throughout the world. To develop and secure the universal adoption of technological and policy standards to defend against, prosecute, and deter cyber crime and terrorism, states should create an international agency, along the lines of the International Civil Aviation Organization (ICAO) but designed to reflect the particular needs and nature of the cyber world. International cooperation must include an effective program to upgrade the capacities of states that lack the technological resources to cooperate in a comprehensive international regime. These measures, though far-reaching by comparison with current policies, can be fashioned to maximize private-sector participation and control, to ensure that privacy and other human rights are not adversely affected and so as not to impinge on the national security activities and interests of States Parties.

1. Scope of the Problem

A summary of the problem of cyber crime and terrorism was presented at the Stanford Conference by Peter G. Neumann, principal scientist at the Computer Science Laboratory, SRI International. He stated:

> We are becoming massively interconnected. Whether we like it or not, we must coexist with people and systems of unknown and unidentifiable trustworthiness (including unidentifiable hostile parties), within the U.S. and elsewhere. Our problems have become international as well as national, and cannot be solved only locally.
>
> Computer-related systems tend to fall apart on their own, even in the absence of intentional misuse. However, misuse by outsiders and insiders and the presence of malicious code . . . present some enormously difficult challenges that are not being adequately addressed at present. . . .
>
> Computers and communications are increasingly being used in almost every imaginable application. However, our computer-communication systems are not dependably secure, reliable, or robust. Reliability, fault tolerance, security, and overall system survivability

are all closely interrelated. There are fundamental vulnerabilities in the existing information system infrastructures, and serious risks that those vulnerabilities will be exploited—with possibly very severe effects.

Our national infrastructures depend not only on our interconnected information systems and networks, but also on the public switched network, the air-traffic control systems, the power grids, and many associated control systems—which themselves depend heavily on computers and communications.

Global problems can result from seemingly isolated events, as exhibited by the early power-grid collapses, the 1980 ARPANET collapse, and the 1990 long-distance collapse—all of which began with single-point failures.

Our defenses against a variety of adversities—from intentional misuse to hardware flaws and software bugs to environmental disturbances—are fundamentally inadequate.

Our defenses against large-scale coordinated attacks are even more inadequate. . . .

The risks of cyber terrorism and cyber crime vastly outweigh our abilities to control those risks by technological means, although technology can help and should be vigorously pursued. There are many important problems, such as providing better defenses against denial of service attacks, outsiders, and insiders. Socio-politico-economic measures must also be considered.[1]

2. Costs of Cyber Crime

The costs of cyber crime are difficult to measure, but by any reasonable standard they are substantial and growing exponentially. The most comprehensive available source of data on costs is compiled annually by the Computer Security Institute (CSI), with the participation of the

---

1. Peter G. Neumann, "Information System Adversities and Risks," presentation at the Conference on International Cooperation to Combat Cyber Crime and Terrorism, Hoover Institution, Stanford University, Stanford, California, December 6–7, 1999, pp. 1–2, 3. As of early 2000, some 210 countries were connected to the Internet, which had about 300 million users; the number of users is expected to rise to one billion by 2005. See Martin Stone, *Newsbytes*, March 22, 2000, which was available at ⟨*http://www.newsbytes.com*⟩.

FBI's Computer Intrusion Squad. The CSI survey for 2000, edited by Stanford Conference participant Richard Power, is based on 643 responses from computer security practitioners in U.S. corporations and government agencies.[2] It establishes that computer security breaches are widespread, diverse, and costly. Respondents are investing heavily in a variety of security technologies, at a cost estimated by the International Data Corporation to grow from $2 billion in 1999 to $7.4 billion in 2003.[3] These investments are dramatic evidence of the huge costs being inflicted by cyber crime. To these amounts must be added the costs of cyber crime insurance, a new coverage for an expanding market.[4]

In spite of the costly defensive measures thus far adopted, CSI/FBI survey respondents experiencing unauthorized use of their computer systems increased from 42 percent in 1996 to 70 percent in 2000; those not experiencing such events declined from 37 percent to 18 percent in the same period. Only 37 percent of all attacks reported in 1996 involved Internet connections; in 2000 this proportion increased to 59 percent, with a corresponding decline in insider attacks. So far, the most serious category of reported financial loss has been through "theft of proprietary information," which appears to include attacks that result in the theft of financial data.[5] Other categories of substantial losses include fraud, virus attacks, denial of service, and sabotage.

Estimating the monetary damage inflicted by cyber crime is diffi-

---

2. See Richard Power, ed., "2000 CSI/FBI Computer Crime and Security Survey," *Computer Security Issues and Trends* 6 (Spring 2000). See also Richard Power, *Tangled Web: Tales of Digital Crime from the Shadows of Cyberspace* (New York: Que/Macmillan Publishing, 2000).

3. Power, ed., "2000 CSI/FBI Computer Crime and Security Survey," p. 3.

4. See Carolyn Batt, "Marsh Offers Policy Against Computer Viruses and Fraud," *The Age*, May 31, 2000: "Such insurance does not come cheap. . . . [P]remiums in the United States . . . ranged from $US15,000 to $US700,000," available at 2000 Westlaw (WL) 21651659. See also "On Message," *The Guardian* (London), June 8, 2000: "A survey conducted by Lloyd's showed 75% of firms have no e-commerce insurance cover against damage caused by computer hackers and viruses"; available at 2000 WL 22777128.

5. See Power, ed., "2000 CSI/FBI Computer Crime and Security Survey," p. 6.

cult but worth attempting, and particularly valuable for tracking relative costs from year to year. The CSI/FBI surveys for the last four years report total losses of about $100,000,000 in 1997, increasing to some $266,000,000 in 2000.[6] Stephen J. Lukasik has found a pattern reflecting a trend in which costs have essentially doubled each year.[7] This progression has been shattered by costs associated with the "I Love You" virus of May 2000, estimated at between $1 and $10 billion. Although the costs reported by respondents include lost time, and may be exaggerated, the reluctance of companies to acknowledge losses tends to result in underreporting.[8] The overall numbers are useful indicators when these uncertainties are taken into account.

3. Transnational Nature of Cyber Crime

At a purely technical level, all messages on the Internet are broken down into "packets" that separate and travel through available routers and servers located throughout the world.[9] Cyber crime goes beyond this technical, transnational dimension and involves senders who deliberately fashion their attacks and other crimes to exploit the potential weaknesses present in the infrastructure's transnational nature. These weaknesses include: (1) a worldwide target pool of computers and users to victimize, or to exploit in denial-of-service or other attacks, which enables attackers to do more damage with no more effort than would be necessary in attacking computers or users in a single state; and (2) the widespread disparities among states, in the legal, regulatory, or policy environment concerning cyber crime, and the lack of a

6. Ibid., p. 9. See also Richard Power, "Estimating the Cost of Cyber Crime," presentation at the Stanford Conference, December 6–7, 1999, pp. 6–11.

7. See Stephen J. Lukasik, "Current and Future Technical Capabilities," Chap. 4 in the present volume.

8. The "FBI estimates that only 17 percent of computer crimes are reported to government authorities." Robert L. Ullman and David L. Ferrera, "Crime on the Internet," *Boston Bar Journal*, Nov./Dec. 1998, n 6.

9. See Robert E. Kahn and Stephen J. Lukasik, "Fighting Cyber Crime and Terrorism: The Role of Technology," presentation at the Stanford Conference, December 6–7, 1999, pp. 6–11.

sufficiently high degree of international cooperation in prosecuting and deterring such crime.

The most damaging cyber attacks thus far experienced have been transnational, originating in many different countries and aimed at computers everywhere. Here are some prominent examples:[10]

- The so-called "Phonemasters," a "loosely-knit," "12-member" international "hacking ring" headed by Jonathan Bosanac of Rancho Santa Fe, California (near San Diego), who, using the on-line name "The Gatsby," developed a method for gaining access to telephone networks (such as MCI, WorldCom, Sprint, and AT&T), credit-reporting databases (such as Equifax), and even the FBI's own National Crime Information Center, which they utilized in a number of countries.[11] "The breadth of their monkey-wrenching was staggering; at various times they could eavesdrop on phone calls, compromise secure databases, and redirect communications at will. They had access to portions of the national power grid, air-traffic–control systems and had hacked their way into a digital cache of unpublished telephone numbers at the White House. . . . [T]hey often worked in stealth, and avoided bragging about their exploits. . . . Their customers included . . . the Sicilian Mafia. According to FBI estimates, the gang accounted for about $1.85 million in business losses."[12]

- David L. Smith, a New Jersey programmer, pleaded guilty in December 1999 of creating the "Melissa" computer virus and

10. For more examples, see Power, ed., "2000 CSI/FBI Computer Crime and Security Survey," pp. 6–7; Richard Power, *Current and Future Danger: A CSI Primer on Computer Crime and Information Warfare*, 3d ed. (San Francisco: Computer Security Institute, 1999), pp. 1–38.

11. See Kathryn Balint, "Notorious Hacker, 'The Gatsby,' Gets 18 Months' Prison," *San Diego Union-Tribune*, March 4, 2000, available at 2000 WL 13951675.

12. See John Simons, "Phone Hex: How a Cyber Sleuth, Using a 'Data Tap,' Busted a Hacker Ring—Audacious 'Phonemasters' Stole Numbers, Pulled Scams, Tweaked Police—A Sex-Line Prank on the FBI," *Wall Street Journal*, October 1, 1999, p. A1, available at 1999 WL-WSJ 24916121.

using an x-rated website to spread it through cyber space via e-mail in March 1999, where it "rampaged personal, government, and corporate computers around the world," "caused worldwide devastation," and was estimated to have done $80 million (or more) in damages.[13]

- From December 1999 through April 2000, five hackers in Moscow stole more than 5,400 credit card numbers belonging to Russians and foreigners from Internet retailers, pocketing more than $630,000 until arrested.[14] The incident pointed up the threat that "Eastern European fraudsters continue to pose . . . for all card issuers, even those with no direct business in the region.[15]

- In 1995–96, from his home in Buenos Aires, a twenty-one-year-old Argentine student, Julio Cesar Ardita, "slipped through the security of . . . systems at Harvard University's

13. See: "Melissa Virus Exposes Computer Users' Vulnerability," *Japan Computer Industry Scan*, April 12, 1999, available at 1999 WL 9642279; "Battling the Cyberspace Superbugs: With 18,000 Viruses Infecting the World's Computer Networks, the Hunt Is on for the Cyber-Criminals Who Put Them There," *Western Daily Press*, May 5, 2000, available at 2000 WL 3236905; "Melissa Virus Creator Pleads Guilty: A Computer Programmer Admitted on Thursday that He Created and Distributed the Melissa Virus," *Newswire*, December 10, 1999: "In the Federal plea, both sides agreed that the damage amounted to more than $80 million"; available at 1999 WL 6824880.

14. See "Suspected Russia Hackers Held," *New York Times on the Web/Breaking News from Associated Press*, April 28, 2000, reported at ⟨http://www.nytimes.com/aponline/i/AP-Russia-Hackers.html⟩. See also "Hacker Reveals Credit Card Data," ibid., January 10, 2000: a hacker, "a self-described 19-year-old Russian using the name Maxim, sent an e-mail" to the *New York Times* "boasting that he exploited a security flaw in the software used to protect financial information" at the website of an Internet music retailer, CD Universe, and posted credit card numbers he stole from the site "after the retailer refused to pay a $100,000 ransom"; reported at ⟨http://www.nytimes.com/aponline/a/AP-Credit-Card-Crook.html⟩.

15. See Jason Fargo, "Card Fraud's New Hotbed?," 13 *Credit Card Management*, April 1, 2000, p. 9698, available at 2000 WL 10684223; reportedly "shoddy practices" at Union Card Processing Company, a Moscow-based firm that processes automated teller machine transactions for Russian banks, "allowed criminals to obtain card data with which they then manufactured counterfeit cards."

Faculty of Arts and Science, the U.S. Defense Department, the U.S. Naval Command, the San Diego-based Control and Ocean Surveillance Center, the Washington-based Naval Research Lab, NASA's Ames Research Center and Jet Propulsion Laboratory, and the Los Alamos National Laboratory in New Mexico."[16] His actions were not criminal in Argentina, and his extradition to the U.S. was refused, although he later surrendered voluntarily.

- Reports of persistent, international attacks on official government websites throughout the world in 1999–2000 appeared with great frequency. Some of the notable ones include: (1) Hackers breaking into the website of the Ministry of Finance of Romania in November 1999 to introduce bogus taxes and to change the official exchange rate of the national currency.[17] (2) Recurrent Taiwan-China "hacker" wars in 1999 and 2000 in which attackers broke into various government and business websites, penetrating protective firewall software with seeming ease.[18] (3) Frequent transnational attacks on sensitive military and other national security networks of many governments, as well as public service websites/infrastructure at the national and local levels.[19]

16. See David Berlind, "Reno's Border Patrol Made Ineffective," *PC Week*, April 8, 1996, p. 78.

17. See "Hackers Alter Romanian Money Rate," *New York Times on the Web/ Breaking News from Associated Press*, November 3, 1999, reported at ⟨http:// www.nytimes.com/aponline/i/AP-Romania-Hackers.html⟩.

18. See "Taiwan-China Hackers' War Erupts," *New York Times on the Web/ Breaking News from Associated Press*, August 9, 1999, reported at ⟨http:// www.nytimes.com/aponline/i/AP-Taiwan-China-Hackers.html⟩; "Taiwan Spy Agency Website Hacked," ibid., March 6, 2000, reported at ⟨http://www.nytimes.com/ aponline/i/AP-Taiwan-China-Hackers.html⟩.

19. See, e.g., Stephen J. Glain, "Blind Arab Brothers, Allegedly Hackers, Disconcert Israel: They're on Trial for Tapping into Defense Phone System to Commit 'Cybercrimes,'" *Wall Street Journal*, October 21, 1999, p. A1; Daniel Verton, "Cyberattacks Against DOD up 300 Percent This Year," reported at *CNN.com*, November 5, 1999; "Swedes Charged with U.S. Hacking," *New York Times on the Web/ Breaking News from Associated Press*, August 16, 1999, reported at ⟨http://

- The "I Love You" virus was propagated from the Philippines in May 2000.[20] Estimates of the damage it caused range up to $10 billion, mostly in lost work time. U.S. investigators pressed to have the suspects in the attack—computer programming students from the Philippines—arrested and prosecuted, and Filipino investigators attempted to do so under a 1998 law prohibiting the use of "access devices," such as credit cards, to defraud. The Chief State Counsel concluded, however, that this law could not be used, since "the intention of a computer hacker . . . is not to defraud but to destroy files."[21] The Philippines adopted a law punishing those who spread computer viruses with up to three years' imprisonment and fines from $2,350 to a maximum "commensurate" with the damage caused.[22] The new law will not apply retroactively, however, so this costly act has gone unpunished.[23]

---

www.nytimes.com/aponline/i/AP-Sweden-Hackers.html⟩; "Hacker Takes Over Hawaii's Website," ibid., July 6, 1999: "We've had to block out the entire country of Brazil because we've had so many crack attempts from so many locations in Brazil"; reported at ⟨*http://www.nytimes.com/aponline/a/AP-Computer-Hacker.html*⟩.

20. See "Report on Love Bug Virus Submitted," *New York Times on the Web/ Breaking News from Associated Press*, June 13, 2000, reported at ⟨*http:// www.nytimes.com/aponline/i/AP-Philippines-Love-Bug.html*⟩. Note that the 2000 CSI/FBI report predates the extreme disruption and costs associated with the rapid spread of the "I Love You" computer virus around the world from the Philippines in May 2000.

21. See "Philippines Seek 'Love Bug' Law," *New York Times on the Web/Breaking News from Associated Press*, May 17, 2000 (remarks of Elmer Bautista), reported at ⟨*http://www.nytimes.com/aponline/i/AP-Computer-Love-Bug.html*⟩.

22. See "Philippines Addresses Web Crimes," *New York Times on the Web/ Breaking News from Associated Press*, June 14, 2000, reported at ⟨*http:// www.nytimes.com/aponline/i/AP-Philippines-Love-Bug.html*⟩.

23. "A lack of applicable laws forced prosecutors to dismiss all charges yesterday against the man accused of releasing the 'Love Bug,' a computer virus that caused billions of dollars in damages worldwide." See "'Love Bug' Suspect Set Free," *Palo Alto Daily News*, August 22, 2000, p. 9; Robert Frank, "'Love Bug' Case Against Student Gets Dismissed As Laws Lag," *Wall Street Journal*, August 22, 2000, p. A20.

4. Weaknesses of the Current System

The open and defiant manner in which hackers currently operate reflects the weakness of the legal, defensive, and investigative capacities of the current system.[24] They plan and discuss proposed forms of attack on websites, exchanging ideas and comments.[25] These activities enabled Thomas A. Longstaff of the Computer Emergency Response Team (CERT)/Coordination Center (CC), Software Engineering Institute (SEI) at Carnegie Mellon University to predict at the Stanford Conference that a new and very harmful, distributed form of denial-of-service attack was the next likely threat. He described precisely the method that was used by hackers in the subsequent worldwide February 2000 attacks—on CNN, eBay, Amazon.com, and others—to plant programs in computers around the globe that enabled hackers to send so many messages to particular IP addresses that they were rendered inoperable. Though law enforcement personnel were able to

24. Hackers adopt nicknames reflecting their intentions and attitudes, such as "Badman," "Masters of Deception," "Legion of Doom," and "Mafiaboy." See "Teen Hacker Appears in Court," *Yahoo! News/Associate Press*, June 6, 2000 (story relating to a 15-year-old Canadian nicknamed "Mafiaboy," who is alleged to have instigated a February 8, 2000, cyber attack on the CNN website, one of a series of attacks that targeted major sites including Yahoo!, eBay, and Amazon.com), at ⟨*http://daily news.yahoo.com/h/ap/20000606/wl/canada_teen_hacker_1.html*⟩.

25. Numerous "hacker" and/or cyber security/cyber attack-related websites exist, with many, varying objectives. Compare, e.g., ⟨*http://www.attrition.org/*⟩ ("a computer security website dedicated to the collection, dissemination, and distribution of information about the industry for anyone interested in the subject") with ⟨*http://phrack.infonexus.com/*⟩ (classified by Yahoo.com as "technical info. for hackers") and ⟨*http://www.hackernews.com/*⟩ ("Our first mission is to deliver the real news from the computer underground *for* the computer underground"). See also, "Crowds Awaited at Hacker Convention," *New York Times on the Web/Breaking News from Associated Press*, July 8, 1999 (story about the 1999 "DefCon," an annual hackers convention in Las Vegas begun with only 100 attendees in 1993, which as of the July 1999 meeting was attracting thousands), reported at ⟨*http://www.nytimes.com/ aponline/f/AP-Hackers-Convention.html*⟩. Also: ⟨*http://www.defcon.org/*⟩ (website for the 2000 "DefCon 8.0").

anticipate this type of attack, they were not able to prevent it, and security personnel at CNN, Yahoo!, Amazon.com, and others could not defend against it. After several months of investigation, in April 2000, the Royal Canadian Mounted Police (RCMP) arrested a Montreal teenager on suspicion of having caused the CNN and other shutdowns, but the extent to which the culprit (or culprits) may be successfully prosecuted is in doubt, and deterrence of those not caught and punished, as well as of other would-be attackers, seems unlikely.[26] These troubling failures stem from serious weaknesses in the authority and capacities of states to protect cyber systems from attacks.[27]

Escalating Dangers of Attacks

New forms of denial-of-service and other destructive types of attack, such as the "I Love You" virus, have been openly discussed, or uncovered, and cyber copycats continue to be active, replicating or modifying attacks into yet more dangerous forms—such as the "Killer Resume" follow-on to "I Love You"—with virtually complete impunity.

Knowledgeable individuals have anticipated new forms of cyber attack that may be even more costly than prior ones. For example, a virus similar to "I Love You," called "Timofonica" (Spanish for "phone prank"), that has been intercepted in Europe is designed to attack cell phones, and can easily be altered to attack pagers and other hand-held devices such as Palm Pilots and Microsoft Pocket PC com-

---

26. See "Teen Hacker Appears in Court," *Yahoo! News/Associate Press*, June 6, 2000; "Hacker 'Mafiaboy' Likely to Face More Charges," *Yahoo! News/Reuters*, June 7, 2000 (the suspect could face "up to two years in a youth detention center and a . . . $675 fine, if found guilty"), available at ⟨*http://dailynews.yahoo.com/h/nm/20000607/wr/mafiaboy_dc_1.html*⟩; "Canadian Hacker Pleads Not Guilty," *New York Times on the Web/Breaking News from Associated Press*, August 3, 2000, reported at ⟨*http://www.nytimes.com/aponline/i/AP-Canada-Teen-Hacker.html*⟩.

27. See generally the excellent report prepared by McConnell International, "Cyber Crime . . . and Punishment? Archaic Laws Threaten Global Information" (December 2000), available at ⟨*http://www.mcconnellinternational.com*⟩.

puters.[28] Vincent Gullatto, director of the AVERT antivirus lab at the San Jose, California–based Network Associates, which makes McAfee antivirus software, has noted that, once hand-held devices become sophisticated enough to use "miniature automation programs known as macros, the potential to wreak havoc will grow."[29] Similarly, as reliance on wireless transmission increases, the danger posed by forms of jamming will grow. An even more threatening development is predicted by Israeli computer security expert Ofer Elzam. In addition to "an increasing number of viruses, worms, and vandals" he expects will populate the cyber world, he anticipates "something far more lethal and threatening—the Trojan horse."[30] These devices, Elzam states, "are smart spying machines or engines that can sit in a PC for years and give anyone access to the most personal information stored on the computer," without creating any sign of damage: "Things are going to get much, much worse in every field of Internet security," in part because "the more complicated things get the more holes there are."[31] It was reported on June 18, 2000, that an undisclosed number

28. See "New Virus Targets Handheld Devices," *New York Times on the Web/ Breaking News from Associated Press*, June 6, 2000, reported at ⟨http:// www.nytimes.com/aponline/f/AP-Cell-Phone-Virus.html⟩

29. Ibid.

30. See Nicky Blackburn and Meir Ronne, "Forget Viruses, the Trojans Are Coming," *Jerusalem Post*, May 28, 2000, p. 8, available at 2000 WL 8258478. "Like its Greek namesake, Trojan horses are weapons hidden within a friendly exterior. They come as seemingly innocuous e-mails or lurk in websites on the Net. A user may receive an innocent-looking e-mail, but embedded within the attachment, or in some cases even the HTML message itself, is a coded page, which connects your PC to a website. From there a small Trojan horse, often as little as 6k, is downloaded into your computer and the hacker, blackmailer, competitor, or just good, old-fashioned enemy is alerted, often through ICQ messaging, that the computer has been penetrated. The hacker can then add however many programs he wants to the victim's computer, allowing him access to the most personal files, be they financial plans or letters to a lover. In some circumstances the hacker can even have remote control of the computer itself, a threat with many worrying implications. The same can happen to a user while surfing the Internet. A user might be lured to a particular site by promises of a free holiday or entry into a sweepstakes and while . . . visiting a Trojan horse or a virus is downloaded to their computer."

31. Ibid.

of America Online (AOL) employee accounts had been compromised by a Trojan horse.[32] The trend toward increasingly dangerous attacks is well established.

The danger of cyber attacks extends to matters of intense public concern. Cyber terrorism has not yet resulted in any public disaster, but attacks on the websites and cyber systems of public agencies are common.[33] Favorite targets include defense and intelligence agencies.[34] Although for the most part these attacks are amateurish and are blocked successfully or result in only superficial damage to websites,[35] a significant number have shut down websites, and some have penetrated much further.[36]

---

32. See "AOL Confirms Hacking of Employee Accounts," *Chicago Tribune*, June 18, 2000, p. 7, available at 2000 WL 3676402. Other scientists have characterized the most highly connected nodes, through which most messages are channeled, as the Achilles' heel of the Internet. See "Scientists Spot Achilles' Heel of the Internet," *HPCwire*, July 28, 2000, which was distributed through ⟨*trial@hpcwire.tgc.com*⟩.

33. See: "Hackers Become an Increasing Threat," *New York Times on the Web/ Breaking News from Associated Press*, July 7, 1999, which was reported at ⟨*http:// www.nytimes.com/aponline/w/AP-Hacker-Threat.html*⟩; Verton, "Cyberattacks Against DOD up 300 Percent This Year," *CNN.com*, November 5, 1999.

34. See, e.g.: "Hackers Attack Army's Internet Site," *New York Times on the Web/Breaking News from Associated Press*, June 28, 1999, reported at ⟨*http:// www.nytimes.com/aponline/w/AP-Army-Hacked.html*⟩; "Taiwan Spy Agency Website Hacked," ibid., March 6, 2000. Hackers have reportedly even disrupted service to the top-secret U.S. Air Force "Area 51" site in Nevada. "Hacker Disrupted Service to Area 51," ibid., April 21, 2000, reported at ⟨*http://www.nytimes.com/aponline/a/ AP-Area-51-Hacker.html*⟩. The FBI has also "acknowledged . . . that electronic vandals" have been able to "shut down its own . . . site for hours." See "FBI Admits Its Site Was Attacked," ibid., February 25, 2000, reported at ⟨*http://www.nytimes. com/aponline/w/AP-Hacker-Investigation.html*⟩.

35. See, e.g., "White House Hacker Faces Prison," ibid., November 22, 1999, reporting that the White House website attack consisted primarily of slight alterations to the site including "the phrase, 'following peeps get some shouts'—hacker slang for 'hello,'" reported at ⟨*http://www.nytimes.com/aponline/w/AP-White-House-Hacker.html*⟩.

36. Consider the 1998 "Solar Sunrise" attack of "young hackers from California and Israel" who "were able to penetrate numerous Department of Defense computers and gain 'root' access, meaning they had the capability to shut the systems down or steal or alter important information." See "Statement of Michael A. Vatis, Director, National Infrastructure Protection Center, Federal Bureau of Investigation, Before the

To classify such attacks as pranks merely because they seem politically aimless is mistaken. Politically aimless conventional attacks on public infrastructure are an established form of terrorism—the hallmark of anarchists. Where such attacks are intended to, and do, cause serious damage, they should, and will, be treated as terrorist acts. Furthermore, when states sponsor such attacks, they take on an additional political dimension; the FBI's National Infrastructure Protection Center (NIPC) appears to believe that state-sponsored acts have already been undertaken.[37] Among the nation's critical infrastructure most vulnerable to cyber attacks are transportation (especially air travel), power, defense, water, and medical care. The Stanford Conference focused on the dangers to civil aviation as exemplifying this danger.[38]

Disparities in National Laws of Protection and Cooperation

A significant weakness in the current system is the disparity among individual states in the laws and practices necessary to permit them to investigate and prosecute cyber crime effectively.[39] Though states may

---

Senate Committee on Judiciary," *Hearing on Internet Security and Privacy*, May 25, 2000, available at ⟨*http://www.senate.gov/judiciary/52520mav.htm*⟩.

37. Ibid.: "Over the past several years we have seen a broad spectrum of computer crimes ranging from defacement of websites by juveniles to *sophisticated intrusions that we suspect may be sponsored by foreign powers*, and everything in between" [emphasis added]. See generally the 1998 Center for Strategic and International Studies (CSIS) report, *Cybercrime, Cyberterrorism, and Cyberwarfare: Averting an Electronic Waterloo* (Washington, D.C.: CSIS, 1998), and Georgetown University Professor Dorothy E. Denning's reactions to it, discussed in Paul Talacko, "Computer Hackers and Cyberterrorists: Close Watch Around the Clock," *Financial Times*, October 4, 2000, p. iv.

38. See the essays in Chap. 3 of this volume. The potential for attacks on the power infrastructure is discussed by Stephen J. Lukasik in "Metrics for Assessing the Vulnerability of the Electric Power Grid to Cyberattack," unpublished ms., Consortium for Research on Information Policy and Security (CRISP), Stanford University, September 11, 1999.

39. See, e.g., "Cyberattackers Target Latin America," *New York Times on the Web/Breaking News from Associated Press*, February 16, 2000: "Internet vandals are wreaking havoc in Latin America's fast-growing cyberspace frontier" where "it's even

have agreements in place to cooperate against and extradite or prosecute for conventional crimes involving the *use* of computers, no international agreement yet exists on such cooperation for criminal attacks on computers and the information infrastructure.[40] In several
highly significant cases, investigations and prosecutions have been
stymied by this deficiency. In 1996, Argentine hacker Julio Cesar Ardita escaped relatively unscathed after having compromised numerous
sensitive and proprietary computer networks, including some in the
U.S. Department of Defense (DOD), from his Buenos Aires home.
Argentina refused to extradite Ardita to the U.S., because his intrusion
did not constitute an extraditable crime. Another very serious series
of attacks on national security sites in the U.S. and Israel—subsequently code-named "Solar Sunrise" by the DOD—was conducted by
"a trio of teenage hackers" in February 1998.[41] These individuals were
identified and were ultimately prosecuted for their criminal conduct,
but not without significant difficulties encountered by U.S. and Israeli
investigators owing to the lack of established commitments and pro-

---

easier to break into many websites because Internet culture is relatively immature and
authorities are generally ill-prepared to respond" and governments "have done little
to address digital crime," reported at ⟨*http://www.nytimes.com/aponline/i/
AP-Latin-America-Hacker-Attacks.html*⟩.

40. This distinction is part of the three-category breakdown of the role of computers in crime found in *The Electonic Frontier: The Challenge of Unlawful Conduct
Involving the Use of the Internet: A Report of the President's Working Group on
Unlawful Conduct on the Internet* (March 2000), Part II.A. Inexplicably, this report
focuses "primarily" on the category of using computers as a tool for crime. It recognizes the need for international cooperation but makes no recommendations for
dealing with crimes against computers—in spite of the following conclusions (in Part
III.E.1 & 2): "When one country's laws criminalize high-tech and computer-related
crime and another country's laws do not, cooperation to solve a crime, as well as the
possibility of extraditing the criminal to stand trial, may not be possible. . . . Although
bilateral cooperation is important in pursuing investigations concerning unlawful
conduct involving the use of the Internet, multilateral efforts are a more effective way
to develop international policy and cooperation in this area. The reason for this stems
from the nature of the Internet itself."

41. See, e.g., William Jackson, "1999: The Year of Computer Security," *Newsbytes News Network*, December 15, 1998, available at 1998 WL 20720335.

cedures. Boaz Gutman, chief superintendent of Computer Crime Division, National Anti-Fraud Investigation Unit, Israeli National Police, detailed some of the difficulties at the Stanford Conference. He noted that, though voluntary cooperation is better than none, the lack of national commitments led to confusion and resentment in the Solar Sunrise case, especially when U.S. personnel became intensely involved in the Israeli investigative and judicial processes.[42] In spite of encountering difficulties like these, the U.S. and other states were no better prepared when the "I Love You" virus was propagated from a state where deliberate computer attacks were not even illegal.

Even states with advanced economies, and heavily reliant on information technology, have failed to take steps necessary to protect themselves and others from attacks, thereby becoming weak links in the chain of security, or places where criminals and terrorists are able to attack other states with impunity. In his keynote presentation at the Stanford Conference, Raisuke Miyawaki, chairman of Ochanomizu Associates in Tokyo, explained how and why Japan had failed to take Internet security seriously, and the risks this created for Japan's economy and for users worldwide:

> The ease with which the origins of cyber attacks can be hidden, and the fact that cyber attacks on one nation can come from anywhere on the globe, mean that cyber crime and cyber terrorism are truly international threats. And Japan's relatively lax cyber defenses mean that Japan is a potentially weak link in the global economic and

---

42. Boaz Gutman, "Constraints on Cooperation," Presentation, at the Stanford Conference, December 7, 1999, pp. 1–3. Michael Vatis, director of the FBI's National Infrastructure Protection Center, testified on July 26, 2000, before the Subcommittee on Government Management, Information, and Technology of the Committee on Government Reform of the U.S. House of Representatives that the lack of laws "that specifically criminalize computer crimes" undercuts investigations in foreign countries. "This means that those countries often lack the authority not only to investigate or prosecute computer crimes that occur within their borders, but also to assist us when evidence might be located in those countries." "Computer Security: Cyber Attacks—A War Without Borders," available at ⟨*http://www.house.gov/reform/ gmit/hearings/2000hearings/000726cybersecurity/000726h.htm*⟩.

security architecture in the event of a major cyber crime, cyber terrorist, or cyber military attack on Japan.[43]

Miyawaki reviewed the rapid increase in illegal network access cases in Japan, as well as several unexplained or unsolved incidents involving break-ins at the national computer research centers, a shutdown of parts of Japan Railway's system in Tokyo, and several shutdowns of the Tokyo Stock Exchange, all caused by computer problems of unknown origin:

> The uncertainty surrounding many of these incidents is troubling. When such network systems crash, they are restored by the company that installed the system, and the problem is not examined by a third party with a special interest in cyber security. Also, unless the crash affects an ATM or other highly visible network that affects customers or everyday citizens, companies don't publicize their computer problems—and, it is said, there are many such incidents that companies don't publicize.[44]

The program Miyawaki recommends to deal with Japan's cybersecurity deficiencies includes the passage of laws making unauthorized access to computer networks illegal (adopted in 1999) and authorizing wiretapping in computer cases (effective August 2000). He also supports Japan's increased involvement in the private-sector and voluntary government programs under way. At the Stanford Conference, he stressed the need for international cooperation, through harmonization of laws and technical issues, emergency response mechanisms, and intelligence sharing. He concluded that, to act effectively against the growing cyber threats, states must in effect form a cyber-defense alliance:

> The goals and tactics and behavior of cyber rogue nations, cyber criminals, and cyber terrorists are threats to all the world's nations. We of the world's leading democratic nations must examine what

43. Raisuke Miyawaki, "International Cooperation to Combat Cyber Crime and Cyber Terrorism," keynote presentation, at the Stanford Conference, December 7, 1999, p. 2.

44. Ibid., p. 6.

has helped us work successfully together in the past, and take lessons from that in preparing for the new era of cyber crime and cyber warfare. Perhaps, we must even create a technologically linked "cyber-defense alliance." And as in so many other matters, the day-to-day sharing of intelligence and information on cyber-security, and the steady building of trust between nations and national officials, will be the bedrock on which international cooperation against cyber crime and cyber terrorism must be built.[45]

The pertinence of Miyawaki's warnings about Japan's vulnerability was fully borne out in January 2000, when a series of humiliating raids on government websites by hackers prompted emergency conditions.[46] His insights are universally applicable.

Vulnerability of Existing Programs

Several participants at the Stanford Conference observed that current computer systems are inherently vulnerable. Robert E. Kahn, president of the Corporation for National Research Initiatives (CNRI), explained that existing systems are unstable and subject to spontaneous failure, even as they are increasingly relied upon for sensitive functions, requiring ever higher levels of complexity.[47] SRI's Peter G. Neumann believes that the unreliability of current technology is by far the greatest danger to cyber security.[48] Vulnerabilities are regularly exploited by hackers and other criminals, and the widespread dominance of highly vulnerable Microsoft programs and services has created a sit-

45. Ibid., p. 11.

46. See, e.g., "Hackers Break Into Japan Government," *New York Times on the Web/Breaking News from Associated Press*, January 25, 2000, reported at ⟨http://www.nytimes.com/aponline/i/AP-Japan-Hackers.html⟩; "Japan Calls Emergency Meeting as Hackers Hit Again," *Yahoo! News/Associated Press*, January 26, 2000, at ⟨http://dailynews.yahoo.com/h/nm/20000126/wr/japan_hackers.html⟩; "Japan Moves to Halt Hackers," *New York Times on the Web/Breaking News from Associated Press*, January 28, 2000, reported at ⟨http://www.nytimes.com/aponline/i/AP-Japan-Hackers.html⟩.

47. See Kahn and Lukasik, "Fighting Cyber Crime and Terrorism," p. 15.

48. See Peter G. Neumann, "Information System Adversities and Risks," pp. 1, 2, 3.

uation of grave risk.[49] Most software designers, concentrating on satisfying customers seeking greater ease of use and functions requiring
greater complexity, regard reliability and security as secondary matters. Enhanced security in cyber systems requires enhanced reliability
and stability, not merely quick-fixes in which vulnerabilities to specific
types of attacks are eliminiated on a case-by-case basis through design
modifications.

The vulnerability of the information infrastructure also stems from
the insufficiency of current security measures. The costly "I Love You"
virus was "a relatively simple Visual Basic script" that operated much
like the "Melissa" virus of the year before, according to Michael J.
Miller of *PC Magazine*: "Melissa was enough of a warning. We
shouldn't be going through this again."[50] Microsoft provided a fix for
the "Melissa" virus, but since it did not change the components targeted by "Melissa," it was still relatively easy to run scripts affecting
the settings in Microsoft's widely used Outlook, Outlook Express,
Exchange, and Windows. Microsoft left these components unchanged
for the same reasons they were designed to be accessible: "convenience
for users and letting corporations create complex scripts that tie Outlook together with other Microsoft applications." As Miller points
out, while anti-virus makers found the "I Love You" virus and came
up with a fix "fairly quickly," this was "not good enough in this era
of Internet time. By the time the virus definitions were ready, the virus
had already spread. The anti-virus makers must come up with a more
generic way of blocking suspicious-looking scripts before they've
spread all over the world."[51] Miller also observes how many computer
users have failed to implement even the limited security measures that
are available for their protection, creating dangers not only for them-

---

49. See Charles Piller, "The Cutting Edge: Focus on Technology Innovation—
Ubiquitousness of Microsoft Opens Window to Trouble," *Los Angeles Times*, June
5, 2000, p. C-1, available at 2000 WL 2247689.
50. See Michael J. Miller, "Forward Thinking," *PC Magazine from ZD Wire*, June
27, 2000, available at 2000 WL 18128008.
51. Ibid.

selves, but also for others, from attacks designed to exploit their inadequate protections.[52]

"Cultural" Vulnerabilities

A subtle aspect of the "culture" of businesses that operate in cyber space is their reluctance to cooperate openly in efforts to suppress cyber crime. The business sector, as Donn B. Parker of Atomic Tangerine (a spin-off of SRI International) explained in his submission to the Stanford Conference, although increasingly reliant on cyber commerce and support, has significantly different incentives from law enforcement with regard to the handling of cyber crime, and consequently with respect to the sharing of information concerning such crime:

> Security is a fundamentally different issue for business than it is for government because the goals of business and government are fundamentally different. Business survives and grows by managing risks, including security risks, to achieve profit and productivity and views security as a necessary enabler to achieve its goals. Security is balanced with other objectives and made as transparent as possible to avoid interfering with or constraining these objectives. Greater security is often promoted and implemented in businesses when it is needed to meet customer expectations or regulator requirements, when losses are occurring, or in attempts to meet standards of due care to avoid negligence. Competing businesses have hidden agendas and sensitive security and loss experience information that would cause them harm if revealed. Business organization public affairs experts reveal cyber crime and security information to the public only when necessary and beneficial under controlled, well-timed circumstances that minimize the negative impact on business objectives.
>
> Governments, and especially military and law enforcement departments, in contrast to business, have security as their goal, and it

---

52. Home and university computers are commonly left easily accessible to infiltration and attack. See "Hackers Had Access to Home Computers," *New York Times on the Web/Breaking News from Associated Press*, June 9, 2000, reported at ⟨*http://www.nytimes.com/aponline/a/AP-Hacker-Attack.html*⟩.

is enforced by law and motivated by significant rewards and penalties. Legislatures, watchdog groups, and news media discover and publicly report losses and security failures within governments, and incidents are vigorously prosecuted. The relationship between business and government organizations is not on a level playing field. Businesses are allowed to fail; governments are not. Governments have hidden agendas that include criminal investigations of businesses and their staffs. Governments may be sued only with their consent. Many government people are sworn officers of the law, have security clearances, and must keep their crime-fighting activities and intent secret.

Governments also have the duty to protect their indigenous infrastructure businesses in the support of commerce and national security and are often frustrated in their efforts to assist reluctant businesses in achieving more effective security. For example, businesses learn from experience that reporting a suspected high-tech crime to law enforcers may result in taking great amounts of valuable employees' time away from business goals to assist in gathering evidence, giving depositions, and acting as witnesses in court appearances.[53]

As Parker concludes, "It is necessary to understand the cultures of businesses and governments to achieve effective security information-sharing and usage among them."[54]

One clear implication of Parker's insights is that cooperation between private and public cyber security experts should occur through voluntary affiliations of businesses, at the national and international level.[55] Parker noted several such efforts, including the International Information Integrity Institute (I-4) and the Information Security Forum (ISF), which serve the information security staffs of many of the world's largest corporations and several governments. Significantly, many of these organizations include present and former government officials, including former law enforcement personnel, who participate

---

53. Donn B. Parker, "Sharing Infrastructures' Cyber Crime Intelligence," paper submitted to the Stanford Conference, December 6–7, 1999, pp. 2–4.

54. Ibid., p. 5.

55. See the discussion of clearinghouses for such cooperation in Chap. 4 of this volume.

in what Parker observes is in effect an "old boys network" and have a high degree of mutual trust. In addition, other more explicit alliances have been developed between business and government.[56] Parker considers these groups—especially those providing informal exchanges—as the most effective vehicles available for partly overcoming the conflicting interests between businesses and governments, which otherwise limit the likelihood of robust cooperation. He believes they should be allowed to evolve internationally, as a supplement to more formal methods of communication:

> The informal method partly solves or at least sorts out the international dichotomy problem of global businesses interacting with national governments' entities. It provides a means for citizens of each country that are employed by international infrastructure businesses to interact with their own governments that may, in turn, share the information obtained with other governments.[57]

The reluctance of private-sector cyber users to cooperate with governments also suggests that governments cannot responsibly expect the private sector to solve the cyber security problem. Speeches and congressional testimony by U.S. Attorney General Janet Reno and FBI Director Louis J. Freeh called upon businesses for assistance in dealing with cyber crime.[58] The response of the Internet Alliance,

56. The FBI's Computer Investigations and Infrastructure Threat Assessment Center (CITAC) has joined InfraGard, a business-controlled organization that plans to have fifty chapters throughout the U.S., one in each area served by an FBI field office. The U.S. Treasury Department is cooperating with the private Financial Services Information Sharing and Analysis Center (FS-ISAC), established and operated for U.S.-licensed banks and U.S.-regulated financial firms. Other efforts include cooperation by the U.S. Department of Commerce and the Critical Infrastructure Assurance Office with the power industry.

57. Parker, "Sharing Infrastructures' Cyber Crime Intelligence," p. 19.

58. See, e.g., Remarks of Attorney General Janet Reno to the National Association of Attorneys General, January 10, 2000, available at ⟨*http://www.usdoj.gov/ag/speeches/*⟩; U.S. Department of Justice Computer Crime and Intellectual Property Section (CCIPS) materials, including "The Electronic Frontier: The Challenge of Unlawful Conduct Involving the Use of the Internet: A Report of the President's Working Group on Unlawful Conduct on the Internet" (March 2000), available at ⟨*http://www.usdoj.gov/criminal/cybercrime/*⟩; "Statement of Louis J. Freeh, Director, Fed-

among others, makes clear that the private sector will reject any effort to overreach and enlist businesses in law enforcement.[59] Businesses will cooperate, but the private sector cannot be expected to perform roles traditionally performed by law enforcement.

The cyber world's culture in fact includes a very significant element of users and participants who strongly oppose virtually any form of government activity. As Stephen J. Lukasik explains below in Chapter 4, the Internet is largely fashioned and run by private-sector experts, some of whom look upon a government role in creating standards mandating or enabling cooperation in law enforcement as a cure more dangerous than the disease of cyber crime.[60] Even as established an organization as the Internet Alliance, composed of representatives from large and powerful cyber and cyber-related businesses such as AOL, AT&T, eBay, Microsoft, Netscape, and Prodigy, has argued that all transnational efforts to control cyber crime should be based on *voluntary* cooperation.[61] In testimony before Congress, businesses have emphasized what Congress should *not* require:

> We must not pass laws of dubious enforceability, risking erosion of the public's confidence in law enforcement and in the Internet. We must resist overreaching, even in the name of security, and make certain that constitutional and statutory protections in the investi-

eral Bureau of Investigation, Before the U.S. Senate Committee on Appropriations, Subcommittee for the Departments of Commerce, Justice, State, the Judiciary, and Related Agencies," *Hearing on Cybercrime*, February 16, 2000, available at ⟨*http:// www.senate.gov/~appropriations/commerce/freehcyber.html*⟩.

59. See "Testimony of Jeff B. Richards, Executive Director of the Internet Alliance, Before the U.S. Senate Committee on Appropriations, Subcommittee on Commerce, Justice, State, and Judiciary," *Hearing on Cybercrime*, February 16, 2000, available at ⟨*http://www.senate.gov/~appropriations/commerce/richards 00.html*⟩.

60. See, e.g., K. C. Claffy, "Traffic Observation in a Stateless Data Networking Environment," presentation at the Stanford Conference, December 7, 1999, available at ⟨*http://www.caida.org/outreach/presentations/Crisp9912/*⟩.

61. See, e.g., the materials posted at ⟨*http://www.internetalliance.org/policy/ index.html*⟩.

gation and prosecution of Internet crimes are observed. . . . [I]ndustry cannot and must not be made an agent of law enforcement.[62]

The notion that voluntary activity alone can create adequate security for cyber activities is simply untenable. First, it is likely that at the national level cyber crime would be even more prevalent and costly had the U.S. government left the area unpoliced; the domestic laws so far adopted that make cyber attacks criminal have at least provided a vehicle by which to arrest—and thereby to stop, punish, and deter— cyber attacks designed to steal, defraud, and destroy.[63] The great majority of users—commercial, educational, individual—favor such laws. Effective government on the international level also depends on adopting laws setting universal standards for misconduct, authorizing investigatory cooperation and extradition, and developing and standardizing technologically advanced methods for detecting, blocking, tracking, and deterring prohibited conduct.

A much broader attack on the regulation of cyber space than that advanced by the business community is based on the notion that cyber space cannot or, in any event, should not be regulated by government. John Perry Barlow's claim in "A Declaration of the Independence of Cyberspace" is that cyber space is "an act of nature," based on collective actions, and beyond the borders of any state.[64] This philosophical effort has been supplemented with legal arguments based on a claimed lack of jurisdiction to regulate cyber space. Both the philosophical and the legal claims are thoroughly addressed by Neil W. Netanel, who explains how "courts and legislators have increasingly applied real world, state promulgated law to cyberspace activity, steadily constricting the domain of semiautonomous cyberspace rulemaking," and why these developments, in principle, reflect sound results based on tradi-

---

62. "Testimony of Jeff B. Richards, Executive Director of the Internet Alliance," available at ⟨*http://www.senate.gov/~appropriations/commerce/richards 00.html*⟩.

63. See, e.g., 18 U.S.C. § 1030, "Fraud and related activity in connection with computers."

64. See ⟨*http://www.eff.org/~barlow/Declaration-Final.html*⟩.

tional liberal democratic theory.[65] Legislators and courts are rapidly coming to regard cyber activities as analogous to other activities already regarded as permitting prescription, investigation, and enforcement on any of the traditional bases for legal regulation.[66]

Resistance to government involvement in cyber regulation is not, however, entirely based on anarchistic preferences or paranoid fantasies; U.S. government actions have undermined trust and strengthened the case for purely voluntary initiatives. The U.S. government has, for example, exerted much effort in attempting to restrict the effectiveness and distribution of advanced encryption, though encryption is widely regarded as one of the most effective tools available for the protection of cyber security and privacy.[67] When the government appeared to have lost its battle to prevent the free transfer and use of encryption, it tried to convince Congress, and later the Internet Engineering Task Force (IETF)—which establishes voluntary standards for Internet Protocols (IPs)—to include "trap doors" in computer security programs so as to enable the government to pursue criminal investigations more easily. The IETF refused to do so.[68] The implementation

65. See Neil Weinstock Netanel, "Cyberspace Self-Governance: A Skeptical View from Liberal Democratic Theory, *California Law Review* 88, no. 395 (March 2000): 2–4.

66. See, e.g., *Governor of Brixton Prison and Another, Ex Parte Levin*, 3 W.L.R. 657 (Q.B. 1996), *aff'd* 1 Crim. App. 22 (1997). See also Jack L. Goldsmith, "Against Cyberanarchy," *University of Chicago Law Review* 65 (1998): 1199.

67. See Michael R. Arkfeld, "E-Mail—Revisiting Security Issues," *Arizona Attorney* 27, no. 12 (Aug./Sept. 2000): "Encryption [is] a useful method to insure privacy in e-mail transmissions. Encrypting data sent over the Internet renders that message unbreakable, except by the most sophisticated of computer decrypting programs. Encrypted files are 'nearly impossible to break.'"

68. See, e.g., "IETF Rejects FBI Pressure to Allow Network Wiretaps," *Network News*, February 16, 2000, available at 2000 WL 7833204. See also Amy Zuckerman, "Task Force Tackles Internet Standards," *Journal of Commerce*, April 19, 2000, available at 2000 WL 4187332: "The IETF isn't beholden to any country." Some additional changes sought by the U.S. government may, however, be entirely appropriate and consistent with existing authority. See "Statement of Michael A. Vatis, Director, National Infrastructure Protection Center, Federal Bureau of Investigation, Before the Senate Committee on Judiciary" (seeking enhancement of "the ability of law enforcement at the federal, state, and local level to address the burgeoning load

of a search engine injudiciously called "Carnivore " enhanced distrust, although the system seems potentially consistent with legal standards.[69]

Distrust on the international level has been generated by the COE's Draft Convention on Cyber-Crime, the most recent version of which (at the time of this writing) was released on November 19, 2000.[70] This draft—the twenty-fourth since the exercise was initiated—includes coverage of copyright offenses, despite the lack of international consensus on the scope and forms of protection of the many types of works potentially covered. The draft also specifies the types of cooperation that may be required under it, not only from States Parties, but also from Internet Service Providers (ISPs) and other entities and individuals. Among other things, ISPs may be required to conduct real-time surveillance of customers (an earlier draft had required them to store at least forty days of customer data), and all entities and individuals could be required to provide passwords (an earlier draft would have used technology to identify each computer on the Internet). Criticisms of the COE's draft convention, which has been substantially revised in recent months, are in many respects unwarranted, and fail

---

of computer forensics"), available at ⟨http://www.senate.gov/judiciary/52520mav. htm⟩.

69. See "Congress Probes FBI E-Mail Snooping Device," *Palo Alto Daily News*, July 25, 2000, p. 10: "Lawmakers of both parties grilled FBI officials . . . over the bureau's use of 'Carnivore,' a device designed to monitor and capture e-mail messages in a criminal investigation." See also "Justice Dept. Seeks Carnivore Review," *New York Times on the Web/Breaking News from Associated Press*, August 24, 2000, reported at ⟨http://www.nytimes.com/aponline/w/AP-Carnivore.html⟩; Will Rodger, "'Carnivore' Unlikely to be Validated," *USA Today*, September 5, 2000, available at ⟨http://www.usatoday.com⟩. For contrary views, see Ted Bridis, "FBI Gets Web Guru Cerf's Support for Carnivore," *Wall Street Journal*, September 7, 2000, B8: "The Federal Bureau of Investigation has largely won over a crucial ally, technology pioneer Vinton Cerf, in its bid to defend the use of its Carnivore Internet surveillance system"; Ted Bridis and Neil King, Jr., "Carnivore E-Mail Tool Won't Eat Up Privacy, Says FBI," *Wall Street Journal*, July 20, 2000, A28; Bruce D. Berkowitz, "'Carnivore' Won't Devour Cyber-Privacy," *Wall Street Journal*, July 19, 2000, p. A22.

70. See "Draft Convention on Cyber-Crime," released for public discussion on November 19, 2000, available at ⟨http://conventions.coe.int/treaty/en/projets/ cybercrime24.htm⟩.

to take into account that all the measures it proposes are "subject to the conditions and safeguards provided for under the domestic law of the Party concerned, with due regard for the adequate protection of human rights and, where applicable, the proportionality of the measure to the nature and circumstances of the offence."[71] But the COE's effort has evoked negative reactions because of its scope and because it seeks to establish standards without allowing for an open process in which the private sector is able fully to participate.

Widespread distrust of the intentions of commercial entities and merchandising groups with regard to privacy also exists among experts and consumers. Commercial entities and service providers have unilaterally developed and used intrusive software and practices that fail to inform consumers adequately or to provide effective methods for opting out of information-collecting programs.[72] Congress and the Federal Trade Commission (FTC) are considering restrictions on merchandising and consumer tracking aimed at protecting privacy.[73] Finally, private-sector decisions to maintain proprietary systems and programs designed for user convenience and accessibility rather than for security are themselves a root cause of cyber vulnerability; the private sector could greatly enhance cyber security by reordering design priorities, without any government involvement.

An enhanced government role need not, however, be one that requires significantly greater domestic powers or more intrusive mea-

---

71. See ibid., art. 14, § 2.

72. "TRUSTe, a privacy advocate organization that runs a privacy seal-of-approval program for retail Web sites and shows companies how to write effective privacy policies, itself has tracked users with means not mentioned in its own policy." See "Group: Web Agency Tracks Users," *New York Times on the Web/Breaking News from Associated Press*, August 24, 2000, which was reported at ⟨*http:// www.nytimes.com/aponline/w/AP-Online-Privacy.html*⟩.

73. See Brian Krebs, "Senate Considers Stronger Anti-Cybercrime Measures," *Newsbytes News Network*, May 25, 2000, reporting on proposed legislation to permit consumers to opt out of programs that collect and use personal information, and on a Federal Trade Commission proposal to allow consumers to view and change any personal information already collected on them), available at 2000 WL 21177763.

sures;[74] rather, the need is for international cooperation to create common standards and practices. In attempting to satisfy these objectives, it is imperative to take into account the legitimate concerns of those who seek to avoid conferring inappropriate or unnecessary powers on governments to regulate and to intrude upon cyber systems, to preserve as far as practicable private-sector control of this uniquely productive and dynamic sector, and to avoid impinging upon national security interests and activities. As Lawrence Lessig has explained, it is illusory to believe that the cyber world cannot be regulated, and to expect that it will not be regulated, for purposes of facilitating commerce, enhancing security, and—one hopes—protecting freedom and privacy.[75] Regulatory power exists in the "code" that governs all cyber activities. But the scope of regulation will depend on the measures adopted, and it is on that front that the battle over the future of the cyber world must be fought.

5. Fashioning a Solution

A program to deal with cyber crime should be based on its characteristics and be limited to the steps needed to address identified weaknesses. The Stanford Conference made clear to many of us the need

---

74. See, e.g., Jennifer Jones, "U.S. Cyberattack Protection Plan Draws Criticism," *CNN.com*, February 3, 2000, reporting on "red flags" raised in objection by the Electronic Privacy Information Center (EPIC), among others, to Clinton Administration proposals for safeguarding critical systems against cyber attacks, which was reported at ⟨*http://cnn.com/2000/TEC...cyberprotection.crit.idg.index.html*⟩. Enhanced national penalties, and greater police powers for the FBI or other national police agencies, seem unlikely to affect, let alone solve, the rash of ever costlier cyber attacks. Longer jail terms in the U.S., for example, as recent legislation proposes, could have a bearing on the conduct only of individuals likely to be subjected to U.S. law. As a reaction to the "I Love You" virus, for example, raising penalties would be a pointless gesture, since Philippine attackers are immune from the application of U.S. law. Only when the U.S. and Philippine governments agree to make cyber attacks crimes for which extradition is promised by both states will the possibility of an enhanced U.S. penalty become even conceivably relevant.

75. See Lawrence Lessig, *Code: And Other Laws of Cyberspace* (New York: Basic Books, 1999).

for some form of international cooperation. Our effort here is to determine what sort of cooperation is called for, and how best to provide it.

First, the transnational nature of cyber crime calls for a transnational response. The actions of individual states are insufficient. Affected states need to agree on the kinds of conduct that should be proscribed and adopt laws making such conduct criminal. Chapter 2 of this volume examines the considerable extent to which an international consensus exists for prohibiting most forms of attacks on computers and computer networks. Considerable consensus also exists on problems of regulating some conventional crimes in which computers are used, including cyber-related child pornography; but as Chapter 6 points out, on many such crimes major differences of political outlook would make a universal agreement impossible. Still, the exclusion of many conventional crimes involving the use of computers from an international agreement is less important than ensuring comprehensive coverage of harmful conduct aimed at computers and their operation, with a commitment to impose substantial penalties.

In addition to ensuring universal condemnation of serious forms of misconduct, any effective system for punishing cyber crime will require the full range of cooperation afforded by states to each other in mutual legal assistance and extradition treaties. The nature of cyber crime also requires national commitments to undertake special efforts to search for, secure, and preserve usable evidence. The speed with which cyber-related evidence can be lost, and the frequency with which it will be located in foreign jurisdictions, makes it necessary to have the consent of states in advance to some forms of searches that reach into their territories, as well as agreements to assist in seizing equipment and other assets and to provide usable evidence and other forms of cooperation. It is insufficient, moreover, for states merely to agree to perform conventional services for each other. They will have to be prepared to implement technologically adequate measures, as these are developed. Participants at the Stanford Conference described efforts under way to enhance the capacity of users, providers, investigators, and prosecutors to deal with the challenges posed by cyber attacks (summarized below in Chapter 4).

Securing agreement from all states connected to the international information infrastructure for these far-reaching forms of cooperation will certainly be more difficult than securing agreement on the conduct to be proscribed. No multilateral consensus yet exists on providing legal assistance and extradition in cyber cases. States must be convinced that such cooperation is in their best interests, as in the areas of civil aviation (discussed in Chapter 3), international banking, money laundering, and narcotics. To overcome claims or fears of improper extraterritorial activities, states should agree that all measures undertaken in pursuing a cyber investigation will be performed in a manner consistent with the law of the state that is asked to perform such services. To overcome claims or fears that cyber investigations or prosecutions could compromise domestic constitutional protections (see Chapter 5), no state should be required by the international commitments it undertakes to compromise its national standards of conduct. In addition, some states, owing to the so-called "cyber divide," will be unable to provide the assistance required by an international agreement. It is very much in the interests of all states to guard against "weak links" in cyber crime enforcement (that could be exploited by attackers). States should agree to a program to assist those states with legitimate needs in this regard, as international agencies do in a number of other arenas requiring technological expertise.

Because cyber systems and programs are designed with efficiency and ease of use rather than security as the primary objective, states should consider adopting technological measures that go beyond investigative cooperation. Technological breakthroughs (of the sorts discussed in Chapter 4) to enhance protection against, and to improve investigation and prosecution of, cyber crimes should be encouraged and widely implemented. To achieve such cooperation will require overcoming the antiregulatory perspectives of private-sector participants who have built and continue to develop the information infrastructure. One necessary response to this resistance is to build private-sector control into the process of developing solutions and formulating standards and practices for enhancing cyber security. This is one of the guiding principles used in designing the multilateral convention presented below in Chapter 6. In addition, the proposed convention seeks to ensure not only that national standards of state conduct related to human rights are preserved, but also that States Parties will provide certain minimum due process rights in the arrest, charging, prosecution, and extradition of suspects, analogous to protections widely regarded as required by international law. Finally, the Draft Convention explicitly makes it inapplicable to national security activities. U.S. officials are justifiably concerned that an international agreement might lead to unwarranted restrictions on defense-related activities. This possibility can be successfully averted, however, as in other treaties potentially bearing upon national security.

A program based on these principles and proposals should eventually overcome resistance to a multilateral convention to deal with cyber crime and terrorism. Escalating damage and the inadequacy of current efforts are increasing the pressure on governments—and through them on ISPs, major companies, and private standard-setting bodies—to respond effectively. Efforts by governments reacting to recent major attacks have focused on seeking (or in the case of legislators offering) new powers, such as stiffer sentences, the right to arrest and/or search without prior judicial approval, and other inadequate and damaging measures.[76] Knowledgeable legislators and industry leaders should eventually turn to more useful and appropriate options.

---

76. See "Statement of Michael A. Vatis, Director, National Infrastructure Protection Center, Federal Bureau of Investigation, Before the Senate Committee on Judiciary" (supporting, among other things, "provisions that would increase the penalties available for those who are convicted"), available at ⟨*http://www.senate.gov/ judiciary/52520mav.htm*⟩. See also Brian Krebs, "Senate Considers Stronger Anti-Cybercrime Measures," reporting on S. 2448, proposed by Senate Judiciary Committee Chairman Orrin Hatch (R-Utah) and Senator Charles Schumer (D-NY), which "would remove the $5,000 damage threshold for prosecuting federal cybercrimes," and noting FBI efforts to more easily obtain "trap and trace" wiretaps "across many different states," available at 2000 WL 21177763.

Apart from the dangers of increasing police powers, relying on prosecutors to plan and implement solutions in a highly technical area in which private control is regarded as a substantial advantage may well be ineffective even in satisfying the need for better security.[77]

Those who support adoption of a multilateral approach to deal with this quintessentially transnational problem must be encouraged by the fact that states have consistently adopted multilateral solutions to deal with technologies that affect populations across national boundaries. As technology advances, new technologies with transnational impact that require transnational controls have repeatedly led to multilateral arrangements; agencies have been created to deal with such international areas as air travel, shipping, and telecommunications. Transnational needs have demanded transnational solutions, which have been satisfied through international agreements on principles, standards, and practices, often developed and proposed by specialized international agencies. States make such arrangements based not upon ideological considerations but on considerations of safety, productivity, and efficiency. They have done so, moreover, with no sacrifice of national sovereignty, and almost entirely on the basis

---

77. It may, in fact, be a mistake to continue to place primary responsibility for coping with cyber crime within the scope of agencies oriented toward criminal investigations, such as the FBI. Prosecutorial agencies are concerned with developing information for their own use, and tracing and capturing criminals. They are not necessarily going to use information to warn the public of attacks or to develop policy and/or technological solutions aimed at making successful attacks less likely. The U.S. General Accounting Office (GAO) report on the NIPC's response to the "I Love You" virus noted that the agency (which is part of the FBI) waited hours after learning of the virus to notify the public, by which time most companies had been infected. See "Statement of Jack L. Brock, Jr., Director, Governmentwide and Defense Information Systems Accounting and Information Management Division, U.S. General Accounting Office, Before the Subcommittee on Financial Institutions, Committee on Banking, Housing, and Urban Affairs, U.S. Senate," *Critical Infrastructure Protection: "I Love You" Computer Virus Highlights Need for Improved Alert and Coordination Capabilities*, May 18, 2000 (GAO/T-AIMD-00-181), available at ⟨*http://www.gao.gov/*⟩. Furthermore, agencies such as the FBI are unlikely to create systemic recommendations, since they are not immediately concerned with relevant private-sector experts or with the internal capacities to develop such plans.

of consensus decisions determined by both self-interest and reciprocity.

The information infrastructure faces analogous challenges. Its security and efficiency will be materially increased through international implementation of principles, standards, and practices specifically designed for this field of activity. The optimum manner of achieving these objectives in this particular field is a multilateral treaty with the necessary commitments to cooperate in investigating and prosecuting an agreed range of conduct, and an international agency with authority to accomplish (through measures analogous to those widely in use by other agencies; see Chapter 6) the legal and technological objectives essential to create a more secure cyber world.

CHAPTER 2

International Responses
to Cyber Crime

Tonya L. Putnam

David D. Elliott

Concerned technical experts well understand that information security issues are inherently and unavoidably global in nature. Judicial and law enforcement officials equally well understand that the means available to investigate and prosecute crimes and terrorist acts committed against, or through the medium of, computers and computer networks are at present almost wholly local and national in scope. The

The material for this chapter is drawn largely from papers prepared for, and presentations made at, Session Two, "International Response to Cyber Crime," of the Conference on International Cooperation to Combat Cyber Crime and Terrorism, Hoover Institution, Stanford University, Stanford, California, December 6–7, 1999. The following persons made especially valuable contributions: Drew C. Arena, Susan W. Brenner, George C. C. Chen, Ekaterina A. Drozdova, Marc D. Goodman, and Dietrich Neumann.

challenge therefore is how to regulate a technology that permits rapid transactions across continents and hemispheres using legal and investigative instruments that are fragmented across jealously but ineffectually guarded national and jurisdictional borders. When one adds to this the rapidity with which the technology itself continues to evolve and the difficulties this poses for designing, updating, and disseminating effective technical security measures, the full complexity of the problem begins to come into view. Recognition of this state of affairs points toward the desirability of arrangements at the international level to overcome these procedural barriers. However, in the short to medium term such efforts will need to build upon, or at least take into account, existing national and regional efforts to combat cyber crime and terrorism.

The International Convention to Enhance Security from Cyber Crime and Terrorism presented in this volume aims to formalize, in the near term, the highest degree of multilateral cooperation feasible. Points of similarity across national-level laws already promulgated by concerned lawmaking bodies in different countries should indicate where, both in substance and scope, efforts to bring about a multilateral arrangement are most likely to succeed. To this end, this chapter will survey a number of existing national laws that establish criminal penalties for various categories of behavior in cyberspace. It will consider whether and to what degree apparent similarities reflect an emerging international consensus[1] on the need for cyber law, on the types of conduct that should be treated as computer crimes, and on the conditions of pursuit and punishment of cyber criminals. In the second part of the chapter, we turn the focus on a brief examination of other multilateral initiatives to combat cyber crime and cyber terrorism, most of which have yet to reach fruition. The objective is to

---

1. "Consensus" as it is used in this discussion is defined broadly as a state of "general agreement." To find consensus on an issue, therefore, does not demand an identity of opinion on every aspect of the question; rather, it merely suggests that there is enough agreement among enough states to permit consideration of a multilateral effort.

demonstrate why a multilateral initiative that can be implemented over the short term, such as the proposed International Convention, is both necessary and desirable in spite of the ongoing parallel efforts of a number of international and regional organizations.

I. National Responses to an International Problem

As argued in the preceding chapter, a growing number of states appear to have recognized that cyber crime and terrorism pose a significant threat to the infrastructure, commercial interests, and public policies of highly industrialized and highly computerized societies. This emerging recognition is reflected most directly in the national legal codes of concerned countries. An examination of the legal codes of fifty countries conducted in mid-1999 by Ekaterina Drozdova, with the help of Marc Goodman, Jonathan Hopwood, and Xiaogang Wang, revealed that nearly 70 percent of the countries for which data were readily found have promulgated, or are planning to promulgate, laws prohibiting a reasonably comprehensive slate of computer-related crimes.[2] The remaining roughly 30 percent of states surveyed had few or no laws against computer-related crimes.[3]

2. Countries in the Drozdova survey found to prohibit, or to be in the process of promulgating legislation to prohibit, most of or all of the computer-related offenses specified as "consensus crimes" in the Draft Convention are: Australia, Austria, Bulgaria, Canada, Finland, France, Germany, Greece, India, Israel, Italy, Japan, Malaysia, Mexico, the Netherlands, Norway, the People's Republic of China, Portugal, Romania, Russia, Singapore, South Africa, Spain, Sweden, Switzerland, the United Kingdom, and the United States. In regional terms, the Drozdova survey encompasses 60 percent of the European countries, 100 percent of the North American countries, several countries in Central and South America and the Middle East, but fewer in Asia and the Caribbean, and very few in Africa. The survey covered roughly 50 percent of world population, including many populous nations such as China, India, Japan, the United States, Russia, and Brazil.

3. These countries are: Argentina, Brazil, Chile, Costa Rica, the Czech Republic, Denmark, El Salvador, Equador, Hungary, Iceland, Ireland, Jordan, Luxembourg, New Zealand, Oman, Panama, Peru, Poland, Saudi Arabia, Trinidad and Tobago, Tunisia, the United Arab Emirates, and Venezuela. The actual state of legal coverage for cyber offenses is, in all likelihood, considerably lower than 70 percent. Although

The Draft Convention discussed in this volume takes an "inductive" approach to determining what kinds of conduct should be considered cyber offenses. That is to say, it seeks to codify on an international scale conduct that all (or nearly all) states that have enacted criminal statutes against cyber crime *already* include among their criminally punishable offenses. The Drozdova survey found that, of the thirty countries identified as having laws against computer misuse, each prohibits, in some statutory form all, or most, of the following acts: (1) unauthorized access;[4] (2) illicit tampering with files or data (e.g., unauthorized copying, modification, or destruction); (3) computer or network sabotage (e.g., viruses, worms, Trojan horses, denial-of-service attacks); (4) use of information systems to commit or advance "traditional" crimes (e.g., fraud, forgery, money laundering, acts of terrorism); (5) computer-mediated espionage; (6) violations against privacy in the acquisition or use of personal data; (7) theft or damage of computer hardware or software. These seven acts will be referred to throughout the chapter as "consensus crimes." (See Figure 1.)

Clearly, the Drozdova data indicate at least some measure of international consensus on the desirability of punishing a small but significant group of acts perpetrated against, or by means of, computers and computer networks. But a great deal of national-level variation at the margins underlies this broad finding. Although points of legal difference in the substantive definition of cyber offenses, and even country-specific gaps in legal coverage, do not necessarily preclude a

---

the survey conducted by Drozdova et al. includes a high proportion of the most highly industrialized and most highly computerized countries, its coverage of the developing world is less thorough owing to limitations on the availability of information about the criminal codes of many of those countries. Insofar as more highly computerized societies have a greater incentive to promulgate laws against computer-related crime, the absence of data for much of Africa, Asia, and the Caribbean is not surprising.

4. Note that throughout this chapter, the term "unauthorized entry" (the formulation used in the proposed International Convention to Enhance Security from Cyber Crime and Terrorism) is used interchangeably with the term "unauthorized access," the preferred formulation in many national cyber laws and international documents.

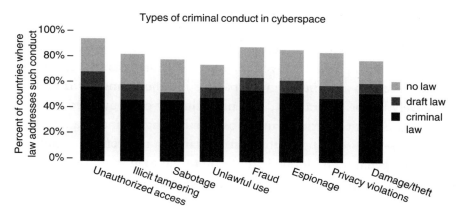

Fig. 1.   Emerging international consensus on cyber crimes: Results of Global Cyber Law Survey of fifty countries in Africa, the Americas, Asia, Europe, the Middle East, and Oceania. (*Source:* Ekaterina Drozdova, prepared for the Conference on International Cooperation to Combat Cyber Crime and Terrorism, December 6–7, 1999, Hoover Institution, Stanford University.)

finding of consensus sufficient to sustain a multilateral effort, the existence of such differences at the very least counsels for closer examination. A country-by-country examination of cyber law on a global scale is, unfortunately, beyond the capacity of a single chapter. Therefore, in this section we examine cyber laws on the books in three geographic regions—the United States, East Asia, and Western Europe—to compile a handful of comparative snapshots of how different countries and regions have responded legislatively to the threats posed by computer and network misuse.

United States

The United States Code contains a number of statutes and statutory provisions to regulate the use of computers and computer technology. Chief among them is the Computer Fraud and Abuse Act (18 U.S.C. § 1030), enacted in 1984, which was "designed to deal specifically with unauthorized use of computers and the alteration and destruction of the records they contain."[5] Unauthorized access to a computer or network without a further offense (e.g., system impairment, obtaining protected information) is per se illegal only with respect to computers used exclusively by the Government of the United States.[6] Unauthorized access to all other computers—for instance, those used nonexclusively by the federal government, including computers containing national security records, and those containing financial and credit records—require some further act or damage to occur in order for criminal penalties to apply. In addition to these offenses, the Act also prohibits use of a computer in interstate commerce to "transmit a program or command which damages a computer system or network," or interrupts the use of a cyber system; "trafficking" in passwords to U.S. Government computers; and the use of interstate commerce to transmit passwords with the intent to defraud.

Under the U.S. federal system, each of the fifty states of the United States is also permitted, within the constraints imposed by federal law, to pass additional substantive criminal laws to regulate computer use at the state level. As Susan Brenner described in her overview of state cyber crime statutes at the Stanford Conference, a number of state legislatures have exercised their ability to further criminalize a wide range of acts involving computers and computer networks. In so doing, these legislatures have provided an interesting demonstration of the degree of substantive variation possible in cyber law, even among entities that share many similarities in their general legal environment. At least as instructive, however, is the degree of coincidence evident particularly with respect to legislative activity on many of the "consensus crimes" identified above.

According to Brenner's research, "crimes involving intrusion and

---

5. Davis McCown, "Federal Computer Crimes" (1995), available at ⟨*http:// www.davismccownlaw.com/*⟩.
6. Under U.S. federal law, unauthorized access includes not only prohibited access from outside a system or organization but also acts in which individuals with authority to access *part* of the data exceed that grant of permission and access nonauthorized data.

damage" are responsible for "by far the largest number of [state] substantive criminal statutes" related to computer crime. Almost all states have trespass and vandalism statutes. Many of these statutes make unauthorized entry a more serious offense when it occurs with the intent or effect of harming data. A substantial number of states outlaw "computer invasion of privacy," which generally entails gaining access to a person's personal financial, medical, employment, or academic information. A handful of states have also added statutes to cover the subsequent use or appropriation of illegally obtained data. Many states also have separate statutes covering use of computers and the Internet to "devise or execute" fraud, theft, and embezzlement. But, as Brenner observed, few states have outlawed computer "forgery," or falsification of data in computer systems; U.S. state legislatures distinguish themselves from the international norm in their uncommon degree of concern with sexual crimes involving computers, which constitute the second-largest body of criminal cyber crime statutes at the state level. In this category, the majority of statutes concern use of the Internet to solicit, entice, or lure minors into a sex act.

On the other hand, few U.S. states currently have statutes that criminalize potentially destructive acts of computer "mischief," such as the creation of viruses, worms, or "malicious logic" programs that can harm the information system or, in many applications, damage the equipment it controls.[7] A handful of states have enacted legislation criminalizing the disruption or denial of essential services, including "a public or private utility, medical services, communication services, or government services." In Brenner's opinion, the lack of activity in this area at the state level is due to a considerable degree to the small number of such incidents reported in the media. In practical terms, a large-scale attack against public or private infrastructure would fall squarely within the purview of federal law enforcement and federal criminal prosecution. However, Brenner argues, there is still room for

7. By contrast, a surprisingly large number of U.S. states have adopted separate statutes to cover the theft and destruction of computer equipment or computer supplies.

state legislatures to act effectively in the criminalization of infrastructure and service attacks.[8] First, state law is necessary for state courts to be able to deal directly with small-scale attacks (that is, those confined to the territory of a single state or portion of a state) against essential services.[9] Second, state law may, under some circumstances, also function as an adjunct to federal prosecution.[10]

Asia-Pacific

George Chen identified categories of computer and network misuse that approach the status of consensus crimes in Asia (Figure 2). These include: unauthorized access; unauthorized use; modifying or damaging data stored on a computer system; theft of money, financial documents, assets, and services by means of a computer; theft of computer software, data, and other forms of information; and damaging or destroying a computer system. Chen cautioned that apparent parallels in the black-letter laws being promulgated in many Asian countries may conceal vastly different modes of interpretation and patterns of enforcement.

In 1997 the Taiwanese criminal code was revised and laws prohibiting computer crimes were added. After a long debate Taiwanese lawmakers decided that merely accessing a computer system without authorization would not be considered an offense unless there was also proof of an additional crime, such as modification or destruction of data. However, the bar on what constitutes an additional offense was set quite low, to include, for example, acts such as reviewing, without consent, e-mail not intended for the intruder. Since 1997, electromagnetic records have been accorded the same protections under Taiwanese law as written documents, including provisions against

8. E-mail correspondence with Susan Brenner, March 6, 2000.

9. The alternative is for a state court to rely upon federal statutes, such as 18 U.S.C. § 1030, to prosecute computer crimes occurring wholly within its territory.

10. Brenner notes, for example, that Oklahoma state law was used in the federal court prosecution of Terry Nichols, one of the suspected perpetrators of the 1995 bombing of the Alfred P. Murrah Federal Building in Oklahoma City.

	Theft of electronic data	Destruction or damage of a computer system	Disclosure of secrets	Computer fraud	Unauthorized access	Forgery of e-document	Defamation/libel	Business disparagement	Obscenity
Taiwan	•	•	•	•	•	•	•	•	•
Hong Kong	•	•	•	•	•	•	•	•	•
China	•	•	•	•	?	•	•	•	•
Japan	•	•	•	•	•	•	X	X	X
Singapore	•	•	□	•	•	•	•	•	•
Thailand	•	•	•	•	•	•	•	•	•
Vietnam	X	X	X	X	X	X	•	•	•
Malaysia	•	•	•	•	•	•	X	X	X

•=prohibited   □=weakly or incompletely prohibited   X=no prohibition   ?=unknown

Fig. 2   Cyber law coverage in selected Asian countries.

forgery and theft, and are likewise regarded as movable property. This feature of the code can be applied broadly in the future to cover everything from transactions involving electronic currencies to interference with the processing of electromagnetic files through, for example, the release of viruses into a system. The Taiwanese code makes it an offense to perpetrate fraud by means of "input [of] false information or commands into a computer or related device, to infringe on copyright, or to appropriate the possessions of others." Other acts that have been criminalized include "libel," "business disparagement," "obscenity," "making threats," "gambling on the net," and "disclosure of secrets."

Under Japanese law, unauthorized access to a computer in which an individual may view secret information is itself a criminal offense, even if there is no damage to the system. The disclosure of secrets that may result from unauthorized access falls under the Business Secrets

Act Against Unfair Competition. Also criminally punishable under Japanese law are "offenses against e-mail," "damage and destruction," "disruption of operations," "computer forgery of electromagnetic documents," and "interception of computer data or files." The current legal trend in Japan is toward making interception of electronic records an offense against movable property, as in Taiwan.

In Singapore, computer crimes are covered by the Computer Misuse Act. Under this Act "unauthorized access," "disclosure of secrets," "destruction or damage of computer systems or electronic data," and "computer fraud" are all prohibited. Although Singapore has no special provisions against defamation or libel, business disparagement, or obscenity perpetrated by means of cyberspace, these offenses are covered under the standard Penal Code. In Malaysia, a Computer Crime Act issued in 1997, though not yet entered into force, covers essentially the same offenses as the Singapore Computer Misuse Act. However, Chen noted, in Malaysia, defamation and libel, business disparagement, and obscenity offenses are subject to civil liability only.

In Hong Kong, computer crimes are, as a rule, governed under the Telecommunications Ordinance. Exceptions include the crimes of "defamation" and "business disparagement," which are covered under the Defamation Ordinance together with Common Law provisions, and also computer obscenity, which is covered by the Control of Obscene and Indecent Articles Ordinance. Under Hong Kong law, "offenses against e-mail," "damage and destruction," "computer fraud," and "theft of electronic data" are all criminal offenses.

In the People's Republic of China, computer-related crimes are covered by Articles 285–287 of the Criminal Code. As Chen explained, the Chinese provisions of which he is aware are notable both for the breadth of their drafting and the severity of the penalties attached. Offenses such as "illegally interfering in the operation of a computer system," for example, are punishable by a minimum sentence of five years in prison, but in 1998 two brothers from Jiangsu Province were sentenced to death after having been convicted of breaking into a bank's computer system pursuant to a robbery. The PRC is also concerned about possible subversive content in network communications, and has undertaken to monitor and criminalize such communications. This effort goes beyond the norms of most other states and is unlikely to find its way into any international agreement.

Finally, in Vietnam and Thailand no law specifically targeting computer crime has been propagated or proposed at the time of this writing. Apparently it is up to prosecutors to stretch provisions in the Criminal Code to cover Internet-related offenses. The general approach has been to attempt to persuade courts in these countries that electronic data should be treated as movable property, thereby extending the protection of existing penal laws against offenses such as theft, fraud, disclosure, defamation, and "mischief." This type of legislative inaction will in all likelihood leave important legal gaps that cannot be papered over with existing statutes. Even supposing that law enforcement and judicial officials in these countries were to take a highly assertive approach to the pursuit of computer crime, the successful prosecution of so-called "pure" computer crimes under existing statutes would demand a high degree of legal creativity and massaging of definitions. In civil code countries lacking a strong tradition of judicial discretion, the chances that such a strategy will prove effective are quite remote.

Europe

The legislatures of Western and Central European countries have been active in promulgating laws prohibiting unauthorized access, computer sabotage, computer espionage, data manipulation, and computer fraud. Though the diversity of national cultures and legal traditions in Europe all but guarantee variation among national laws in this group of states, the European Union (EU) operates in this, as in other fields, as a force for legal harmonization across national approaches.[11]

11. A thorough account of the national laws of all fifteen Member States of the European Union is beyond the scope of this chapter. For more information, consult

All EU Member States, with the exception of Austria, have enacted laws prohibiting some form of unauthorized access to computers and computer networks. Although most EU Member States have statutes prohibiting "mere access" of systems without authorization, some states attach further requirements in order to trigger criminal penalties. In Germany and the Netherlands, for example, the law against unauthorized access protects only "secure systems" for which some effort has been made to inhibit open access. In Spain, some damage to the penetrated system must occur for criminal sanctions to apply. Ulrich Sieber has noted that some general antihacking provisions, such as those in the United Kingdom and Finland, have a built-in progression from a "basic" hacking offense to more serious forms of conduct implicating "ulterior" offenses.[12]

One area in which the national laws of European countries are significantly in agreement is that of computer sabotage, which encompasses purposeful damage to the integrity of computers, computer networks, and computer data. Variation in the extent of protection afforded to computer-stored data (CSD) among the criminal laws of European states is, according to Sieber, rooted in varying requirements of intent and degree of damage caused that underlie vandalism or criminal mischief statutes more generally.[13] States with statutes specifically protecting CSD include Austria, Denmark, Germany, Finland, France, Luxembourg, the Netherlands, Spain, Sweden, and the U.K.; so far in Europe, the enactment of laws prohibiting computer sabotage and the destruction of data includes only a small number of national provisions directed specifically against the creation or distribution of destructive programs, such as viruses, worms, or Trojan horses. Italy, Sweden, and the Netherlands are among the handful of countries that have included such provisions in their respective criminal codes. Only

---

"Legal Aspects of Computer-Related Crime in the Information Society: COMCRIME Study" (1998), prepared for the European Commission by Dr. Ulrich Sieber, University of Würzburg, Germany.

12. Ibid., p. 72.
13. Ibid., p. 78.

Germany and Italy have promulgated laws directed specifically against forms of computer sabotage "leading to the obstruction of business or national security."[14]

The degree of protection afforded by national laws of EU Member States against computer espionage has in many cases been achieved by extending the coverage of laws protecting trade secrets to computer and data processing. Denmark, Germany, the Netherlands, Sweden, and the U.K. have all enacted provisions to reinforce trade secret protection. Civil provisions aimed at discouraging unfair competition in Europe have attained a significant measure of harmonization through First Pillar initiatives in the European Union. By contrast, the criminal sanctions that underlie those policies are anchored in varying national traditions relating to the legal protection of various types of property, including intellectual property, and thus exhibit greater variation. Sieber notes that, whereas intellectual property is an established category in the common law tradition, the civil law (or "continental law") tradition "does not regard information as per se protectable."[15] The situation is similar with respect to computer fraud and computer forgery. While all Member States of the European Union criminally sanction fraudulent acts in general terms, not all have statutes specifically directed against computer fraud.[16] European states that have promulgated laws against computer forgery include Germany, Finland, France, Greece, Luxembourg, and the U.K. Sieber explains that

14. Ibid.

15. For example, civil law states tend to take a much narrower view of the exclusive ownership rights that accrue under copyright, trademark, and patent law. Ibid., p. 75.

16. The countries that have enacted computer fraud statutes include: Austria, Denmark, Germany, Finland, France, Greece, Luxembourg, the Netherlands, Spain, Sweden, and the U.K. Sieber notes that the absence of a computer fraud statute can complicate catching fraud by means of financial manipulations, because many national statutes, including those of Italy and Germany, require deceit of a "person," which leaves untouched a host of offenses involving electronic misappropriations. The fraud statutes in Belgium and France require an "abuse of confidence" as a trigger. Normally, abuse of confidence is understood to apply only to actors in high positions and may not extend to low-level programmers and operators. See ibid., pp. 82–83.

many of the remaining states have forgery statutes that can be extended without difficulty to cover computer forgery. However, in Austria, Belgium, and Italy—none of which has computer forgery statutes— the traditional forgery statutes in force limit protection to "visually readable" documents, thereby excluding electronic and computer stored data from protection.[17]

A survey of national legal initiatives in Europe would not be complete without a few words regarding European Union–level initiatives that increasingly place important limitations on the legislative autonomy of EU Member States. The Council of the European Union has been the most important engine driving EU Member States toward a harmonized approach to combating computer-related crime, but combating computer-related crime inside the European Union is complicated by the fact that the issue straddles important divisions in the EU structure. Issues mainly commercial or economic-regulatory in nature, including, for example, telecommunications, fall within the purview of the European Community, which forms part of the First Pillar of the EU's three-pillar structure.[18] Harmonization in the criminal legal sphere, together with questions of law enforcement and judicial cooperation, are handled under the Third Pillar, Justice and Home Affairs. Whether a matter is handled as a First Pillar or a Third Pillar issue is key to determining the available mechanisms for attempting to bind Member States to a common course of action. The situation is further complicated by the fact that one and the same body, the

17. Ibid., p. 81.
18. The three-pillar structure was established in 1993 under the Treaty of the European Union (TEU) signed at Maastricht. Under this treaty, the First Pillar contains three components, the most important of which is the European Community (EC) (formerly the European Economic Community). The other two components are the European Coal and Steel Community (ECSC) and the European Atomic Energy Community (Euratom). The Second Pillar of the European Union structure is Common Foreign and Security Policy (Title V, TEU). Justice and Home Affairs forms the Third Pillar (Title VI, TEU). See Josephine Shaw, *Law of the European Union*, 2d ed. (London: Macmillan, 1996).

Council of the European Union, can operate under either set of rules, depending upon the question at hand.

Under the Third Pillar, the Council of the European Union acts as an intergovernmental body of national representatives, and not in the legislative capacity it serves under the First Pillar. This means, for example, that when acting in a Third Pillar capacity, the Council operates under a "unanimity" decision rule, as opposed to the "qualified majority" rule normally used for First Pillar affairs. In addition, under the First Pillar, the Council is empowered to issue, in accordance with the rules of co-decision with the European Parliament, Directives and Regulations that are binding upon Member States, and enforceable by the European Court of Justice. By contrast, under the Third Pillar constraints, Council decisions are more akin to traditional international agreements and are therefore not directly enforceable through First Pillar mechanisms. However, the gulf between First and Third Pillar capacities is narrowing slowly as European integration progresses. Under Article 34 of the Amsterdam Treaty adopted in 1997, the Council, acting in its Third Pillar capacity, acquired the power to issue legally binding framework decisions. With regard to the national laws discussed above, this means that the Council may now affirmatively require Member States to bring national legislation into concordance with EU standards in areas where the EU chooses to "occupy the legal field," thereby overcoming at least those points of national difference that inhibit realization of the EU policy.

And the EU has chosen to act in this area. Dietrich Neumann explained that the work undertaken in the European Union in the field of cyber crime has not been directed toward drafting a unified legal instrument.[19] Rather, the EU approach has sought to take into account and, where possible, to complement initiatives in the Council of Europe, the OECD, and the G-8.[20] Neumann points out that one way

---

19. Dietrich Neumann, Stanford Conference, Session Two, pp. 6–7.

20. Drew C. Arena identified the primary legislative measures specific to computer crime enacted by the EC and the EU, as the 1995 and 1997 Directives on Data

forward could have been to formally associate EU efforts with work in other international forums, without developing separate EU initiatives in order to avoid a duplication of effort. However, he argues, "the legislative and regulatory system of the EU allows much more effective action than would have been possible in other forums." Accordingly, the strategy adopted is to associate with existing initiatives where it makes sense and to develop EU instruments where necessary."[21] In concrete terms, these efforts have ranged from the promulgation of new legislation, to funding law enforcement training for investigation of high-tech crime, to initiatives to encouraging more regular coordination between First Pillar and Third Pillar institutions (for example, between telecommunications and law enforcement).[22]

Common Concerns

States in the international system differ widely in their vulnerability to criminal activity perpetrated against or by means of computers and computer networks.[23] They also differ widely according to the degree of threat they face from criminal and terrorist attacks, both domestically and internationally.[24] To a considerable extent, the observable variation in states' reactions to the growing potential for cyber crim-

---

Protection, the 1995 Council Resolution on the Lawful Interception of Telecommunications, the 1997 Council Resolution on Illegal and Harmful Content on the Internet. Pending measures include a Joint Action or Framework Decision on Child Pornography on the Internet and a Directive concerning electronic commerce. More recently, however, computer crime has been addressed at the strategic level in the European Union under the rubric of actions being taken to combat organized crime.

21. D. Neumann, p. 3.

22. See "Action Plan to Combat Organized Crime," adopted by the Council of the European Union on April 28, 1997, Official Journal C 251, 15/08/1997, pp. 0001–0016; see also Council document 11893/2/98, CRIMORG 157 REV 2, a 1998 statement outlining the EU approach to high-tech crime in ten strategic guidelines.

23. A state's vulnerability to computer crime and computer terrorism is a "technical issue" directly related to the degree of computerization of each state's national economy and infrastructure.

24. The "threat" posed to a state by cyber criminals refers to the motivation (economic, ideological, or otherwise) of others to exploit a given state's level of vulnerability, and therefore constitutes a factor distinct from mere vulnerability.

inal and terrorist activity can be explained with reference to these two dimensions.

The sizable group of states that have, or will soon have, laws directed specifically against cyber crime include the most highly industrialized countries, which, as a rule, are also the most dependent upon computers and computer networks. This group also includes a number of countries less dependent upon information technology (IT) that nevertheless share important economic and trading relationships with the IT giants.[25] Not surprisingly, the least computerized societies have been the slowest in passing national legislation against computer crime. Among countries in the Asia-Pacific region, for example, the toughest and most detailed cyber crime laws have been passed in states with the most highly industrialized and highly computerized economies, as exemplified by Taiwan, Japan, and Singapore.[26] States with little or no legislative action on cyber law have low levels of computerization and low reliance on network infrastructures, and they face little or no internal vulnerability from acts of high-tech crime and terrorism. But the very lack of vulnerability to cyber attack among states with low IT dependence is cause for concern in states that perceive a high threat of cyber attack, since the absence of internal vulnerability to cyber attack correlates strongly with a failure to take national legislative action to criminalize such offenses. Network attack

25. Arena pointed out in his Stanford Conference paper that even within this group, consensus on the recognition of the threat is quite new. He related that "only a few years ago, as the United States attempted to discuss the need for protection of critical infrastructure from cyber attack with colleagues from other very developed (but not as IT-dependent) countries I was often politely told that our concern was reminiscent of those who worried [in 1968] that student radicals would spike U.S. urban water supplies with LSD."

26. Although the cyber laws in the People's Republic of China are notable for their "toughness," as Chen pointed out, they are drafted more broadly than those of Taiwan, Japan, and Singapore, which makes them applicable in a wider set of potential circumstances. This difference in approach is probably explained by the greater degree of direct control maintained by the PRC government over most forms of private and public communications. Note that no information on South Korea was included in Chen's research.

can be launched from virtually any geographic location against any other with an international telephone connection, and some countries can become legal operating bases and safe havens for cyber criminals in their attacks against IT-vulnerable states.

Addressing the failure of some states to respond to the threat of cyber crime and cyber terrorism will almost certainly demand differentiated tactics and incentives. In some instances, traditional political pressures at the regional or international organizational level may be sufficient to prompt legislation to bring the laws of less IT-dependent states into line with international minimum standards. Among the least economically well-off states, forging policy may require more tangible incentives along the lines of development assistance and technological transfers already familiar in other areas of international coordination. Even among states that have chosen independently to adopt legislation criminalizing cyber offenses, effort is needed to coordinate national responses both in terms of specifying offenses and in applying the laws that are enacted to cross-border illegal acts. Without measures that actively coordinate national actions and policies at the international level, the amalgam of national cyber laws and policies is unlikely to result in a coherent framework for the identification, investigation, and prosecution of computer crimes occurring within or affecting multiple jurisdictions at any time in the near future.

2. In Search of a Working Consensus

How, then, is it possible to recognize when consensus is present to a degree that could lead to an internationally acceptable but nevertheless substantive prohibition regime? The search for a working consensus demands both finding specific points of agreement and determining an overarching structure within which to frame those points. The purpose of the following survey is to suggest what the points of existing consensus might be and to contextualize them within a larger view of what, ideally, has to be done so that the level of consensus that exists can be put into effect.

In this section we identify two areas in which some level of consensus is necessary if law enforcement and judicial actors working from within various national jurisdictions are to be effective in identifying, investigating and prosecuting computer offenses. The first area is that of specifying what conduct will be treated as a criminal offense. Because this area shows the most potential for formal agreement in the short term, it is the main focus of the Draft Convention. The second area concerns points of existing consensus on what rules and procedures should dictate the scope and extent of operational powers enjoyed by law enforcement and judicial authorities inside their respective spheres of jurisdiction.

Condemnation of Specific Conduct

To cooperate across national borders, whether at the level of bilateral contacts in the course of an actual investigation or in the context of multilateral negotiations to establish a framework agreement, legal systems must agree that certain acts should be prohibited and punished. Particularly in the criminal sphere, international law enforcement and judicial cooperation depend upon at least general agreement on what conduct should be regarded as punishable offenses. The principle of double criminality, for example, prohibits extradition of a fugitive to a requesting state unless the offense charged is a crime in both states. In practice, this principle also extends to mutual legal assistance in gathering evidence in the course of a criminal investigation, particularly when the acts of discovery in question are considered intrusive.[27] Without a minimum basis for agreement, therefore, multi-jurisdictional computer crimes will not be fully investigated, and, as a consequence the perpetrators of those crimes will in many cases go unidentified and unpunished.

Several multilateral efforts to coordinate national responses to the

27. U.N. *Manual on the Prevention and Control of Computer-Related Crime* (1994), ¶ 270. See ⟨*http://www.ifs.unvie.ac.at/~pr2gq1rev4344.html/*⟩ (visited March 17, 2000).

threat of cyber crime have devoted considerable attention to the specification of offenses. The Council of Europe (COE),[28] the Organization for Economic Cooperation and Development (OECD), Interpol, the United Nations Committee on Crime Prevention and Criminal Justice,[29] and the European Union have all been active in various capacities. Additional organizations are becoming involved at a rapid rate: the Commonwealth Secretariat, the Organization of American States (OAS), and the Association of Southeast Asian Nations (ASEAN) have all recently initiated projects on international harmonization of law relating to computer crime among their members.[30] Drew Arena points out that these groups, many of which have overlapping memberships, have taken some pains "to exchange views and avoid duplication or conflicting approaches" in addressing international shortfalls associated with computer-related crime.[31]

The Council of Europe is so far the only organization to have made considerable progress toward negotiating an international multilateral agreement for the specification and criminalization of an enumerated

28. The Council of Europe was formed in 1949 as a standing forum for the promotion of democracy, human rights, and the rule of law among its members. In 1989, the organization's membership began to expand from the original ten Western European states to its current total of forty-one states, which includes many of the newly independent former Soviet republics and former Eastern bloc states. The COE should not be confused with either the European Council or the Council of the European Union, both of which are components of the entirely distinct European Union treaty structure. Unlike EU bodies, the COE has no power to issue binding instruments for its members. Instead, the COE operates primarily through negotiated conventions, roughly 160 to date, that its members are encouraged to adopt and implement.

29. According to Drew Arena, the primary contribution of the UN Committee, to date, has been the publication of its "Manual on Computer-Related Crime" in 1994.

30. The efforts of the Group of Eight, whose most noteworthy contributions have been in the sphere of procedural coordination, are discussed in the following subsection.

31. In Arena's words: "For example, representatives of the Eight and the EU Commission participate in the Council of Europe Committee; the Council of Europe has an observer in the G-8 Subgroup, and the EU hosts annual meetings of the Council of Europe, G-8 and OECD groups."

set of cyber offenses.[32] The Draft COE Convention on Computer-Related Crime concentrates largely on crimes directed against the "confidentiality, integrity and availability of computer data and systems"—"c.i.a.-offenses" for short. These offenses, which Arena also refers to as "pure" computer crimes, are qualitatively "new" offenses that are not readily classifiable under old statutory categories, particularly in countries without some experience in dealing with offenses against nontangible forms of property.[33] The five "consensus crimes" discussed by COE members are: (1) illegal access, (2) illegal interception, (3) data interference, (4) system interference, and (5) the production and distribution of illegal devices that may be used in the commission of any of the first four acts. Offenses against the possession (that is, taking without violating confidentiality), authenticity, and utility of information, although not spelled out explicitly in the Convention, are covered under Article 7 (computer-related forgery). A consensus has also emerged among COE members condemning certain offenses related to child pornography.[34] The aiding and abetting of

32. The UN General Assembly has also created an Ad Hoc Committee to draft a Convention on Transnational Organized Crime before the end of 2000. Arena notes (p. 2) that "in addition to certain references to computer-related issues in the draft text (for example in the context of mutual legal assistance) many states feel that eventually a protocol to this convention specifically addressing cyber crime should be negotiated."

33. Offenses such as "computer fraud" and "computer forgery" essentially entail the application of a new technology to commit an old crime and are therefore easily caught by existing fraud and forgery statutes, but the fact that so many lawmaking bodies in cyber law states have seen fit to promulgate statutes specifically outlawing *computer* fraud suggests that there may be some merit in a distinctive approach. As noted in the *U.N. Manual on the Prevention and Control of Computer-Related Crime*, "the criminal codes of all countries have, up to the present, predominantly protected tangible and visible objects" (¶ 84). Protection for intangible forms of property, such as "intellectual property" and copyright evolved over the course of the twentieth century but has been robustly enforced only in a relatively small number of countries. Even in jurisdictions accustomed to regulating intangible property, the extension of those protections to electromagnetic data and the integrity of information has necessitated new legislative responses.

34. Dietrich Neumann observed that even this modest degree of consensus around a content offense is rather remarkable given the range of opinion regarding the boundaries of free speech among Council Member States and around the globe. Content-

computer offenses is also punishable under the Council of Europe
Draft Convention, as is the attempt to commit a criminal act, although
detail regarding the contours of these latter offenses has yet to be
enumerated.

Still, after more than three years of negotiation, the Draft Convention on Computer-Related Crime has yet to reach final approval.[35]
Thus, although there is much to recommend the thorough approach
of the Council of Europe's Draft Convention, the effort will require
several additional years of negotiation before entering into force. In
the meantime, the threats posed by cyber criminals and terrorists will
continue to mount internationally as the vulnerability to attack grows.

The Council of the European Union,[36] in its ongoing effort to
bridge Council of Europe efforts, issued its "Common Position of 27
May 1999 on negotiations of the European Union relating to the Draft

---

related offenses are particularly difficult to standardize and harmonize because they
implicate some of the most closely held values on which different nations are constructed. For example, in Germany and Italy, both states with fascist periods in their
past, legal tolerance for hate speech is low. By contrast, in the United States, the First
Amendment to the Constitution establishes an extremely high barrier against government censorship on the content of speech, so much so that it protects the dissemination
of information (scripts, codes, and the like) needed to perpetrate many of the crimes
under discussion.

35. The project was launched in 1997 on the initiative of the Council's Committee
of Experts on Cyber Crime. Committee members include Member States of the European Union, Central and Eastern European states, and also a number of active
observer states, including the United States, Canada, and Japan.

36. The Council of the European Union, also known as the Council of Ministers,
is a body of officials holding ministerial positions within their states who are empowered to commit their governments on policy matters. The Council of the European
Union carries out its work mainly through specialized subcommittees. It holds primary
control over approval of the EU budget and also has the power to conclude international agreements between the EU and third states and international organizations. It
functions as the coordinating body for police and judicial cooperation among EU
Member States. As noted earlier (note 28) the Council of the European Union should
not be confused with the European Council, which is the body consisting of the heads
of state of the EU members, plus the president of the European Commission and the
European Parliament that meets only at "European Summits" held biannually.

Convention on Cyber Crime."[37] In this document, the Council articulated what it perceived to be specific points of emerging consensus,
including agreement on features most in need of future inclusion in
the Council of Europe Draft Convention. The Council of Europe/
European Union effort has sought, in Neumann's words, "ways to
overcome, or at least reduce procedural obstacles that hamper international computer crime investigations and which partly relate to the
principles of territoriality and national sovereignty." This effort is
helped by a number of general measures instituted by the EU to facilitate police cooperation at the operational level[38] and to simplify requirements for the extradition of criminal fugitives among Member
States.[39] The European Union has also encouraged its Member States
to enact national legislation to facilitate mutual legal assistance in the
search and seizure of evidence from organized crime and high-tech
crime.[40]

The OECD has also been an active player in efforts to achieve

37. See Official Journal of the European Communities No. L 142, June 5, 1999,
p. 1.

38. See, e.g., Joint Action of November 29, 1996, adopted by the Council on the
basis of Article K.3 of the Treaty on European Union, concerning the creation and
maintenance of a directory of specialized competences, skills, and expertise in the fight
against international organized crime, in order to facilitate law enforcement cooperation between the Member States of the European Union (96/747/JHA); Joint Action
of June 29, 1998, adopted by the Council on the basis of Article K.3 of the Treaty on
European Union, on good practice in mutual legal assistance in criminal matters (OJ
L 191, July 7, 1998, pp. 0001–0003); Act of the Management Board of Europol of
October 15, 1998, concerning the rights and obligations of liaison officers (OJ C 026,
January 30, 1999, pp. 0086–0088); and the Draft Council Act establishing the Con-
vention on Mutual Assistance in Criminal Matters between the Member States of the
European Union (OJ C 251, September 2, 1999).

39. See Council Act of March 10, 1995, adopting a simplified procedure for
extradition (OJ C 78, March 30, 1995).

40. See, e.g., "Council Act of March 12, 1999, adopting the rules governing the
transmission of personal data by Europol to third states and third bodies," Council
Document 10888/99; Council Resolution of January 17, 1995, on the law interception
of telecommunications (OJ C 329, November 11, 1996).

harmonization in the cyber laws of its Member States.[41] Like the approach adopted by the Draft Convention presented in this volume, the OECD initiative has sought to identify and build upon existing areas of international consensus. However, the OECD has not attempted to draft a formal agreement, instead confining its efforts to issuing recommendations and guidelines for action. In 1986 the OECD released its first report on cyber offenses, "Computer-Related Crime: Analysis of Legal Policy," which surveyed existing laws and proposed a minimum list of five substantive offenses that it recommended strongly for criminalization by OECD members. Those offenses are (1) unauthorized access, (2) illegal computer transfer of data or funds, (3) forgery, (4) interruption of service, and (5) illegal appropriation and exploitation of data or software. In 1992 OECD issued "Guidelines on the Security of Information Systems" together with a mandate for a periodic review of those guidelines every five years. The most recent set of guidelines, issued in March 1997, is a set of Cryptography Policy Guidelines, together with an extensive comparative report on cryptography policy.

Several of the Stanford Conference panelists cautioned that apparent patterns of coincidence in the choice of rules and terms may not represent a true consensus but may instead mask widely varying patterns of practice. Laws that appear to be similar or identical from a drafting perspective may be enforced differently by law enforcement and criminal justice officials acting entirely in good faith, owing, for instance, to differing interpretations of key terms or different views regarding the law's intended scope.[42] The potential for variation in practice, they argued, is heightened by the absence of a common vocabulary with which to discuss issues of cyber crime and cyber terror-

41. Arena describes the OECD as having been "active in the field since at least 1980 when it issued its Guidelines on the Protection of Privacy of Transborder Flows of Personal Data."

42. The *U.N. Manual on the Prevention and Control of Computer-Related Crime* notes that there is no globally accepted general definition of computer crime and, consequently, functional definitions are customary for international initiatives (¶ 21).

ism. Marc Goodman noted in his conference presentation that because many national laws do not define basic terms, such as "computer network," "protected system," or "data interference," the laws in which those terms appear have uncertain scope of application.[43] But since this condition obtains in virtually every multilateral legal agreement between sovereign states, and it is not preclusive of a functional international regime. Given the relatively small number of major cyber attacks to date, we simply do not know whether and to what degree these ambiguities may pose problems for international cooperation. Nevertheless, we do know that similar obstacles have been successfully overcome in regulating international intercourse on the open sea and in international air traffic.[44]

More problematic from the perspective of international consensus-building are laws that define the scope of their coverage very narrowly. This point is illustrated by comparing some laws that prohibit "unauthorized entry" into computer systems. In the People's Republic of China, for example, the relevant law makes it a criminal offense to "access computers without permission," particularly computer systems important to state security; in India the law makes it an offense to enter "protected systems" only. In the United States, the federal law has broadened over time from protection of "government computers," to protection of "federal interest computers" and eventually to protection of "computers involved in interstate commerce." It is not difficult to imagine how loopholes and gaps can arise—for instance, in translating the American concept of a "federal interest computer" into a Chinese or Indian equivalent for purposes of extradition, or to request permission for search and seizure of data. In some cases, the narrowness of a formulation chosen by a national legislature is in-

---

43. By contrast, the entire first chapter of the Council of Europe's Draft Convention on Cyber Crime concerns the definition of the terms that will be used, "such as 'computer system,' 'data,' 'service provider,' 'traffic data,' 'search and seizure of data,' and many more."

44. See Chap. 3 of this volume for a detailed discussion of the development of the latter of these regimes.

tended to stimulate a particular response among private entities claiming protection under the law. Germany's statute against unauthorized access criminalizes only the penetration of "specially protected computers."[45] Statutes of this kind are drafted to induce system owners to take proactive steps to protect their systems against outside access, rather than placing the entire burden of deterring criminal acts on *post hoc* legal remedies, as is the case under federal law in the United States. The Draft Convention proposes a definition that would require system users to make clear they intend to restrict access.

Finally, the narrowness of statutes may in some cases be due to practical considerations of enforceability rather than to failure to appreciate wider levels of threat. More broadly drafted laws would in many cases implicate, on a systematic basis, actors and assets located in other jurisdictions, thereby complicating the process of application and enforcement. This suggests that actual levels of consensus regarding computer-related crime may be broader than is immediately apparent from a textual survey of legal codes.

Administration and Operation of Cyber Law

As difficult as reaching consensus on issues of substantive law appears to be, the difficulties multiply when the discussion turns to administration and procedure.[46] Whereas the purpose of substantive law is to

45. Sec. 202 a, Penal Code Computer espionage: Unauthorized procuring of data not meant for the offender or specially protected against unauthorized access; penalty is up to three years' imprisonment or a fine. (Attempt: not punishable.) The term "data" is explained in the comments on Sec. 303a of the Penal Code. "Procuring" data does not imply knowledge of the data. The offense also covers procuring data for a third party. The offender must have acted without the necessary authorization by the party entitled to dispose of the data. The "specially protected" criterion (required to constitute the offense) is not defined by the law. The victim must make his interest in keeping the data secret clear by providing a certain level of access security. Prosecution is subject to a complaint lodged by the victim. The provision protects not only stored data but also data in the course of transmission or processing.

46. In practice, procedural issues are never entirely detached from the substantive specification of an offense. The specification of the elements and seriousness of the offense are important in determining whether the system in question will take cogni-

delineate what private citizens may or may not do, the purpose of procedural law is to regulate what law enforcement and judicial officials may or may not do in administering and enforcing substantive law. Though encouraging a country to incorporate a small number of computer-related offenses into its criminal code is unlikely to have a large impact on the character of the system as a whole, the altering or carving out of exceptions to procedural rules in order to facilitate the identification or investigation of computer-related crimes may have important implications for the national legal systems in question.

The enforceability of laws against cyber offenses enacted at the national level becomes complicated when, as is frequently the case, the source, object, or path of an attack has its physical nexus in more than one country. The main procedural difficulty is not, as some early commentators suggested, the absence of territorial *nexi* in crimes committed via cyberspace, but rather the *plurality* of national connections, each of which may carry its own jurisdictional claims.[47] Even among the several United States, Susan Brenner found that questions of who has jurisdiction to do what with respect to investigating and prosecuting computer crimes in which state lines are crossed in cyberspace are hotly contested.[48] Arena illustrates the types of issues that may crop up even in a relatively straightforward scenario:

> Consider a corporate Internet [host] used by employees of a foreign company in a U.S. city with the system server in another country. U.S. agents obtain a valid warrant to search the computers at the U.S. office for particular evidence of fraud. If the evidence was entered from the site in the U.S. and is still accessible from there, does or

zance of a suspected violation, and, if so, what level of intrusiveness will be permitted during investigation.

47. For an excellent summary and discussion of this debate, see Jack L. Goldsmith, "Against Cyber Anarchy," *University of Chicago Law Review* 65 (Fall 1998): 1199.

48. This is not to say that such questions are entirely unsettled. A large body of jurisprudence, termed the "Conflict of Laws," is directed precisely at resolving jurisdictional contests in a rule-bound fashion in situations where a number of entities have colorable claims to jurisdiction. However, the Conflict of Laws is a notoriously muddy area of the law, in both its domestic and international application, not easily distilled into a set of reliable general guidelines.

should the location of the server matter? What if the location of the server is unknown? Should the U.S. authorities have to seek help from the authorities in the country where the server is located through an international letter rogatory or a Mutual Legal Assistance Treaty to obtain the evidence? Or may they rely on their U.S. search warrant to access and download [the information] at the U.S. site?

Arena points out that the scenario could be easily complicated by the addition of other common considerations, notably "the number of nations involved, the presence or absence of extreme urgency, the existence of consent and its voluntariness, and the extent to which the data sought is protected by firewalls, passwords or encryption." He argues further that a government's opinion as to whether a particular search should be allowed quite frequently depends upon whether it is part of the "searching" state, or the state on whose territory the search will take place. Again, although Arena rightly identifies these factors as impediments to law enforcement and judicial action, such impediments do not, in many respects, constitute new problems for transnational law enforcement.

Officials at the national level have developed mechanisms, in the form of mutual legal assistance treaties (MLATs), to facilitate transnational law enforcement and judicial cooperation generally. Experts at the Stanford Conference agreed that standard mutual legal assistance procedures designed for access to paper documentation are necessary but insufficient for conducting investigations in cyberspace.[49] Dietrich Neumann explained that under the standard approach, formal requests must be addressed to the relevant authority in the home country, which then forwards the request to the appropriate authority in the recipient country, which must then approve and execute the request. Depending on the circumstances, the process can take weeks, months, or even years to complete. By contrast, traffic data and other potentially important sources of information about particular cyber

---

49. For example, identification of the source of a cyber attack can be made most efficiently while the criminal is still on-line, thereby necessitating an extremely rapid response on the part of investigators.

attacks are stored only temporarily in most servers and may become irrecoverable if not seized quickly. Two possible remedial approaches have emerged. The first is to find ways to accelerate traditional mutual legal assistance processes for the investigation of computer-related crimes in which rapid response is key. The second approach anticipates a qualitatively new regime of mutual legal assistance that would, for example, permit law enforcement officials limited powers of direct, cross-border search and seizure, subject to the post-search notification of the searched state.

Although attractive in theory, solutions that would require a drastic overhaul of the existing structure of mutual legal assistance may be beyond political reach, at least in the near future. Even in Europe, with its fairly robust consensus regarding substantive offenses, the COE Committee has made no significant progress on the search and seizure issue, leaving its draft article on transborder search "to be determined." Neumann summarizes the European situation succinctly: "Consensus has emerged where the more traditional concepts of mutual legal assistance were used for drafting provisions of this [COE] Convention. Agreement could also be reached when it came to defining consensus crimes. Difficulties arise, however, where the Convention tries to widen the traditional concepts and therefore enters into conflict with principles such as national sovereignty and territoriality." Thus, the COE has limited itself to constructing the obligation to cooperate "to the widest extent possible" on procedural matters out of broad formulations. These include the "General principles relating to international cooperation" (Art. 20 of Draft No. 18) together with specific provisions on "Extradition" (Art. 21), "Mutual Assistance" (Art. 22), and provisional measures for the expedited preservation of stored computer data (Art. 24). In the European Union, the Council of the European Union's Common Position of May 27, 1999, took a further extraordinary step of endorsing, in general terms, the need for a provision permitting, in exceptional cases, transborder computer searches with post-search notice to the State Party. However, attempts to negotiate this point reportedly became ensnared by differing visions regarding the details and conditions of its use.

Outside the European context, the Group of Eight (G-8), and in particular the High-Tech Subgroup of the Senior Experts on Transnational Organized Crime, have been at the forefront of the multilateral effort to improve international cooperation in obtaining evidence of computer-related crimes.[50] In October 1999 the G-8 ministers adopted "Principles on Transborder Access to Stored Computer Data."[51] The first section of this document requires states to react quickly to requests for the preservation of electronic data, "in particular data held by third parties such as service providers, and that is subject to short retention practices or is otherwise particularly vulnerable to loss or modification." The second section concerns expedited handling of requests to search data thus seized. The idea, in Arena's words, is a "quick freeze, slow thaw" arrangement by which law enforcement and judicial bodies can fulfill their procedural obligations under domestic law for release of information to foreign law enforcement or judicial officials without risking the loss of critical data. Although the principles may appear "fairly modest" in terms of resolving the overall problem, Arena maintains that the G-8 principles lay the basis for an effective interim international regime for the preservation of electronic data.

The third section of the G-8 Principles, "Transborder Access to Stored Data Not Requiring Legal Assistance," addresses the question

50. Arena notes that the Subgroup was created in 1997 at the beginning of the U.S. Presidency of the G-8, and was chaired initially by Scott Charney, then chief of the Computer Crime and Intellectual Property Section (CCIPS) of the U.S. Department of Justice. The group of Senior Experts antedates the Subgroup by only two years. It is often called the "Lyon Group" on the basis of a group of 40 Recommendations on Combating Transnational Organized Crime that were adopted at the group's 1996 summit in Lyon, France. In 1998, a set of Ten Principles and a Plan of Action were announced by the Justice and Interior Ministries of the G-8 members at the Washington meeting, and were subsequently ratified at the 1998 Birmingham Summit.

51. Arena notes that "the Subgroup is currently working on the problem of locating and identifying computer criminals in a global environment, and will hopefully be able to develop principles in this area."

of whether *any* direct penetration of foreign jurisdictions via cyber-space is permitted by outside law enforcement officials in the context of a criminal investigation. The answer in the affirmative specifies that "a State need not obtain authorization from another State when it is acting in accordance with its national law for the purpose of: a) accessing publicly available (open source) data, regardless of where the data is geographically located; b) accessing, searching, copying, or seizing data stored in a computer system located in another State, if acting in accordance with the lawful and voluntary consent of a person who has the lawful authority to disclose to it that data." The sole procedural requirement that attaches to such searches is a post-search notification of the searched State that a search has occurred. In sum, the progress achieved by the G-8 demonstrates that significant steps can be taken to facilitate the investigation of computer-related crimes within the context of traditional mutual legal assistance. At the same time, the third section of the October 1999 G-8 Principles suggests that incremental advances toward a more ambitious transnational investigative regime are possible even now.

3. Toward International Consensus?

The information surveyed in this chapter suggests that a significant degree of consensus exists regarding certain types of prohibited conduct in cyberspace. The roster of prohibited acts enjoying a measure of de facto international consensus runs the gamut from "pure" offenses against the confidentiality, integrity, and availability of computers and computer networks to traditional offenses like fraud and larceny in which computers are a material element. The level of consensus identified in this survey is not particularly "deep" in the sense that, in many instances, it probably does not extend to a detailed specification of computer-related offenses or to common definitions of the "objects" or instruments involved. However, in the opinion of the authors of the Draft International Convention, it is enough to permit formalization on a meaningful level.

The successes and failures apparent in the ongoing efforts of international and regional organizations, considered together with the cyber-crime laws that have been promulgated by concerned states, reveal a great deal about where short-term agreement may be possible, and where it is not. If ratified by a significant number of States, the proposed International Convention to Enhance Protection from Cyber Crime and Terrorism could constitute a meaningful step in coordinating the promulgation and enforcement of existing laws against computer crime and in further closing off legal loopholes and eliminating safe havens for cyber criminals. Indeed, the most persuasive argument in support of a formal, multilateral effort at this juncture is the magnitude of the threats and vulnerabilities against which these measures are directed. In this recognition lie the seeds of effective international action, even as differences in national law and traditional repertoires of transnational law enforcement and judicial cooperation constrain the menu of short-term responses. Experience is showing that national governments are increasingly willing to cooperate in foreign investigations. Director of the National Infrastructure Protection Center Michael A. Vatis reported that in the investigation of the February 2000 e-commerce denial of service attack, "for the first time . . . investigators had sought and received cooperation from foreign governments."[52]

As for the multitude of offenses that fall outside the set of "consensus crimes" identified here, Arena maintains that a lack of consensus may for the present actually be a desirable state of affairs. Absence of consensus lends itself to legal and technical experimentation, which in turn increases the likelihood of happening upon effective solutions that may be foreclosed by premature formalization at the international level. Although this chapter has dealt primarily with proposed short-term steps in the legal sphere, the legal-deterrence approach can and should be reinforced by further developments on the technical side. In the technical realm, harmonization is likely to be helped by the fact

---

52. Matt Richtel, "Official's Testimony Hints at Slow Progress on Internet Attacks," *New York Times*, March 1, 2000, p. A16.

that the technology of security and enforcement is likely to have its source in only a few states. Arena echoed the arguments of Peter Neumann and Richard Power at the Stanford Conference, in positing that the way through the international political maze will probably be found in the free market. Increasingly reliable measures of how much high-tech crime in electronic commerce is costing at the enterprise level have already begun to drive demands for better IT security. Improved cost measurements will also increase awareness of the costs associated with the inefficiencies of transnational fight against computer crime due to outdated agreements for mutual legal and judicial assistance.

In the meantime, progress on the difficult questions can be helped along by demonstrated successes in areas where consensus already exists. Experimentation in transnational law enforcement and judicial cooperation will undoubtedly proceed by means of bilateral agreements among states with similar interests, and through practical lessons learned from investigating and prosecuting cyber offenses. It is to be expected that the de facto regime of multilateral cooperation and consensus will continue to expand and may, over time, pave the way to more comprehensive international legal solutions.

CHAPTER 3

The Civil
Aviation Analogy

PART I

International Cooperation
to Protect Civil Aviation Against
Cyber Crime and Terrorism

Seymour E. Goodman

One of the most frightening images of cyber terrorism is a scenario in which terrorists take over the air traffic control system to cause an aircraft to crash or two planes to collide in flight. H. H. Whiteman, director general for Security and Emergency Preparedness of Transport Canada, places this possibility at the worst-case extremity of a wide range of ways in which information systems could be used to interfere with civil aviation operations.

Transportation systems are important national and international infrastructures that are especially attractive targets for malicious or reckless attack with potentially serious casualty and economic consequences. They have been favored targets of terrorists and criminals for decades. They are also becoming increasingly dependent on information systems, and this dependency is a source of vulnerabilities for hostile information operations. For four important reasons, civil air transport could be singled out for particular attention with respect to international cooperation to combat cyber crime and terrorism:

1. Civil aviation is one of the most widespread and extensively interconnected international infrastructures. It is one of the primary industries for interconnecting and integrating the world, and it spans almost every country on earth. In the United States alone, according to Vidyut Patel of the U.S. Federal Aviation Administration (FAA), almost 300,000 passenger aircraft took flight during 1999, not counting cargo, military, and noncommercial private planes. Each day, this transportation sector is entrusted with millions of lives. The direct and indirect—that is, as a supporting infrastructure for the activities of businesses and governments—economic value of this sector is enormous.

2. The civil aviation infrastructure is extraordinarily dependent on computer-telecommunications information systems. Some of the most prominent and widely used systems include those for air traffic control, navigation, reservations, and aircraft flight control. Others are used extensively for airport and airline management. Individual flights can now be tracked on the Internet in close to real time. Patel stated that more than 180 different information systems have gone through the FAA security certification process. Increasingly, these information systems have become critical to the complete spectrum of activities in this industry. Peter Neumann of SRI believes many of these systems are poorly designed with respect to security and are at risk to GPS jamming, electromagnetic interference, denial of service, Trojan horses, disgruntled employees, and other threats.

3. Civil aviation has a long history of being a target of terrorists. Aircraft and airports have been threatened and attacked all over the world over the course of decades. The extensive vulnerabilities and dramatic consequences of attacks against civil aviation make for very high profile events. The extensive use of, and dependence on, information systems provide the potential for new forms of both crime and

terrorism. Although few well-known events have occurred so far, they include a range of prospective failures from chaos created in baggage-handling systems to an in-flight collision. Industry and governments are extremely sensitive even to the appearance of threats and vulnerabilities. A collapse of public confidence in civil aviation safety, and a failure to manage public expectation, may have serious and widespread economic and social consequences.

4. There are near-universal international forums for cooperation already in existence concerning air transport. Prominent among these are international agreements that go back to 1919, with the dawn of international commercial aviation immediately after World War I. Even then, the unique vulnerabilities of aircraft and the potential for the loss of life resulted in cooperative agreements to improve safety. As Mariano-Florentino Cuéllar, of Stanford's Consortium for Research on Information Security and Policy (CRISP), describes, these ultimately have expanded to include a major new focus on the intentional acts of criminals and terrorists to interfere with air transport either in the air or on the ground. Around 180 sovereign countries are signatories to these agreements, putting them among the most universally accepted of international agreements. They have arguably been very effective in that they have denied havens to attackers and served as umbrella agreements for other cooperative efforts that have collectively done much to curtail physical terrorism and to apprehend and punish people who engage in attacks against civil aviation.

For all these reasons, we believe that it would be timely and prudent to devote attention to developing explicit forms of international cooperation to deal with the vulnerabilities of and prospective threats to this infrastructure. It is a good example of an important sector whose protection can be pursued quickly and within the context of an existing and near-universal international regime that has already proved itself effective against similar problems over a long period of time. Dealing with the problems of cyber crime and terrorism in one major sector may also serve as a useful example and precedent for others, or for international cooperation more generally.

To these ends, Whiteman presents a comprehensive overview of the problems of security in civil aviation. These include an overview of threatening information operations and a description of important forms of international cooperation, including the constructive roles played by the International Civil Aviation Organization (ICAO), which was created under the 1944 Chicago Convention and now operates under the United Nations. He pays particular attention to issues of prevention. Cuéllar then reviews the existing international agreements for the protection of civil aviation against terrorist attacks. He identifies some problems related to attacks via information systems that are not covered by existing conventions and, in keeping with a focus on international agreements elsewhere in this volume, proposes a draft extension to the 1971 Montreal Convention to rectify these problems. Both Whiteman and Cuéllar make it clear that civil aviation safety and security have greatly benefited from an effective and sustained regime of de facto cooperation under the framework of an extensive international treaty structure. We would hope this will be explicitly extended to cover information systems.

The Civil
Aviation Analogy

PART II

Cyber Terrorism and
Civil Aviation

H. H. Whiteman

Often, when cyber terrorism is addressed in the media, one of the examples provided to illustrate the potential damage that can be done is the possibility of downing aircraft in flight or tampering with air traffic control in ways to cause aircraft to crash. This image of civil aviation as a potential target for cyber terrorists is a chilling one, but it paints a worst-case scenario that, in many respects, misses the point about cyber terrorism. Is there a threat? The answer is yes, but with many qualifications.

I. Cyber Terrorism and
Information Operations

If we view cyber terrorism in a narrow sense, it essentially becomes an extension of traditional terrorism into the realm of information technology. Although there is no internationally agreed-upon definition of traditional terrorism per se (the term used in civil aviation is acts of unlawful interference), central characteristics include politically or otherwise motivated use of violence directed at civilians by a group or individual in order to influence public perceptions. Terrorism in this sense can and does apply to the cyber world. There is clearly the potential for individuals with political and/or religious motivations to make use of information technology tools to abuse, tamper, or corrupt IT-based data or control processes, which could result in severe injury or death—rail-switching systems for example. Yet if we limit ourselves to the realm of what I shall refer to as traditional terrorism, we risk focusing on highly unlikely occurrences that constitute the worst-case scenarios. Such focus adds little value in developing a risk-management approach to dealing with the problem.

Cyber terrorism must be considered to include the full range of threats, vulnerabilities, risks, and technological matters that anyone employing IT systems at the core and even on the periphery of their business must contend with today. In Canada, the term that has been adopted to reflect this range of issues is Information Operations, or IO. The current Canadian definition explains IO as "actions taken in support of national objectives which influence decision-makers by affecting others' information while exploiting and protecting one's own information."[1] This definition is admittedly broad and limits itself to addressing national objectives, but it does point to realities that in essence constitute a qualitatively different operational environment that contains many more uncertainties than the one we were function-

---

1. See *Canadian Forces Information Operations*, Doctrine Document B-GG-005-004/AF-032 (April 15, 1998), and the Canadian Forces policy document on IO.

ing within only ten to fifteen years ago. Some of the characteristics of this IO environment include:

- information and decision-making architectures not usually included in information technology security are brought into play as potential sources of vulnerability[2]

- traditional conflict and warfare situations, nontraditional forms of conflict, and peace time environments are within the scope of inquiry

- potential scale of harm is huge

- adversaries are anonymous and include everything from individual recreational hackers to organized state-led initiatives

- there is a multiplicity of targets, traditional and nontraditional

- technology employed for attacks is simple, cheap, and widely available

- early warning indicators of attack are available only when voluntarily provided

- remedies or countermeasures are poorly defined and not readily available

- political, temporal, and geographical boundaries disappear

2. The types of threats involved and their sources vary considerably and both are estimated to be growing at an accelerated pace. See *Critical Foundations: Protecting America's Infrastructures*, Report by the President's Commission on Critical Infrastructure Protection, p. 9, released in October 1997, on increases in information technology expertise and tools. The report is available in its entirety at http://www.pccip.gov/pccip. For a discussion of types of threat and their sources, see *Information Warfare and the Canadian Forces*, document no. 1350-004-D001, Version 1 (May 9, 1996), prepared for Lcdr R. Garigue SITS/ADM(DIS) and T. Romet GDInt/J2 Scientific and Technical, National Defence Headquarters, Ottawa, Ontario, available at ⟨*http://www.dnd.ca/diso/library/lib_e.htm*⟩.

- technological advances create an extremely fluid threat environment[3]

The range of potential perpetrators and intentions in the IO environment is probably the most troubling aspect of this new reality. The availability on the Internet of easy-to-use tools to disable, disrupt, or corrupt systems is astonishing. In addition, the anonymity provided by the Internet may facilitate or encourage individuals to engage in activity or behavior that they otherwise avoid, and there is litle likelihood of being caught. Several high-profile cases involving concerted attacks directed against American government systems were what appear to be the work of thrill-seeking teenagers. The IO environment, therefore, is one of multiple, often unknown attackers, and a wide array of targets, whereas cyber terrorism per se represents a small but potential growth area.

2. Civil Aviation Security, IO, and Critical Infrastructure Protection

The quality of a country's infrastructure is vital to the prosperity and well-being of its citizens. It can be understood as the physical and informational frame upon which an economy depends. Its components include: transportation, energy production and storage, water supply, emergency services, government services, banking and finance, and telecommunications.[4]

The following figures illustrate the critical nature of the transportation sector in Canada. The transportation sector accounted for 3.9 percent of Canada's GDP in 1998 and directly employed approxi-

---

3. This list is inspired by the discussion of the nature of information warfare in *Information Warfare: Legal, Regulatory, Policy and Organizational Considerations for Assurance*, 2d ed., Joint Campaign (July 4, 1996), pp. 1-17–1-18. Available in its entirety at ⟨*http://www.infowar.com/mil_c4i/joint/joint.html-ssi*⟩.

4. This follows in part the breakdown used in the October 1997 *Critical Foundations: Protecting America's Infrastructures*, the report by the President's Commission on Critical Infrastructure Protection.

mately 730,000 people, accounting for a 6.4 percent share of total employment. Government spending (all levels) on transportation for the 1997–98 fiscal year was $17 billion; investment in transportation by governments and businesses averaged $18.8 billion per year between 1993 and 1996. In 1997, tourist spending in Canada totaled $44 billion, 40 percent of which was on transportation.

Threats to and the protection of components of the national infrastructure, both physical and informational, have long been part of defense planning and operational activities in both peace and conflict. Over the last few decades, technological advances have brought qualitative changes to large segments of the infrastructure, particularly in the manner in which they operate, the way they are managed, and the extent to which they are interdependent. These changes have resulted in important gains in efficiency of service, lowered costs, and expanded markets, but they have also increased the number and types of vulnerabilities within the infrastructure, particularly from an information management perspective.[5]

One way to view the increased vulnerability of the infrastructure is to examine the change in the context within which the infrastructure operates. It is in this light that the concept of IO becomes useful in

5. The term National Information Infrastructure (NII) is frequently used to describe the dependency on information that exists in the functioning of the various components of the infrastructure. The United States Army gives the following definition: "A series of components, including the collection of public and private high-speed, interactive, narrow and broadband networks. NII is the satellite, terrestrial and wireless technologies that deliver content to home, business and other public and private institutions. It is the information and content that flows over the infrastructure in the form of databases, the written word, television, computer software, etc. It is the computers, televisions and other products that people employ to access the infrastructure. It is the people who will provide, manage and generate new information, and those that help others to do the same. The NII is a term that encompasses all these components and captures the vision of a nation-wide, invisible, seamless, dynamic web of transmission mechanisms, information appliances, content and people. The global accessibility and use of information in the NII is especially critical given the increasing globalization of markets, resources and economies." From FM 100-6, *Information Operations*, U.S. Army Training and Doctrine Command (October 2, 1995), quoted from *Information Warfare and the Canadian Forces*, document no. 1350-004-D001, Version 1 (May 9, 1996).

analyzing infrastructure vulnerabilities. Much of what has changed in the infrastructure is the way operations are performed, controlled, and monitored. Increasingly, various components of the infrastructure are automated and rely on remote monitoring and control, such as Supervisory Control and Data Acquisition (SCADA) systems, in the conduct of operations. Another aspect of automation in the infrastructure has been the increasing reliance on commercial-off-the-shelf (COTS) information technology products to replace aging custom-engineered systems such as those used in air traffic control.

For decades, the automated systems in use in civil aviation were custom engineered, designed to fail-safe in crisis or unusual circumstances. Although this still holds true today with respect to highly robust system designs, the progressive inclusion of COTS technology in large systems, combined with the greater access and easy-to-use tools that can permit interference (point-and-click virus labs, "how to" guides to hacking, etc.) have raised concerns about how secure civil aviation systems really are.

The short and immediate answer is that, currently, civil aviation systems are quite secure. First of all, most systems still have significant custom-engineered components not easily accessible or understandable even by adept attackers. Civil aviation systems are also inherently robust, having strong backup mechanisms, either built-in or alternate (human), which are regularly tested in the course of circumstances such as power cuts to control towers and erroneous automated flight data. And new systems are, more often than not, engineered or configured within an elaborate security architecture meant to reduce to a minimum the potential for improper use or willful interference. One more very important consideration—related to the robustness aspect—is that the possibility of system failure or breakdown is a central feature of the design in that it is always a consideration and is addressed through the inclusion of redundant or parallel systems and subsystems. Systems are designed with the requirement that there be no single point of failure. In this sense, civil aviation systems are considered extremely hard targets for an IO attack, regardless of its origin.

There is, however, another set of challenges to the vulnerability of civil aviation systems—what has been termed "the insider problem." This has long been a concern in "traditional" aviation security, and one can recall several incidents in which airline or airport employees, or persons posing as such, facilitated or perpetrated acts of unlawful interference with civil aviation. The IO concern that arises is that of the potential for tampering with or modifying source code or specifications included in installation or maintenance manuals, embedded components, and flight management systems, for example, by people having intimate knowledge of a given system. Modifications could be introduced at several points during the manufacturing or maintenance processes, and could result in system failure not addressable by existing backup systems and procedures. The IO issue, in other words, expands the range of potential failures to include some that are not addressed in normal system design. Although such occurrences are deemed to be highly unlikely, windows of opportunity exist and could be exploited by entities on the high end of the threat spectrum—that is, states or terrorist organizations possessing a high degree of technical sophistication.

Some of the specific areas where such opportunities could be exploited include flight management system data, software-based flight control systems (flight control logic), parts manufacturing (specification modification), and maintenance specification modification. Yet, though windows for unlawful interference with these systems do exist, many if not most of them, particularly those involving actual aircraft operations, are extremely well protected, not only by their design and the sheer level of expert knowledge involved but by the administrative processes that are integrated in the elaboration of these systems (multilevel certification by external bodies).

There exists yet another order of potential IO problem areas with regard to civil aviation. These are areas that may be more easily targeted by a recreational or casual hacker or a determined and organized attacker (state or terrorist group)—areas that, if successfully targeted, could disrupt civil aviation operations on a broad scale. These are power distribution, communication lines (telephone), and administrative systems. Some examples of critical, while not particularly complex, systems, include electric power to the control tower (failure over extended period); phone lines, both for tower communications (emergency services access—fire, ambulance, police, weather conditions) and radar (radar data runs on dedicated rented phone lines); electric power for airport lighting, ventilation, etc.; computer reservation systems; passenger manifest data; physical access control; and passenger/baggage matching systems.

Disruption in these areas can have an immediate and significant impact (ripple effect) on the civil aviation system. Given the highly interdependent nature of an infrastructure that often extends beyond national borders, localized disruptions can severely affect larger systems. Disruptions at a major hub such as Toronto can have grave consequences for national systems in terms of flight reassignments and delays, which can result in significant financial losses for the industry as well as potential longer-term effects on passenger and public confidence in the system as a whole. In addition, such disruption can affect the operations of the entire range of service providers and other transportation sector players that feed into the civil aviation system, either directly or indirectly, such as air navigation system, catering, mail and cargo delivery, passenger rail, and cruise ship operations.

In summary, it is clear that IO threats are a matter of concern for civil aviation. The greatest potential threat is not the threat posed to aviation-specific systems, but rather the threat to those systems that support them, such as electrical power distribution.

3. Prevention—Canada's Way Ahead

One of the first questions a policymaker faces is where to focus limited funds and resources to obtain the best result. In addressing current IO challenges, there are two general paths followed, most often in conjunction: (1) to focus on identifying and prosecuting perpetrators, bringing them to justice in the face of tremendous hurdles (technolog-

ical, jurisdictional); (2) prevention, whereby vulnerabilities are identified and possibly corrected, in areas of information technology and
management. Ideally, both the preventive and prosecution components should be pursued, but the preventive route yields potentially
greater immediate results in that it ultimately reduces the overall vulnerability of the infrastructure by eliminating system holes and by
educating users. Raising awareness levels is a critical component in
pursuing the preventive agenda. The degree of sophistication of an
attacker needs to be greater in the face of a more secure system that is
managed with sound security administration practices (password
change schedule, strict access permissions control, personnel screening, etc.).

One question that arises in pursuing the preventive agenda is the
possibility of conflict between its objectives and those of the prosecu-
tion/administration of justice agenda. Information gathered in the
course of an investigation, particularly relating to technical methods
and approaches, can often be critical in addressing vulnerabilities, but
the necessity of protecting evidence prevents it from being released. In
such cases the potential benefits in terms of awareness and the elimi-
nation of vulnerabilities can be greatly reduced. Policymakers have to
address this issue and develop mechanisms that permit greater access
to and distribution of investigation-based information.

Although Canada has not yet issued a definitive policy on critical
infrastructure protection, the focus in most departments, other than
enforcement bodies, appears to be on prevention within the limited
budgets available—on vulnerability assessments, system mapping, reviews of IT security system policies, standards, and practices in order
to improve the government's preventive posture. Several business-
related initiatives are also under way in government that are likely to
further the preventive agenda, including the Public Key Infrastructure
(PKI) initiative, which will give the government the security it needs
to conduct its business electronically in order to improve service delivery. This initiative ties into Canada's e-commerce strategy, which aims
to create the conditions for national e-commerce to grow. Some other

components of the e-commerce initiative are a policy on cryptography, establishment of a legal framework for digital signatures and electronic documents, and legislation governing the protection of personal information in the cyber domain.

A preventive approach has also been adopted to address threats in the civil aviation security area. Work with the civil aviation industry has been done to ensure that there is at the very least a recognition that the operational environment has changed and that some thought needs to be given to a number of previously unheard of threats that may constitute problems in the future. In Canada, most of the transportation infrastructure is in private hands, and therefore the elements that drive the risk management process in industry are somewhat different from what they are in government. The challenge with industry currently is that of demonstrating a clear threat. While there are few precedents that would compel industry or even Transport Canada to act in order to modify the preventive security posture of civil aviation in Canada, there are certainly enough data (mostly of U.S. origin) to investigate what the IO environment needs in the long run. The point that has to be made to industry is that, though catastrophic failure resulting in mass casualties is unlikely, there may well be incidents that will have some serious economic impact.

Looking at the various arrangements that exist for effective international cooperation in general, the work and structure of the International Civil Aviation Organization (ICAO) provide much food for thought.

4. The International Civil Aviation Organization as a Model for International Cooperation on Cyber Terrorism

The International Civil Aviation Organization was established in 1944, by means of the Chicago Convention, to develop international standards and recommended practices for the aviation industry. Now, over 180 states are parties to this Convention. Its basic objective is the development of safe (including secure), regular, efficient, and economical air transport. Acts of unlawful interference such as terrorism are a primary area of concern, and security is one of its official priorities.

The Chicago Convention as a multilateral international convention specifically addresses preventive security practices for international civil aviation in its Annex 17, adopted by the ICAO Council in 1974. The security standards and recommended practices contained in Annex 17, together with the implementation guidance contained in the ICAO Security Manual, essentially establish the preventive security regime for civil aviation. Once standards are developed, states parties must file a public difference if they do not agree.

Besides the ICAO, there are other multilateral international security conventions in place that deal with response to acts of unlawful interference against aviation. These include the Tokyo Convention of 1963, which established criminal jurisdiction; the Hague Convention of 1970, which removed safe haven and freedom from prosecution; and the Montreal Convention of 1971, which extended the range of offenses that could be pursued. The Convention on the Marking of Plastic Explosives for the Purpose of Detection, which came into force in June 1998, constitutes a departure from these conventions in that it focuses on the prevention aspect.

At this time there is probably little in terms of incidents or trends that would move the ICAO AvSec (Aviation Security) Panel to address the issue of cyber terrorism as a priority, but ICAO has nonetheless achieved much in terms of cooperation and consensus that may be helpful in supplying best practices and guidance for cooperation in the IO field. In fact, the two areas, civil aviation and the information technology infrastructure are similar in many ways: they present major challenges to safety and security; they represent a serious threat to their users if attacked; they have become critically important to national and international commerce; and neither can be contained by national boundaries. The similarities are useful to keep in mind when going over what type of preventive security regime has been achieved by ICAO.

The major elements in the preventive security program that states parties to ICAO Annex 17 observe are the establishment of national organizations, cooperation with other states, establishing preventive security measures, managing response to unlawful acts, and establishing security-related planning and training. As the record indicates, the efforts of ICAO member states appear to have had a positive impact on the state of civil aviation security (Figure 1).

A more detailed analysis of Annex 17 shows that the agreed-upon framework offers many concrete measures, the structure of which could potentially be applied or adapted to counter IO threats.

Establishing national organizations to develop and implement plans and procedures. The national organization should participate by: designating an administrative authority, establishing a security program, reviewing national threat level and adjusting as necessary, defining and allocating tasks between state, operators, etc., establishing airport security committees, ensuring the development of contingency plans, ensuring the development of training programs, conducting background checks on those implementing security, requiring operators providing service to implement security programs, and promoting security R&D. Many of these measures could be applicable in the establishment of a national IO security program. A national organization would be necessary to manage, guide, and focus development and to provide a conduit for information exchange. An international organization, similar to the ICAO, would of course also be required in order to harmonize and coordinate the efforts of national organizations.

Cooperating with other states to adapt their security programs: by making written programs available to other states, including appropriate clauses in bilateral agreements, meeting requests of other states for special measures, cooperating in the development of training programs, and cooperating in security R&D. These measures, in addition to fostering compatibility and adding the benefits of world-class knowledge and experience, would promote participation and cooperation and help to ensure that less privileged states reap the same security rewards as wealthier or more technologically advanced states.

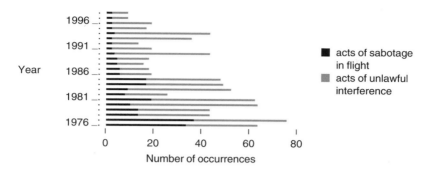

Fig. 1.   ICAO figures, 1976–1996.

Establishing preventive measures to prevent weapons, explosives, and other dangerous devices from being introduced by any means whatsoever: by preventing unauthorized carriage of weapons; conducting pre-flight checks to discover suspicious objects; surveying, inspecting, and testing to ensure security implementation; controlling transfer of passengers and goods to prevent introduction of weapons; establishing identification and access control procedures; and ensuring that design and construction of facilities take account of security needs.

This is probably an area where the IO threat would pose the most challenge. Concrete measures that address operational issues must be developed if an international convention is to mean anything. The pace of technological change makes this requirement particularly difficult to address, and this is where increasing awareness through structured programs focusing on industry/government consultations and cooperation can produce significant results, such as standard industry-wide strategies to present and address issues and problems.

Managing response to unlawful acts: by taking measures for safety of persons subject to acts of unlawful interference, exchanging information on incidents with other states, providing the ICAO with information as soon as possible after such incidents; expeditiously notifying all implicated states and the ICAO; and reevaluating security to remedy weaknesses subsequent to incidents. It is imperative to mitigate harm caused by incidents as expeditiously and efficiently as possible.

These measures are meant to ensure that response by the concerned community is as swift and complete as possible.

Miscellaneous measures from other ICAO Annexes that are relevant to security: broadcasting warnings if subject to unlawful interference; establishing training programs to minimize the consequences of unlawful interference; permitting tax/duty free importation of security equipment; assisting, on a priority basis, aircraft subject to unlawful interference; notifying rescue centers, operators, other aircraft operating in the vicinity; establishing emergency plans for threats, fires, sabotage, natural disasters, etc.; and periodically testing plans and revising them as appropriate.

The first thing to examine if ICAO is to be considered, if not as a model, then certainly as a source of best practices and lessons learned, is what forms the basis for consensus. Why has ICAO been successful in obtaining consensus and building agreement on security issues? There is general agreement that unlawful interference with civil aviation is deemed by all to be contrary to the public good and to the main objective of preserving human life. The stigma of terrorism is a long-lasting one for any state or industry associated with it (e.g., *Achille Lauro*—U.S.$ 300 million immediate direct loss), and those that carry the stigma pay a heavy price. This general, unconditional agreement—that terrorism is to be done away with and its perpetrators brought to justice—is the fundamental underpinning of consensus building within ICAO on the security front.

A consensus analogous to the one that exists on civil aviation terrorism is difficult to achieve in the area of IO threats, in spite of the similarities noted above. A consensus for IO may be more difficult because of the remoteness of the threat to human life: the existing body of incidents that can clearly make the link between IO-type attacks and the loss of life is probably not sufficient to make the case in favor of basing consensus on the protection of human life. Moreover, we do not have any internationally accepted definition of what constitutes IO threats or even cyber terrorism.

Yet there are sufficient data to support at least a partial agreement on the basis of the potential for serious harm—individual, social, and/ or economic. The case can be made that potential widespread disruptions in economic activity brought on by an infrastructure attack, regardless of source, are serious enough to pursue international cooperation.

It is also noteworthy that ICAO has been successful in building consensus on commercial matters. One positive result has been the harmonization of minimum regulatory standards and practices (in no way related to security) that facilitate international aviation. The underlying consensus-building motivation on commercial issues has been a belief in an open system in which interoperability is the norm. The creation of an international voluntary regime that would establish minimum standards for a secure infrastructure environment might go part of the way in addressing a common response to IO-type threats, permitting the establishment of a baseline for managing risk in the IO environment. Some examples of elements that could constitute this sort of regime include consumer protection laws extending to the cyber domain, the existence of a national IO threat information clearinghouse, making cyber crime a punishable offense under law, having open access to strong encryption, and having information and data handling and storage standards.

The list of ICAO preventive security measures becomes relevant here. An international regime could take the form of an ISO-type approach to basic quality standards that businesses and/or countries could strive for. This would in effect create a preventive regime framework standard against which companies and countries could be assessed.

The IO threat is so broad and the interdependencies it underscores (power distribution, telecommunications) so numerous that addressing it sectorally, such as in an ICAO-type forum, may not be practical. Because the IO operational environment cuts across all economic activity, it could probably be best addressed in an international forum with a broad mandate, and in international organizations such as the International Organization for Standardization (ISO) and the International Telecommunications Union (ITU). Nonsector-specific business organizations could also be considered, although the grounds for consensus may be somewhat at odds with what could be possible within an international state-based entity. Some business organizations that are currently addressing issues surrounding e-commerce include the Alliance for Global Business (AGB) and the International Chamber of Commerce (ICC).

5. Government and Industry

One of the difficulties in addressing the issue of IO-type threats and, by extension, critical infrastructure protection in Canada is that most of the components of critical infrastructure are now managed not by government but by private entities. The main thrust in Canada for commercializing the management of much of the infrastructure was to increase efficiency and to have the users of the systems—not all taxpayers—foot the bill. This push has also included an effort to reduce the regulatory burden on these entities. So the challenge we face in Canada at this juncture is to convince industry, without resorting to regulation, that IO threats are a problem and that critical infrastructure protection is a new part of the equation of doing business. This places the onus on industry for action and requires that government act not as a regulator and enforcer but as an enabler and facilitator. This is certainly the route the Canadian government has taken with regard to electronic commerce.

The transportation industry in Canada recognizes that IO threats, at the very least, are one more item to consider in managing risks. The problem is that very few probably realize the extent to which these threats could rapidly become serious problems affecting their operations. Keeping industry abreast of these developments through security awareness and consultation forums is part of our role as a government; where danger to the public is not voluntarily addressed by the private sector, government can implement enforceable requirements.

Cooperation with industry is central to developing a workable approach to tackling the IO issue. This not only includes those areas dealing directly with infrastructure but also must involve manufacturers and providers of IT services. Consultation forums involving all levels of government and a cross-section of industry may prove beneficial for airing problems, devising common approaches, and sharing best practices. This strategy worked very well for Canada in preparing for and addressing the millennium-bug problem. Raising awareness in government, industry, and the general population was key to achieving the critical mass necessary for significant remedial action to be undertaken and central coordination permitted to maintain focus. The same sort of vehicle could be considered for the IO issue.

Canada is in the process of developing a national policy on critical infrastructure protection that will very likely include a significant role for private industry in supplying expertise and guidance to government and those entities that manage our critical infrastructure. The policy is also likely to support the creation of a Computer Emergency Response Team or CERT-type body that could serve as a clearinghouse for information and advice on system vulnerabilities and solutions. None of this is yet defined or agreed upon, but one thing is clear: government and industry will have to work in partnership to address this issue successfully.

CHAPTER 3

The Civil
Aviation Analogy

PART III

Past as Prologue:
International Aviation Security Treaties as
Precedents for International Cooperation
Against Cyber Terrorism and Cyber Crimes

Mariano-Florentino Cuéllar

The rise of cyberspace may seem unprecedented, but in some respects it bears a striking resemblance to the development of aviation—a technology that also effectively shrank the world and altered life during times of war and peace.[1] In less than a century, civil aviation went

---

1. The dictionary defines cyberspace as "the online world of computer networks." (*Merriam-Webster's Collegiate Dictionary*, 1997). For the purposes of this paper, the term "cyberspace" denotes the multifaceted global network of computerized information exchange (including the Internet) made possible by information technology. "Cyber crime" refers to crimes committed within the scope of (or greatly facilitated by) cyberspace. Descriptions of aviation technology suggest the similarities with cyberspace. Martin Sharp, upon completing a flight in the first jet airliner (the de Havilland Comet), declared, "One arrives over distant landmarks in an incredibly

from being exotic to being essential. In the process, states with considerable political, economic, and legal differences were forced to cooperate to improve the security of civil aviation. As the following pages discuss, the extent of this cooperation was unprecedented.

I. Overview

Over the years the system of international law protecting civil aviation security has developed three features, all of which are deeply relevant to the international challenge of policing cyberspace. First, the system combines regulatory authority and criminal enforcement. Second, the system has expanded over time to encompass new threats affecting the security of the network (in this case, civil aviation), and to include an ever growing cluster of nations. Third, the system exhibits what economists term "path dependence": initial focused steps favoring legal cooperation made the system safer, which increased the system's economic value and thereby encouraged countries to take further steps toward legal cooperation even in the face of domestic political opposition. Airspace and cyberspace are obviously different, but certain institutional characteristics of cyberspace mirror those of the international civil aviation network in critical ways. In both cases, the relevant economic activity takes place in a decentralized, interdependent network that needs to be policed in the face of rapidly changing technology. For this reason, the system of international legal cooperation to promote aviation security serves as an engaging precedent for the modern challenge of international cooperation against cyber threats.[2]

---

short time but without the sense of having traveled." Quoted in ⟨*http://www.skygod.com/quotes*⟩, accessed July 15, 1999.

2. The focus on aviation is the result of a survey of international cooperation and treaty law conducted to evaluate suitable models for cooperation. Among other areas, we surveyed cooperation against narcotics trafficking and money laundering, nonaviation-related terrorism, and economic cooperation in postal services, telecommunications, and resolution of the Year 2000 computer problem. The international law framework governing civil aviation security appeared especially promising as a

Yet, ironically, these emerging cyber threats also point to the short-comings in the existing aviation security system. Civil aviation depends on networked technology infrastructures to provide electric power, remote sensing capabilities, and communications. All these infrastructures are vulnerable to cyber threats; a disruption in one can cause fatalities as surely as an explosive charge nestled in the belly of an airliner. Accordingly, cyber threats are not materially different from the threats that spurred adoption of the aviation security treaties in the first place. For all the present system's laudable achievements, the framework of international law protecting civil aviation is not fully prepared to address the emerging cyber threats made possible by increasingly accessible technologies. Given that deficiency, draft treaty language is proposed herein that would provide enhanced coverage of cyber offenses targeting civil aviation. In addition to addressing specific threats in the sector, the proposed language illustrates a promising approach to addressing international cyber threats by focusing on an infrastructure that has already garnered considerable international legal attention and by expanding the existing framework to cover the most prominent and unpredictable new threats from cyberspace.

To make these arguments, this part of Chapter 3 proceeds as follows. Section 2 focuses on the structural barriers to international cooperation that states have overcome to build a legal framework improving aviation security. Section 3 describes what legal mechanisms states have used to overcome these barriers in the case of civil aviation security, focusing particularly on the advantages of developing both an enforcement and a regulatory component to improve security. Section 4 concentrates on why the aviation issue gave states a distinctive reason to overcome structural barriers through innovative legal approaches to cooperation. Section 5 then discusses the short-comings of the system in addressing cyber threats, and proposes draft treaty language to address these shortcomings. Finally, section 6 con-

---

model for cooperation against cyber threats. See sect. 2 below for a fuller discussion. For additional discussion of international legal arrangements that serve as effective analogies for international cooperation against cyber threats, see Chap. 6.

cludes by observing that the use of explicit treaties (as opposed to informal agreements) has given the international civil aviation security system a means to promote deterrence, grow international consensus, and enhance technical cooperation against threats. When existing treaties lay such a foundation, advocates for international cooperation against cyber threats can achieve considerable gains by amending treaties dealing with specific infrastructures (such as aviation) to encompass cyber threats. In contrast, advocates of a comprehensive international accord on cyber threats face far greater obstacles, because even in the twenty-first century, states continue to harbor concerns that broad international crime treaties arouse domestic political opposition and encroach on their sovereignty.

2. Structural Barriers to Achieving International Cooperation

To build an effective international system protecting civil aviation security, states have overcome a number of structural challenges.[3] Both domestic and transnational political developments alter the context for cooperation, often encouraging states to prefer flexible informal agreements instead of explicit treaty obligations. The framework under which international cooperation can achieve a particular goal must frequently contend with technological complexity and innovation. Moreover, all cooperative arrangements are subject to enforcement challenges. Below, I analyze these challenges and explain why the use of explicit treaties—an approach that has characterized civil aviation security—is likely to produce more lasting results.

An initial challenge is the reluctance of states to bind themselves legally through the formal use of an explicit treaty rather than an informal agreement. In civil aviation security, informal agreements have always been supplemented by treaties. It may seem self-evident that a treaty is preferable to an informal agreement: after all, formal

---

3. In sect. 4, I argue that international cyber crime cooperation faces many of the same structural challenges that have been overcome in civil aviation security.

treaties have been the hallmark of the civil aviation security system and are frequently the capstones of international negotiation to address transnational challenges ranging from environmental protection to migration.[4] Yet informal agreements and cooperative ventures have played an important role promoting cooperation, for several reasons. Informal agreements are more flexible, allowing countries more latitude to change their observance of terms in response to evolving domestic and transnational political developments. In the criminal context, only significant criminal offenses—such as murder and large-scale narcotics trafficking—have been considered extraditable crimes. For a variety of other offenses, a host of organizations and actors still have significant incentives to cooperate through informal agreements. For example, there is no significant multilateral agreement specifically focused on combating credit card fraud. Nonetheless, domestic law enforcement agencies, the private sector, and consumers still have strong incentives to cooperate in addressing such fraud. Although credit card fraud is still a nettlesome problem, some law enforcement agencies and analysts report that projected increases in these offenses have not materialized.

As an example of the advantages and limitations of informal agreements, consider the case of money laundering. In spite of an apparent consensus on the deplorability of money laundering and narcotics trafficking and a great deal of international interest, the international agreements covering these activities have not proved to be entirely suitable models for international cyber crime cooperation. The major international mechanism currently addressing money laundering enforcement is the Organization for Economic Cooperation and Development's (OECD's) Financial Action Task Force (FATF).[5] Under OECD auspices, the work of FATF centers on promoting the adoption and implementation of a basic document containing forty major recommendations to enhance laws against money laundering. This doc-

4. See sect. 3.
5. For a discussion of the creation of the FATF, see FATF, Tenth Annual Report, July 2, 1999.

ument does not have the binding force of a treaty, but a large number of OECD members (including the world's ten largest economies) have made a political commitment to implementing the forty recommendations.

Although FATF has achieved some noteworthy results, money laundering presents a striking opportunity for countries to expand formal cooperation to address the problem meaningfully. Among its achievements, FATF has developed a standard definition of the money laundering offense (though not all its predicates), and has provided technical assistance to members and nonmembers attempting to develop anti-money laundering measures; it has also instituted a system for mutual evaluations of member countries. The use of an international agreement such as FATF does not mean that treaty law gives states carte blanche with respect to dirty money, but the absence of a treaty means participants retain considerable flexibility to choose their enforcement strategies. After all, money laundering can have a large number of predicate crimes, including terrorism, narcotics trafficking, fraud, and arms trafficking. And without a specific treaty-defined conception of predicate offenses, combating laundering activity can mean different things to countries depending on their predicate offenses. Moreover, the financial system has grown increasingly global and efficient in transacting its business. Although FATF's membership constitutes an important bloc, international movements of money allow numerous jurisdictions with smaller economies and strict bank secrecy laws to play a role in money laundering, and even the members of FATF themselves vary in the strength of their bank secrecy laws. As a result, it has become more difficult to control illicit financial flows through regulation or criminal investigation that targets a single national financial system.[6] At the same time, lucrative criminal activity

6. Examples of transnational money laundering activity abound, but a simple hypothetical case serves to illustrate the principle. As long as money laundering within and across national borders persists—activity that can take place in Japan, Switzerland, and a myriad other locations—financial regulation and investigation targeting only Japan could hardly dent such a system. The best that such a domestic strategy

has a more global scope, and can spread its negative externalities over a greater proportion of countries.

The persistent reliance on international agreements arises because obstacles to cooperation counterbalance incentives for treaty use. Although crimes such as money laundering have negative externalities for many states (where crime becomes more profitable), the activity can generate large returns for other states, especially bank secrecy havens whose bank balances swell with potentially ill-obtained money. Finally, economic interests (in this case financial institutions) within the states can perceive a threat from treaties that explicitly or implicitly impose additional requirements on their behavior. As a result, significant multilateral treaties to control money laundering have been out of reach, and interested parties have instead turned to informal agreements. Thus, although the FATF recommendations serve as an auspicious beginning, most recently extending even to Internet banking transactions and Internet gambling, they lack a reliable enforcement mechanism even for member states, let alone for nonmembers. For these reasons, this paper supports treaty language to complement the preventive system in the aviation context (discussed in section 5 below), and a broader treaty (discussed in Chapter 6 of this volume) to cover cyber threats beyond aviation.[7]

Technological complexity and change can also become structural obstacles to cooperation, making specific treaty language harder to define and exacerbating the need for preventive as well as enforcement approaches. In light of these obstacles, centralized technical organizations, though they do not guarantee success, make an important contribution to the advancement of safety and security goals. In the context of aviation security, the International Civil Aviation Organi-

could achieve would be to increase the costs of the initial placement of resources in a domestic financial institution.

7. Even the preventive system that characterizes aviation has a nexus to treaty law (see sect. 2 above). Both the civil aviation context and the other areas of international cooperation surveyed in this project suggest that treaty commitments change states' political incentive and encourage cooperation even beyond the provisions of a treaty.

zation plays such a role. The ICAO lacks the power to sanction members for noncompliance with treaties or its own regulations, but it serves as a forum of exchange and consultation.[8] With more and better information, key member states can then coordinate their activities or act unilaterally. Generally, treaties dealing with civil aviation and other commercial matters, such as telecommunications, postal cooperation, and the commercial aspect of civil aviation, give rise to an international organization of some type.[9]

Compliance is a further obstacle to cooperation. In this regard, it appears that specific, narrowly drawn offenses have created a regime where compliance is the subject of less controversy. Information is easier to gather and analyze when offenses are clearly defined—compare aviation, for example, to narcotics enforcement, where offenses are wide-ranging but where even a system of "certification" by the United States (backed by threatened sanctions) does not appear to lead to long-term enforcement solutions in countries that are the source of narcotics. Consider also the difficulty of monitoring a country's adherence to the FATF's 40 Recommendations against money laundering. The recommendations are quite broad, and although it may be possible to monitor cash flows, information on aggregate money laundering activity is notoriously difficult to obtain.[10] Since the variable of most direct interest to compliance cannot be monitored directly, assessing compliance requires an analysis of countries' policies against money laundering. Yet even this is not enough, because policies as they exist in theory and as they are implemented in practice may vary considerably, so that a team of experts has to travel to a country to

8. The history of the ICJ provides an apposite illustration of this difficulty. See, e.g., Shabtai Rosenne, *The World Court: What It Is and How It Works* (Norwell, Mass.: Kluuwer Academic, 1989), discussing the limitations faced by the ICJ in building legitimacy for its interpretation of ambiguous provisions in treaties.

9. Hence the Chicago Convention, discussed below, led to the ICAO.

10. See, e.g., Vito Tanzi, "Money Laundering and the International Financial System," IMF Working Paper no. 96/55 (1996). Although the FATF recommendations are not a binding obligation on the same order as those of a formal treaty, countries may have an interest in complying for diplomatic and economic reasons.

find out how a policy is being implemented. The breath of the agreement (that is, its inclusion of financial institution regulation as well as criminal investigation as an aspect of anti-money laundering policy) increases the work of the evaluation team and also the probability that its evaluation will not be accurate.

Finally, the threat of international sanctioning activity can play a positive role in achieving common goals. For example, although the G-7 (now G-8) is not formally empowered to enforce treaty obligations, it coordinated to punish countries that do not comply, as in the 1982 G-7 punishment of Afghanistan by denying it landing rights when it failed to extradite or prosecute the hijackers of a Pakistan International Airlines plane that landed in Afghan territory. As we shall see below, these threats of unilateral or multilateral sanctioning also help enforce ICAO standards and recommended practices, given the organization's lack of extensive tools to compel members to implement the guidelines.[11]

3. International Cooperation to Achieve Civil Aviation Security

Since the time aviation became commercially viable, air safety has been a compelling objective for a large number of states around the world.[12] Given the magnitude of the structural challenges discussed above, it is hardly surprising that the architecture of the current international civil aviation system took shape over most of the twentieth century, beginning with blanket agreements that established a frame-

11. See Pierre de Senarclens, "Governance and the Crisis in the International Mechanisms of Regulation," *International Social Science Journal* 50 (1998): 91, arguing that effective global governance depends on the coordinated action of states in support of international regulatory regimes, since most international organizations are not powerful enough to induce compliance by themselves.

12. Mark W. Zacher with Brent A. Sutton, *Governing Global Networks: International Regimes for Transportation and Communications* (New York: Cambridge University Press, 1996), p. 94: "In probably no other international industry is safety or the prevention of accidents a bigger issue than it is in air transport."

work for international air travel.[13] But if the scope of what was considered to be a safety concern changed over the years, the concern over safety did not change. Early in the twentieth century, countries sought to limit dangerous accidents and commercial crimes.[14] By the middle of the century, terrorism had become a threat throughout the world.[15] The interest in reining in aviation-related terrorism resulted in an incremental series of treaties beginning with the Convention on Offenses and Certain Other Acts Committed on Board Aircraft in 1963 (the Tokyo Convention). Although the present cooperative regime provides a coherent framework for extradition, investigative and regulatory cooperation, and technical assistance, the process that has produced these arrangements thus far suggests that the system may continue to change over time. In succeeding decades, states turned their attention to activities that upset the idealized framework chiseled early in the century. The first such agreements were concerned with airborne threats to aircraft in flight. Later, states agreed that threats to aircraft in flight need not originate in the air, and they developed conventions addressing threats to aircraft preparing for flight, navigation systems, and airports.

13. This discussion only highlights the most significant international civil aviation agreements. For a more all-encompassing discussion of relevant agreements through the late 1980s, see Paul Stephen Dempsey, *Law and Foreign Policy in International Aviation* (Dobbs Ferry, N.Y.: Transnational Publishers, 1987).

14. Commercial crimes were a concern long before terrorism was. For a discussion of the role of commercial crime control in nurturing the infant aviation industry, as it had nurtured crime control in the marine shipping and rail transport domains, see Frederick C. Dorey, *Aviation Security* (New York: Kluuwer, 1983), pp. 106–9.

15. Aviation-related terrorist activity was at first more common in Soviet-bloc countries, but by the late 1950s, Western nations increasingly became the targets of such terrorism. Robert A. Friedlander, *Terrorism: Documents of International and Local Control* (Dobbs Ferry, N.Y.: Oceana Publications, 1984), p. 324, describes the growing interest of the United States and Western Europe in safeguarding aviation security following high-profile aviation security breaches targeting them.

Early Cooperation: Paris and Chicago Conventions

The Air Navigation Convention of 1919 (the Paris Convention) was the first major attempt to develop rules for international civil aviation. The principal objective of the Paris Conference was to establish a system for major countries to consult each other and agree on standards governing transnational civil aviation.[16] To this end, it was attended by representatives from nearly every region of the world, although the initial agenda was set primarily to reflect the interests of European countries.[17] In fulfilling its objective, the Paris Convention had three major substantive concerns. First, it settled much of the ambiguity concerning countries' rights to their airspace; although the treaty included language emphasizing the importance of rights-of-access to nonhostile aircraft, the right of a country to control its airspace was recognized as well. Second, it established a framework for allowing civil flights to occur between countries.[18] Third, it authorized the creation of the International Commission for Air Navigation (ICAN), and airlines created the International Air Traffic Association, to develop safety and technical standards. Significantly, the Paris Convention continued the approach taken in the law of the sea, which distinguished between civil and military vessels requiring access to ports. Like many treaties dealing with economic activity, the treaty depended crucially on countries' interests in maintaining positive reciprocal relations.[19] Unilateral and multilateral sanctions against noncompliance were contemplated.

The Paris Convention was amended several times after it came into force. Because its primary focus was overall cooperation, it did not create obligations that could have any direct relevance to cyber crime

16. Air Navigation Convention, Paris, October 13, 1919, 41 Stat. 1687.

17. Ramon de Murias, *The Economic Regulation of International Air Transport* (Jefferson, N.C.: McFarland, 1989), emphasizes the interest of European nations in creating a reliable system to transport cargo and people across medium-haul routes.

18. This early system preserved virtually all authority that each country had to regulate civil aviation within its borders.

19. This is the case absent greater, countervailing, interests.

or other types of criminal offenses; nonetheless, the parties confirmed that states had jurisdiction to address offenses taking place in their airspace. In instances where offenses occurred over international waters, the country of registry was granted jurisdiction.[20] The system of international cooperation established under the Paris Convention set the stage for future arrangements that targeted criminal offenses against aircraft.

The Convention on Civil Aviation in Chicago in 1944 (the Chicago Convention) sought to fill in the gaps left by the Paris Convention (and its amendments) in establishing an international regime to facilitate transborder civil aviation activity.[21] Negotiated along with the creation of the United Nations' International Civil Aviation Organization (ICAO), the Chicago Convention and its various components constitute the major international civil aviation convention still in force for the United States. As with the Paris Convention, the primary safety-related objectives of the Chicago Convention concerned the prevention of accidents.

The safety measures contemplated by the Chicago Convention were far-reaching. The accord addressed air navigation rules, and led to the further development of the ICAN through the creation of an Air Navigation Commission. It also established a framework to promulgate and evaluate rules on technical equipment, practices for transporting dangerous goods, rescues in cases of accidents, joint investigations of accidents, and even joint financing of air navigation facilities

20. Given the early stage of aviation and the still-nascent concept of airspace, the simple approach to jurisdiction over crimes taken in early civil aviation conventions is understandable.

21. Convention on International Civil Aviation, Chicago, December 7, 1944, 59 Stat. 1693, 84 UNTS 389. Technically, this is only one of several agreements reached in Chicago at the gathering known as the Conference on International Civil Aviation, but it is the broadest in scope. The other three agreements include: (1) the Interim Agreement, dealing with provisions having effect before the Convention took effect; (2) the International Air Transport Agreement; and (3) the International Air Services Transit Agreement—collectively referred to as the "Chicago Convention." See, e.g., Stephen D. McCreary, "The Chicago Convention: Article 22 and the SFAR 40 Episode," *Journal of Air Law and Commerce* 54 (1989): 721, 722.

in Greenland and Iceland. Yet in the area of crime control, the Chicago Convention merely affirmed the Paris Convention's assignment of jurisdiction over criminal acts on board aircraft. If the act was committed while the aircraft was flying over a country's airspace, that country had jurisdiction; if the aircraft was flying over the high seas, which was considered international airspace, the country of registry had jurisdiction. The structure of the Chicago Convention resembled that of the Paris Convention, although the Chicago treaty included a provision allowing an international organization—the ICAO—to issue the equivalent of advisory regulations, known as "Standards and Recommended Practices" (SARPs).[22] In the period following World War II, the system provided enough flexibility to encompass a significant growth in international cooperation to prevent accidents. Just as the growing reliance on cyber systems has engendered broad interest in protecting the integrity of cyberspace, the marked increase in aircraft size and in the volume of air travel played an important role in spurring such cooperation.[23]

The issues addressed at the Chicago Convention highlight some of the similarities and differences between international civil aviation and cyberspace. In both cases, countries have had to overcome technical hurdles to promote efficiency in the network and to reduce accidents. In the aviation context, countries supported the establishment of an international organization (the ICAO) as a means of marshaling, analyzing, and maintaining technical information to service the international civil aviation system.[24] Of course, one significant difference

---

22. See Eugene Sochor, "From the DC-3 to Hypersonic Fight: ICAO in a Changing Environment," *Journal of Air Law and Commerce* 55 (1989): 407, describing the regulatory nature of ICAO SARPs and their evolving effect on the international aviation industry.

23. Zacher with Sutton, *Governing Global Networks*, p. 92, explains the effect of the growing economic importance of civil aviation on international efforts to regulate damage control problems in the field.

24. Certain specialized international organizations exist to deal with specific aspects of cyberspace policy, such as the registration and regulation of domain names on the Internet.

between cyberspace and airspace is that the latter is more obviously linked to a country's physical territory.[25] Computers allow information to travel without obviously impinging on a state's physical sovereignty; aircraft penetrate the airspace of more than one country in the course of international flights. As a result, the Chicago Convention adopted an approach that was protective of countries' rights to their airspace.[26]

The Growing System of International Civil Aviation Security

By the mid-twentieth century, countries began to express concern about the security component of the international aviation system. Yet these concerns remained secondary to the development of an efficient economic network to manage air traffic. Cold War divisions also hampered any sustained focus on civil aviation security. Even in its first half-century, commercial air travel yielded considerable economic

25. Nonetheless, although transactions in cyberspace may appear to take place in a domain that is devoid of links to countries' sovereign territory, in fact they are taking place in real space. The difference is that the jurisdictional rules in force determine precisely where in real space the transactions have taken place. Depending on the rule, a legal system could recognize that the transactions occurred in the physical location of the user(s) who initiated the transaction, in the location of the server(s) containing the software that received the transaction information, or in the location of the server(s) used to access the Internet. In some respects, the issues raised in resolving such conflicts are no different from the issues raised in the Paris and Chicago conventions concerning countries' jurisdiction over crimes occurring on board aircraft. For an analogous discussion of how existing conceptions of jurisdiction can effectively resolve even complex disputes about the control of cyberspace, see Jack L. Goldsmith, "Against Cyberanarchy," *University of Chicago Law Review* 65 (1998): 1199, who argues that, analytically, there is no difference between working out conflict of law issues and jurisdiction issues in real space or cyberspace.

26. Indeed, in some respects the degree of recognition over sovereign airspace even trumped concern over safety. Sovereignty over national airspace could interfere with safety if an aircraft is forced to adopt longer or more dangerous routes when a country denies access to its airspace (or certain portions of it). Although the Chicago Convention does express in general terms that countries should allow innocent passage to civil aircraft attempting to shorten routes, the principle is subject to numerous exceptions, consistent with the concern over sovereignty.

benefits.[27] Unfortunately, commercial aviation also provided a sterling opportunity for militants to call attention to their causes through terrorist acts. The physical isolation of aircraft allows offenders to attempt to wrest control from the pilots—which, because of the technical complexity of modern aircraft, can place hundreds of passengers at risk. As instances of criminal activity on board aircraft mounted—particularly targeting Western countries—the inadequacy of existing international law on the problem became evident.[28] The Tokyo Convention was the first major effort in international cooperation to turn attention directly to terrorism targeting aircraft.[29] Because it was the first such effort and because of the exacerbated sensibilities that countries possess about criminal enforcement, the Tokyo Convention's objectives were limited to offenses taking place on board aircraft in flight. In essence, it required states to take control of an aircraft that had been unlawfully seized, and to return the aircraft to the control of its lawful commander. Significantly, however, the treaty did not clearly specify the obligations of the signatories beyond simply taking control of the aircraft: the state taking custody of the aircraft was not obligated to punish the hijackers or to surrender them to a state requesting extradition. The Tokyo Convention depended on its signatories to

27. See, e.g., Betsy Gidwitz, *The Politics of International Air Transport* (Lexington, Mass.: Lexington Books, 1980), who emphasizes the degree of political interest in civil aviation that was stimulated by the economic consequences of rapid, relatively safe, routine air travel.

28. Between 1949 and 1985, over 1,500 persons were killed in nearly 90 separate bombings and explosions on aircraft. Indeed, in the period 1970–1979 alone, criminal acts against civil aviation resulted in 1,255 deaths, as well as 1,013 wounded and 33,097 persons who were taken hostage. See Henrik Gam, "Liability Damages for Injuries Sustained by Passengers in the Event of Hijacking of Aircraft and Other Violations of Aviation Security," *Lloyds Maritime and Commercial Law Quarterly* 217 (May 1988). The striking figures for the 1970s (accounting for approximately 80 percent of total deaths) help to explain the continuing salience of the issue even after the flurry of treaties negotiated between 1961 and 1971.

29. Convention on Offenses and Certain Other Acts Committed on Board Aircraft, Tokyo, September 14, 1963, 20 U.S.T. 2941. Although other conventions had dealt with crime issues to settle jurisdictional matters, the major safety concern in previous treaties was the prevention of accidents, not the punishment of willful, malevolent actions affecting the international civil aviation system.

police themselves.[30] As was the standard practice, disputes were meant to be settled by negotiation or arbitration. If two countries were unable to agree on an organization to perform the arbitration within six months of the request for arbitration, then either party could submit the dispute to the International Court of Justice (ICJ), consistent with its statute. Because of the added breadth of later conventions (the Hague Convention and the Montreal Convention), the Tokyo Convention has not drawn significant enforcement interest from signatories.

The Convention for the Suppression of Unlawful Seizure of Aircraft (Hijacking) of 1970 (the Hague Convention) sought to extend the reach of the Tokyo Convention and to provide for a less porous enforcement system for arresting and prosecuting hijackers and related offenders.[31] Nonetheless, the Hague Convention still focused primarily on hijackings, to the exclusion of many other offenses that could potentially affect the safety of the civil aviation system. Whereas the Tokyo Convention simply required states to take offenders into custody, the Hague Convention required parties having custody of the offenders either to prosecute or to extradite them. The Hague Convention further obligated parties to criminalize the act of unlawfully taking control of an aircraft, or attempting to do so.[32] These offenses were to be punishable by severe penalties. Finally, parties were required to assist each other in connection with criminal proceedings instituted under the treaty.

---

30. Of course, a state might still punish or extradite the alleged offenders if it chose, but it faced no legal requirement to do so.

31. Convention for the Suppression of Unlawful Seizure of Aircraft (Hijacking), The Hague, December 16, 1970, 22 U.S.T. 1641.

32. The convention makes it an offense for any person on board an aircraft in flight to "unlawfully, by force or threat thereof, or any other form of intimidation, seize or exercise control of that aircraft." Hague Convention, art. I, 22 U.S.T. 1641, at 1644 (1970).

The Montreal Convention and Modern Developments

By 1971, it was apparent that hijacking was not the only threat, or perhaps even the major threat, to the international civil aviation regime. Terrorists could forgo the technical difficulties involved in hijacking a plane, and could threaten passengers and aircraft through interference with the air navigation system, or while planes were on the ground. The 1971 International Convention for the Suppression of Unlawful Acts Against the Safety of Civil Aviation (the Montreal Convention) had the goal of broadening the scope of international legal authority to deal with terrorism targeting civil aviation.[33] In particular, the Montreal Convention sought to protect air navigation facilities and aircraft (along with their passengers) on the ground from terrorist attack. It went considerably further in specifying aviation-related offenses to be criminalized, to include unlawfully and intentionally performing an act of violence against a person on board an aircraft in flight if the act is likely to endanger the safety of the aircraft. Parties also were required to criminalize the placement of explosive devices on aircraft, the destruction or damage of air navigation facilities, and communication of information known to be false that could thereby affect the safety of an aircraft in flight.[34] Whereas the premise for the Hague Convention appeared to be that the most dangerous threats to aviation safety were inside the aircraft, the Montreal Convention recognized that aircraft were simply elements of a civil aviation system that could be disrupted in a number of different ways; damaging an air navigation facility or providing false information to a pilot could be just as lethal as harming the pilot while the plane was in flight. As in the Hague Convention before it, parties were required to apply severe penalties to these offenses, to prosecute or to extradite

33. Convention for the Suppression of Unlawful Acts Against the Safety of Civil Aviation (Sabotage), Montreal, September 23, 1971, 24 U.S.T. 564.

34. The Convention also bound parties to criminalize any attempt at such offenses or acting as an accomplice.

the offender, and to assist each other with relevant criminal proceedings.

Because of its somewhat broader scope compared with other treaties on international civil aviation safety, the Montreal Convention could have greater applicability to cyber crime than earlier conventions. Its concern with protecting air navigation systems could be applied to the deliberate use of computers to sabotage an information network essential to the proper function of a navigation system.[35] Since the Montreal Convention also covers offenses involving the provision of deliberately false information to aircraft with the objective of affecting their safety, then certain offenses involving the use of computers to provide false information to aircraft could also be covered.[36] Yet for all the foresight of the Montreal Convention, some potential cyber offenses might well fall outside its coverage, such as a cyber attack designed to cause delays and inconvenience rather than specific disruptions in safety.

Addressing Gaps in Coverage or Enforcement

Over the years, the world has seen a decline in terrorist acts targeting civil aviation.[37] Although general improvements in safety practices and technologies have contributed to the decline, it is likely that the antiterrorism treaties have also yielded some results. They reflect a nearly global consensus deploring aviation-related terrorism. What had be-

35. An "air navigation system" includes sensing equipment, radio and communications equipment, and related technology.

36. Subsequent amendments to the Montreal Convention explicitly criminalize offenses targeting airports (even if these do not directly affect air navigation systems). Protocol for the suppression of unlawful acts of violence at airports serving international civil aviation, supplementary to the convention of September 23, 1971. Montreal, February 24, 1988, TIAS.

37. Michael S. Simons, "A Review of Issues Concerned with Aerial Hijacking and Terrorism: Implications for Australia's Security and the Sydney 2000 Olympics," *Journal of Air Law and Commerce* 63 (1998): 731, 732, indicating that, although terrorism remains a threat for civil aviation and other critical infrastructures, the incidence of annual terrorist activity targeting civil aviation has declined.

gun as a passing reference to crime in early treaties dealing with civil aviation grew to encompass offenses against aircraft in flight, aircraft on the ground, air navigation systems, and airports. The system of treaty law addressing these offenses grew in fits and starts, amid considerable substantive disagreement between countries, some of whom occasionally sympathized with the political goals of offenders.[38] Nonadhering countries have been reluctant to extradite or punish their own citizens, or individuals whose goals are admired.[39]

Countries most concerned about civil aviation–related terrorism have responded to the situation in two ways: through unilateral action and through cooperation with countries that share the degree of concern over terrorism. Unilateral action involves the threat of restricting the access of offending countries to domestic airports, as well as notifying domestic and international passengers using U.S. facilities about airports judged to be unsafe (based on the home country's own safety standards). The U.S. Department of Transportation notifies passengers in U.S. airports when certain airports are not in compliance with a predetermined antiterrorism safety standard, and the Secretary of Transportation possesses legal authority to block air traffic between the U.S. and a certain jurisdiction if that jurisdiction's safety violations are significant enough. The U.S. has also been viewed as part of a de facto enforcement system in instances where states decide not to accept safety and security regulations arising from the ICAO standard-setting process. In a similar vein, the G-8 countries have undertaken a coor-

38. Of course, in most cases, a country that is not in compliance will present a treaty interpretation under which the noncomplying country has in fact discharged its obligations. See, e.g., *Case Concerning Questions of Interpretation and Application of the 1971 Montreal Convention Arising from the Aerial Incident at Lockerbie, Libyan Arab Jamahiriya v. United States of America*, 1992 I.C.J. 114, 1992 WL 190214 (Request for Provisional Measures) (where Libya argued that its refusal to extradite suspects involved in the destruction of a Pan American Airlines flight over Lockerbie, Scotland, was in compliance with the Montreal Convention).

39. For example, offenders' goals could be popular with key domestic constituencies. Hence, a country's leadership may prefer to violate international law instead of strictly adhering to the existing conventions, especially when there is ambiguity in the text.

dinated effort to deny landing rights to airlines from countries that do not cooperate with measures against civil aviation–related terrorism, particularly those that fail to comply with obligations under the Hague Convention and the Montreal Convention. The threat is not idle. As noted earlier, in 1982, the then G-7 punished Afghanistan by denying it landing rights when the country failed to extradite or prosecute the hijackers of a Pakistan International Airlines plane that landed in Afghan territory. The threat of denied landing rights in G-7 countries also played a role in pressuring South Africa to prosecute hijackers who attempted a coup in the Seychelles in 1981.[40]

These reactions to gaps, or compliance problems, in the existing civil aviation treaty regime are instructive in two ways. First, compliance issues recur even when countries ordinarily recognize the value of a particular goal. Second, countries occasionally use access to an international network as a means of furthering safety-related goals. In the case of civil aviation, the network is the international system of conventions and the denial of access is the denial of landing rights. These insights are relevant for the regulation of cyberspace, a context where the ability and willingness of states to regulate varies considerably.

4. Why Aviation Is Distinctive

We have chronicled how governments gradually moved from a safety-centered approach in protecting international civil aviation to a concept focusing increasingly on security against willful, destructive activity.[41] The concept of security itself then evolved from one focused

40. John F. Murphy, *Punishing International Terrorists: The Legal Framework for Policy Initiatives* (Totowa, N.J.: Rowman & Allanheld, 1985), pp. 18–20.

41. Of course, the complexity of the international aviation system ensures that there is always a relationship between safety and security. Since accidents can cause failures in the system, governments have cooperated to develop a comprehensive system to reduce the probability of accidents. Security breaches against the system can then attack either the underlying technology of the system (that is, hijacking an airplane) or the procedures and technologies designed to reduce the safety risks in the system (providing false information to air traffic controllers). Thus some of the efforts to reduce safety problems can have a collateral, if indirect, effect on reducing security

primarily on protecting aircraft to one focused on protecting the technological network on which aircraft depend to operate safely and efficiently.

Looked at in the context of international cooperation in other areas involving safety and security, aviation security seems to be distinctive, in five ways. (1) This area of international law has steadily grown over time to encompass more offenses. (2) The responsibilities imposed on signatories are very specific and the network being protected is technologically complex. (3) As a matter of law, the system has both a prevention and a law enforcement component. (4) A growing number of countries have signed on to the regulatory regime. (5) Finally, acceptance of the treaties has coincided with greater security.

Here is some of the evidence: at first, countries were most interested in the basic rules of airspace; they could not agree on how the system should function under the best of circumstances, let alone on how they should cooperate to address intentional damage to the system. This was the subject of the Paris Convention in 1919. Through Annex 17 to the Chicago Convention of 1944 (which created ICAO), states have committed to observing ICAO's standards on preventive security—unless they specifically and publicly reject them. ICAO may lack direct capacity to enforce its guidelines, but the information it generates allows key countries with large aviation markets to impose (or threaten) restrictions that serve as a de facto enforcement mechanism. About 180 countries and 23 international organizations participate in ICAO, which provides technical assistance for preventive security measures.[42]

Since 1989, ICAO has offered technical assistance on aviation security to 132 states. Because the framework exists and appears to work, these programs are funded by donor states. Fifteen such states have contributed nearly $5 million to the program since 1989. In 1963, the Tokyo Convention only went as far as to establish criminal juris-

threats. The context of cyber crime and security may involve similar relationships between safety and security.

42. ICAO, The International Civil Aviation Organization: Annual Report 1999.

diction over the interference with aircraft while they were in flight,[43] but there is now also a law enforcement component to the system, enacted by the Montreal Convention, now signed by 174 countries. Indeed, since treaty membership is usually the most controversial element of any legal regime, this level of membership may understate the total number of countries that voluntarily cooperate in aviation security–related law enforcement—contrast this to the 79 countries that have signed the Hostages Convention, and the 144 countries that have signed the Narcotics Convention.[44] Since adoption of the civil aviation treaties, sabotage and acts of unlawful interference have steadily declined; in 1998, for example, ICAO reported only about ten acts of unlawful interference and basically no acts of sabotage.

Aviation is distinctive for both psychological and economic reasons. The psychological reasons include the ready availability of graphic images, high casualty to incident ratio, and high mortality to casualty ratio. There are at least three economic reasons why civil aviation security engenders considerable international interest: (1) the growing economic significance of international air transportation in absolute terms, (2) the indirect benefits of air transportation, and (3) network externalities.

During the last four decades, air transport has become an increasingly important economic sector in terms of total revenue.[45] Civil aircraft manufacturers in the U.S. and Europe have become major industries. Security threats afflicting civil aviation place these economic sectors at risk. Moreover, civil air transport provides indirect economic benefits by lowering transportation costs, increasing the diffusion of labor, and allowing for redundancies that allow transport to proceed when surface or seaborne routes are blocked. Finally, the

43. U.S. Department of Transportation, FAA Website, International Programs, ⟨*http://www.faa.gov/international*⟩ (accessed June 19, 1999).

44. United Nations Convention Against Illicit Traffic in Narcotic Drugs and Psychotropic Substances, December 20, 1988, T.I.A.S., 20 I.L.M. 493 (Vienna Convention).

45. See, e.g., Dempsey, *Law and Foreign Policy in International Aviation*, and de Murias, *The Economic Regulation of International Air Transport*.

principle of network externalities applies to international civil aviation, thereby raising the value of a portion of the network to the extent that the entire network grows.[46] The notion of network externalities is straightforward. Certain goods and services increase in value to the extent that a greater number of users are included in the network. For example, the value of telephone networks increases as more people can be reached on the network. The value of e-mail communication also increases as the number of e-mail users grows. In the aviation context, if certain portions of the network are considered unsafe, the remaining portion of the network loses value; so that if there is a spate of terrorist attacks on airports in Africa, for example, and aircraft flying to Africa, then the entire international civil aviation network is less able to provide efficient transportation to Africa. This makes the network itself less valuable.[47] Even beyond the economic considerations, aviation security is an appealing objective because of the psychological significance of breaches in aviation security, due in part to the sense of empathy that many people who use the international aviation system feel when confronted with an aviation disaster.[48]

To some extent, these elements of the aviation sector have analogues in the context of cyber crime. Cyber networks are growing in economic value.[49] And as the networks grow, the economic activity beyond information technology is increasingly dependent on cyber

46. Although passengers may not feel network externalities when they buy a ticket to fly between two geographic points, everyone else in the system benefits from network externalities. An airline investing in aircraft finds these more valuable if there are more safe airports that they can fly to, and governments can secure a similarly greater benefit (at the margin) when investing in aviation infrastructure as the network grows in size and scope.

47. See generally, Nicholas Economides and Lawrence J. White, "Networks and Compatibility: Implications for Antitrust," *European Economic Review* 38 (1994): 651, discussing network externalities in the context of antitrust analysis.

48. For a review of the psychological research on the salience of aviation versus other types of disasters, see Richard Nisbett and Lee Ross, *Human Inference: Strategies and Shortcomings of Social Judgment* (Englewood Cliffs, N.J.: Prentice-Hall, 1980).

49. For example, as of June 2000, the stock market capitalization of information technology companies in the U.S. far surpasses the price-earnings ratios that many financial analysts consider most acceptable.

networks. Moreover, network externalities almost certainly play a significant role in the development of information technology networks. Although cyber crime does not necessarily inspire analogous psychological reactions, certain developments could be framed in a manner that would help the public perceive the salience of cyber security breaches and the implicit threat to their safety.[50] The perception of cyber insecurity decreases the network's value. Users of information technology could be "hijacked," and in the midst of a cyber attack they might feel as helpless as if they were on an aircraft that had been hijacked. A plane could crash when given faulty information. Water could be poisoned though interference with purification systems. Policymakers can emphasize the analogy between civil aviation security and cyber security to help build the domestic political consensus that often serves as a precursor for international cooperation in damage control.

5. Applying the Civil Aviation Precedent to Cyber Threats

The existing framework of international law covering civil aviation security is laudable but not entirely adequate to address cyber security breaches. In civil aviation there are indeed ways in which cyber threats could elude coverage under the existing legal framework. But there may be ways in which we can bring such threats under the scope of the international treaties protecting civil aviation.

Filling the Gaps in Existing Aviation Security Treaties

The growth in the scope of the international civil aviation security system illustrates a gradual progression that filled in gaps left by previous accords. For instance, the Montreal Convention finally reflected

---

50. For a discussion of the psychology of framing information in a manner that increases its salience, see, e.g., Daniel Kahneman and Amos Tversky, "Choices, Values, and Frames," *American Psychologist* 39 (1984): 341.

the growing international consensus that aircraft safety could be indirectly threatened by undermining air navigation systems. Yet, although the international civil aviation system has achieved impressive results, the existing legal framework does not provide coverage against all major cyber threats. Today the advent of cyberspace and the increasing relevance of information technology again creates a gap between what the treaties cover and the nature of the threat.

Some of the existing civil aviation security treaties could be found to impose legal obligations relevant to cyber crime. For example, the Montreal Convention specifically covers instances where a person "communicates information which he knows to be false, thereby endangering the safety of an aircraft in flight."[51] More generally, it requires members to punish offenders who interfere with the safety of the air navigation system, which includes the sabotage of an air navigation system through computer viruses, transmission of inaccurate information, or related technologies. Other malicious attacks against aircraft in flight or on the ground, or against air navigation systems, are also covered.

Nonetheless, in most cases such obligations are quite circumscribed in comparison to the range of offenses targeting civil aviation that could arise through, or benefit from, information technology. In particular, the current treaties generally do not cover the use of computers to target critical infrastructures necessary for the security of civil aviation. As with virtually all international terrorism treaties, the focus is on malicious—not reckless—conduct. Thus, for example, two academics who recklessly and unlawfully interfere with an air navigation system would not necessarily commit an offense under current treaty law.

Moreover, the current international treaty law does not cover reckless or malicious cyber attacks against critical infrastructures collaterally affecting civil aviation security.[52] Such attacks could signifi-

---

51. Montreal Convention, art 1(d), 24 U.S.T. 564.
52. The only exception to this is if the attacks were considered de facto attacks on the air navigation system.

cantly and adversely interfere with the commercial or economic efficiency of the international civil aviation system, and thereby interfere with safety. If, for example, a cyber attack penetrates airline reservation systems, terrorists could learn the identity, destination, and itinerary of any passenger, allowing individuals to be targeted while they make their way through the network.[53] Reckless or malicious cyber attacks could also affect collateral infrastructures, upon which the international civil aviation system depends, such as electric power grids.

Although gaps in the system exist even beyond cyber terrorism, cyber offenses are particularly threatening in terms of their potential to damage a number of the infrastructures upon which civil aviation depends. In many cases, computers pose a new enforcement challenge. Illegal information or reproductions (of currency, for example) can be transmitted throughout the world in seconds. The combination of expertise and malevolent intent can disable the vital computer networks. Accordingly, it could be argued that cyber crimes merit enhanced punishments and increased provisions for transnational law enforcement cooperation. For these reasons, it is probably easier to reach international consensus on the cyber offenses than on changes to other aspects of international law governing civil aviation security.

Specific Changes to the International Treaty System

Minor changes to an existing treaty could address cyber threats currently not covered. The Montreal Convention provides a vehicle to achieve this, because it already presents a politically sustainable and legally coherent framework concerning prosecution or extradition.

---

53. Interference with airline computer systems could also put passengers at risk by changing air traffic patterns, concentrating passengers in certain locations, and interfering with maintenance schedules and crew assignments. A recent computer malfunction at Phoenix's Sky Harbor Airport highlights the damaging consequences of problems with maintenance and pilot crew schedules. The computer malfunction delayed flights on one airline for nearly a day.

Although using an existing treaty is not the only way of achieving this result, it is the most straightforward.[54]

The language below would go a considerable distance to address the core cyber threats not currently covered. Although the format I offer is designed to follow Section 1 of Article I in the Montreal Convention, the language easily could be adapted to stand on its own:

> 2. Any person commits an offense if he unlawfully, and intentionally or recklessly,[55] engages in any of the following conduct to commit an offense specified under section one of this Article[56] or to adversely interfere with a significant aviation infrastructure without legally recognized authority, permission, or consent, if such an act is likely to endanger the safety of the civil aviation system:[57]

54. The goal of this language is not the Montreal Convention per se, but rather the body of international law that pertains to civil aviation security. Another alternative that achieves this result would be a separate treaty, though such a vehicle would probably attract more attention and political debate than an amendment to the Montreal Convention.

55. The addition of the word "recklessly" extends the provision to instances where individuals unlawfully engage in prohibited conduct, mindful of the danger it poses yet with a complete (that is, reckless) disregard of the consequences of their actions. Example: two college professors of computer science seek to test whether a new theoretical approach to breach computer security works as predicted; they infiltrate a computer network used to transmit air traffic information and hinder its ability to rapidly transmit information. The professors are so eager to complete the test that they put aside their knowledge of the activity's risk to civil aviation. Even if the professors did not undertake the activity with malice (that is, with the general intent of causing harm), their recklessness would constitute an offense under this language if damage results.

56. This refers to the first section of the article defining offenses in the Montreal Convention. The goal here is to extend the recklessness standard to instances where cyber systems are compromised in the course of committing one of the original offenses in the Montreal Convention, such as "destroy[ing] or damag[ing] air navigation facilities or interfer[ing] with their operation." Montreal Convention, art. 1 (d), 24 U.S.T. 564.

57. The "significant aviation infrastructure," defined in detail below, refers to critical infrastructures that, if compromised, would adversely affect civil aviation. Although civil aviation security would be threatened even by a noncyber attack to such an infrastructure, cyber attacks against these infrastructures deserve coverage in an international treaty for two reasons: (1) cyber attacks can be more easily undertaken across national boundaries; (2) a cyber attack against these infrastructures can have more insidious consequences for aviation safety because it could be timed, localized,

(1) creates, stores, alters, deletes, transmits, diverts, misroutes, manipulates, or interferes with data or programs in a cyber system with the purpose of causing, or knowing that such activities would cause, said cyber system or another cyber system to cease functioning as intended, or to operate with a significantly reduced capacity to perform its intended function;[58]

(2) enters into a cyber system for which access is restricted in a conspicuous and unambiguous manner;

(3) interferes with tamper-detection or authentication mechanisms.[59]

The following definitions would complete the picture:

1. "Cyber system" means any computer or network of computers used to relay, transmit, coordinate, or control communications of data or programs.[60]

2. "Adversely interfere" means any conduct with a meaningful likelihood of causing a "significant aviation infrastructure" (defined below) to cease functioning as intended, or to operate with a reduced capacity to perform its intended function.[61] A "meaningful likelihood" means an identifiable and nontrivial change in probability beyond what would arise in the normal course of operating the civil aviation system or a "significant aviation infrastructure."

3. "Significant aviation infrastructure" means any interconnected network of physical devices, pathways, people, and computers used to maintain, power, supervise, or operate air navigation facilities or airports, and without the proper function of which civil aviation security would be adversely affected; including but not limited to electric power grids, meteorological equipment, water and fuel

---

and coordinated to exert maximum damage on aviation. Example: interrupting an airport's access to electric power is always dangerous, but it is far more so in the case of a crowded airport, at peak periods of take-offs and landings, on a rainy evening.

58. This clause focuses on direct interference with cyber systems affecting civil aviation, either directly or collaterally (through interference with other critical infrastructures).

59. These two clauses allow coverage of offenses involving breaches of security, even when data are not significantly altered.

60. This defines the potential target of cyber attacks.

61. The goal of this definition is to explain the most worrisome type of interference with critical infrastructures that indirectly affect aviation. Note that the definition of adverse interference here parallels Section 2 of the proposed treaty language.

supply networks, airline reservation systems, and information systems used to transmit information relevant to civil aviation safety.[62]

    4. "Civil aviation system" means any aircraft in flight, or preparing for imminent flight, air navigation facilities, and airports.[63]

In conjunction with the existing prohibitions of the Montreal Convention and its previous amendment (extending coverage to airports), this new language addresses the two major cyber security problems with the existing international treaty system. First, the new language makes clear that cyber attacks interfering with infrastructures that affect aviation, such as electric power, constitute offenses under the treaty. Even interference with computer reservation systems would be covered, as long as such interference placed safety and security at risk. Second, because of the unique threat posed by cyber attacks, the new language specifies that an unlawful cyber attack endangering the civil aviation system is covered under the treaty even if the perpetrator is reckless rather than malicious.

Although this last element is controversial, a growing number of intentional cyber attacks may have been undertaken recklessly rather than maliciously, yet caused (or had the potential to cause) significant damage to critical infrastructures. The legal standard of recklessness involves a deliberate disregard of the risk involved in a certain action even when it is known, which involves an element of deliberateness far beyond that involved in negligence.[64] The goal of this language is to address enforcement through prosecution and extradition rather than regulation, but the proposed changes extend the reach of this

---

62. This definition specifies what critical infrastructures are protected by the treaty language. The objective is to strike a balance between wide coverage (including most infrastructures on which civil aviation depends) and narrow application (maintaining focus on civil aviation).

63. This is just a convenient shorthand to refer to the specific aspects of the civil aviation system that are already covered by the Montreal Convention (aircraft in flight and air navigation facilities) and a previous amendment (airports).

64. In common law systems, negligence is generally viewed as the failure to consider a risk that a person should reasonably have considered. Civil law legal systems make analogous distinctions.

regime to matters that are regulated outside transportation agencies. Accordingly, this proposal would also require states to build domestic consensus among government agencies charged with protecting non-aviation infrastructures such as energy and telecommunications.

This proposal illustrates the selective expansion approach in action. The proposal's expansion of international criminal liability is consistent with the objectives of established treaty law. The focus on cyber threats is consistent with cyber technology's potential to lower the cost of threatening a key economic infrastructure. The focus is international because the protected infrastructure (civil aviation) is, and because the nature of cyber technology poses the threat that criminals and terrorists might stretch an offense across geographic boundaries and political borders. To address the threats, the selective expansion approach uses the same path-dependent logic that resulted in the international aviation security laws that the proposal seeks to enhance. Treaties of narrow scope reduce initial opposition and encourage signatories to change their prevention, safety, and enforcement practices. States enhance prevention and observe the treaties to avoid politically costly controversies over treaty interpretation, or sanctions that might impede their use of a valuable technological network such as the international aviation system. In contrast, proposals to radically expand international criminal liability for cyber offenses would be far more likely to arouse opposition on sovereignty grounds.[65] Once the precedent is established with narrower treaties, politicians are likely to find it less costly to support further expansions of international criminal liability, regardless of whether such expansions protect airspace or cyberspace.

---

65. See Dan M. Kahan, "Gentle Nudges vs. Hard Shoves: Solving the Sticky Norms Problem," *University of Chicago Law Review* 67 (2000): 607, arguing in favor of incremental changes in criminal liability to reduce the prevalence of "sticky norms" against the imposition of the new liability.

6. Conclusion

The international experience with aviation security indicates that, even though treaty law is not infallible, it is nonetheless an important component of international enforcement and prevention. Covering certain offenses with a treaty furthers the applicability of a legal standard and encourages participants to share information. This leads to specific political consequences that advance underlying goals of safety and security:

- *Deterrence of specific offenses.* Treaty law allows for extradition or prosecution to loom larger, marginally enhancing deterrence against cyber terrorism and cyber crimes targeting civil aviation. Potential offenders would find it marginally harder to assume that jurisdictional difficulties would allow them to evade punishment if they are caught.

- *International consensus for legal cooperation.* Treaty law reflects international consensus, encouraging law enforcement and security cooperation, for which still other treaties provide the framework. If a treaty defines an offense, the authorities of signatory countries are more likely to cooperate in addressing the offense.

- *Enhanced prospects for technical cooperation beyond the confines of the treaty.* Treaty law is a starting point to encourage international consensus on objectives for technical cooperation to avoid the offenses in question, even if such cooperation is beyond the scope of any single treaty. If countries sign a treaty recognizing certain conduct as offensive, it is probably more likely that both public and private research will focus on developing solutions to the offenses.[66]

---

66. Separate arrangements dealing exclusively with technical and investigative cooperation also exist.

These benefits arise from more than the normative impact of treaty law. Rather, there is a political connection between expanded treaty law and some of the objectives highlighted above. Once expanded prohibitions are legally in place, it is difficult for countries to retreat from them. Because gains and losses tend to be perceived asymmetrically—meaning that people value the avoidance of a loss more than the corresponding gain—a country is more likely to suffer greater scorn for terminating recognition of offenses than for not initially recognizing them.[67] Interest groups supporting cooperation (such as security and safety firms, special prosecution and investigation units, and transportation firms) develop in response to new opportunities. Finally, since countries are sensitive about their sovereignty on criminal justice matters, and extradition or prosecution of offenders poses complications in the context of domestic politics, countries develop a strong incentive to improve prevention approaches.

Thus, the regulation of cyberspace raises difficult but surmountable challenges. The universe of users is expanding far more rapidly than in the case of other communications technologies developed during the twentieth century, such as television, radio, and the telephone.[68] Hardware and software change vertiginously in months, and transactions can take place over a multitude of national jurisdictions. Given these developments, there is room for original and principled thinking in policing cyberspace. Such thinking played an indispensable role in negotiating the treaties that govern civil aviation security, and as with aviation, part of the challenge is a political one—generating a consensus that a certain network is valuable enough that everyone might be adversely affected if it suffered at the hands of criminals or terrorists.

---

67. To see this, just imagine what the international response would be if a current member of NATO seceded from the NATO constitutive treaty. Presumably, the consequences would be much more severe in terms of political, economic, and diplomatic costs than if the country had not joined in the first place. This intuition is consistent with the research of cognitive psychologists on how gains and losses are valued by people. See, e.g., Kahneman and Tversky, "Choices, Values, and Frames."

68. See, e.g., David R. Johnson and David R. Post, "Law and Borders: The Rise of Law in Cyberspace," *Stanford Law Review* 48 (1996): 1367.

The case for a multinational convention covering the entire range of threats is very strong. In the meantime, states should use the selective expansion approach to extend twenty-first century legal protections to civil aviation, a critical infrastructure that has all but defined the twentieth century.

CHAPTER 4

Current and Future Technical Capabilities

Stephen J. Lukasik

Information systems are vulnerable to attack, as evidenced by the rapidly growing number of system intrusions. Current protection capabilities allow for relatively limited degrees of defense or deterrence, making attack relatively easy and defense relatively difficult. This chapter outlines technical measures that could help to identify and track intruders into computer systems and networks. But in addition to deploying specific technologies, a new international regime will be required to reduce the ability of intruders to hide behind the frequently slow and incompatible processes under which defenders must operate when different sovereign nations are involved in the investigation of an intrusion.

Some of what is suggested will require explicit agreements among nations, but there are other steps that, without government-to-government agreements, will fit naturally into the open and cooperative environment that has characterized the Internet to date. Such measures, undertaken directly by the users who, by definition, live in "Internet-time," can be accomplished more rapidly than those where formal international agreements must be agreed to and implemented. Thus, in spite of the rapid rate of growth of system intrusions, there is the prospect of being able to make significant improvements in system security on a time scale that matches that of the problem.

The focus here is on criminal violators, including terrorists who seek to attack and destroy elements of society. A different, and potentially more severe, threat is where the attacker is a sovereign state. That class of attack, constituting what is called information warfare, is beyond the scope of the discussion here and of the Draft International Convention presented in Chapter 6.

1. The Internet and Its Governance

The Internet provides the basis for the global information infrastructure, and it increasingly provides connectivity for a wide range of other infrastructures. To the extent that the Internet manifests vulnerabilities that cannot be addressed through unilateral measures, changes in its governance may be desirable. This requires examining existing mechanisms that can effect change. To the extent that these change mechanisms prove to be incapable of protecting the Internet, other approaches will be needed to protect this global resource.

Internet Structure and Function Are Determined by its Developers

The Internet is governed through the voluntary activities of the technical people who develop and extend its functionality.[1] Internet users

---

1. See Michael A. Erlinger, "Internet Protocols for Protection Against Cyber Crime," presentation at the Conference on International Cooperation to Combat

adopt its protocols to be able to communicate with others; vendors implement its protocols in their hardware and software products because the user market requires it; technical experts extend the Internet based on their research and analyses. Thus, although the provision of Internet services has become a major business, the Internet's core specifications and their implementations are maintained and developed by its users acting through a governance structure that is little changed in concept from the way its founding academic researchers proceeded thirty years ago. Even the businesses that use the Internet or provide its communication facilities are not, as organizations, part of the group that develops and maintains the Internet's technical specifications, although those specifications must change to keep up with new technologies that are deployed. This may be changing, as more constituencies demand to be heard, but the fundamental processes through which the Internet operates have stood the test of time and are not likely to be abandoned lightly.

The Internet runs on the basis of network protocols, agreements on how information should appear in a message, how that information is to be interpreted, and the format of that message. The Internet is managed, developed, and operated by a hierarchy of volunteer organizations. The Internet Architecture Board (IAB), the Internet Engineering Task Force (IETF), the Internet Engineering Steering Group (IESG), and the various IETF Working Groups are the primary groups responsible for the development of the Internet.

The IETF, the engineering, development and standardization arm of the Internet Architecture Board (IAB), is a self-organized group dedicated to the continued development of the protocols and standards that form the basis of the Internet. The IETF's mission includes: identifying and proposing solutions to operational and technical problems in the Internet, specifying protocols and architecture to solve such technical problems, making recommendations to the Internet Engi-

Cyber Crime and Terrorism, Hoover Institution, Stanford University, Stanford, California, December 6–7, 1999.

neering Steering Group (IESG) regarding the standardization of protocols and protocol usage in the Internet, and providing a forum for the exchange of information within the Internet community.

The IETF is organized into eight areas of interest, one of which is security. Each area is headed by an Area Director, who oversees the various working groups—the creators of Internet specifications—that consist of all parties having a stake in the protocol under consideration. A charter sets the agenda and timetable for the group's work. Working groups focus on developing a protocol specification, but sometimes they serve to delineate some current practice. Working groups are established based on a recognized need and they terminate when the work called for by their charter is completed.

The IETF standardization process is well defined.[2] The process starts with a working group producing a series of documents called Internet Drafts that are posted on the WorldWideWeb[3] with notification to the IETF mailing list. Based on comments received, the working group can decide that an Internet Draft reflects a consensus view. At this point the working group asks the IESG, through its Area Director, to make the Internet Draft a Proposed Standard RFC.[4] A Proposed Standard specification is advanced only if it is stable, represents the resolution of known design choices, is well understood, has received significant community review, and appears to enjoy enough community interest to be considered valuable. Thus a Proposed Standard RFC is viewed as the initial specification from which implementations should be developed.

After a minimum of six months the working group can ask that the Proposed Standard RFC be moved to the level of Draft Standard RFC. The requirement for such a change is based on the existence of two independent and interoperable implementations from different code bases and on sufficient successful operational experience. Such

---

2. See S. Bradner, "The Internet Standards Process—Revision 3," RFC 2026 (October 1996), available at ⟨*http://www.ietf.org/rfc/rfc2026.txt*⟩.

3. See ⟨*http://www.ietf.org/ID.html*⟩.

4. See ⟨*http://www.ietf.org/rfc.html*⟩.

implementation experience may well uncover the need for changes to the specification. It is the implementation and experience requirement that differentiates the Internet standardization process from other standards activities. Implementations are used to prove the utility and precise operation of the specification.

After a minimum of four months a Draft Standard can be moved to an Internet Standard. Internet Standards are characterized by a high degree of technical maturity and by the understanding among its developers that the specified protocol or service provides significant benefit to the Internet community. This process is shown in Figure 1. Security issues were not of concern for the original Internet specifications. Cyber crime per se is not currently an IETF agenda item. Addressing cyber crime would have to be stated as an issue in protocol design.

The Internet Involves Both Physical and Information Architectures

There are two views of Internet architecture. The most common is that the Internet is a set of linked computer hardware, software, and communication facilities.[5] In this view, security is a matter of protecting that hardware and software against theft, damage, or denial of service. A second view is that the Internet links a collection of information. Though not as easily understandable as that of physical architecture, certain features of its information architecture are becoming clearer. First, just as the physical Internet embodies a meta-architecture that embraces the interconnection of heterogeneous networks through the processes described above, so does the information system embody a meta-architecture that embraces heterogeneous information systems. Robert Kahn and Robert Wilensky in their introduction to this general notion describe the digital object as the basic architectural element in

5. See Robert E. Kahn and Stephen J. Lukasik, "Fighting Cyber Crime and Terrorism: The Role of Technology," presentation at the Stanford Conference, December 6–7, 1999.

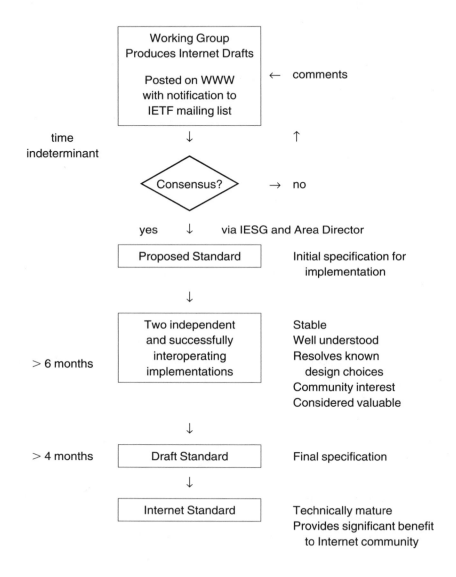

Fig. 1.   The Internet standardization process.

the global information system, with each object having a unique and persistent identifier.[6]

Finally, the architecture assumes the existence of certain systems that can speak with authority on specific information issues. For example, is the following digital object subject to a claim of copyright in the United States? Or, regarding authenticity, what is the following organization? Or, are the bona fides of this organization accurate? While some entities may have their authority conferred by law, others will develop it by superior performance in the marketplace.

Given the existence of a meta-architecture for information systems, the Internet will embrace many of them, all different in some aspects. Today, the most widely used information systems are those that rely on access to files on specific machines. The older File Transfer Protocols (FTP) and the current Web protocols are examples of information system protocols, but because neither one allows for persistent access over time through unique identifiers, one can expect the spectrum of information systems in the future to range from those that are strictly informal, with possibly transitory information, to those that have more formality.

Defining the Internet

The broad term "information infrastructure" covers a range of private, public, and national capabilities. I focus here on the information systems that constitute the Internet and exclude separate national systems used by sovereign nations for the operation of their government, and facilities owned or operated by private entities that are separate from public facilities. I do, however, include both physical aspects and the information and service aspects that are not necessarily physical.

---

6. See Robert Kahn and Robert Wilensky, "A Framework for Distributed Digital Object Services," available at ⟨*http://www.cnri.reston.va/cstr/arch.html*⟩; see also "The Handle System," available at ⟨*http://www.cnri.reston.va/cstr.html#archi tecture*⟩.

Within the United States, the Federal Networking Council has adopted the following definition of the term "Internet":[7]

> Internet refers to the global information system that:
>
> (i) is logically linked together by a globally unique address space based on the Internet Protocol (IP) or its subsequent extensions/follow-ons;
>
> (ii) is able to support communications using the Transmission Control Protocol/Internet Protocol (TCP/IP) suite or its subsequent extensions/follow-ons, and/or other IP-compatible protocols; and
>
> (iii) provides, uses, or makes accessible, either publicly or privately, high level services layered on the communications and related infrastructure described herein.

An important element of this definition is the reference to "subsequent extensions/follow-ons." The dynamic character of networking technology suggests the need for a continuing review mechanism to ensure that basic conceptual underpinnings are not inadvertently changed with the passage of time. A second important element is the inclusion of high-level services within the definition. More than simply the physical devices and telecommunications capabilities that constitute the underlying network, one must view the global information system in its totality.

Abusing, Misusing, and Attacking the Internet

The Internet, after undergoing a twenty-year period of development and use by academic researchers, took on a different aspect when it was opened up to commercial users in the late 1980s. The environment quickly changed from one directed to the open and cooperative use of its information resources and services by a narrowly defined set of users to one where the new users sought privacy in their communications, and protection of their intellectual property, and expected to receive a choice of reliable services at costs set competitively.

7. See Federal Networking Council, October 24, 1995, available at ⟨http://www.fnc.gov⟩.

The new users display a varied set of behaviors. Some are business competitors or bargain-seeking consumers who are not above stealing intellectual property or services. Others are irresponsibly playful, and they set loose viruses and other malicious code or they deface web sites or destroy data files. Still others are criminals who use the Internet to perpetrate fraud, theft, and extortion. Terrorists, noting the increasing dependence of many societies on the Internet, may use it as a target or channel for the expression of their views, or to harass, coerce, or destroy social institutions. National security analysts translate these same concerns into the domain of strategic attacks on sovereign states. Such abuses and attacks may use the Internet to reach other targets, or they may target the Internet itself. The first category uses the Internet to attack defined entities, such as a particular computer, the information contained within it, or the service it provides, thereby causing harm to those dependent on those entities. The second category, attacking the Internet itself, intends to degrade or deny parts of its contents and capabilities to large numbers of users.

Compounding these difficulties are several related factors. As information technology becomes increasingly powerful, so do the attack tools that become available. These tools are distributed to would-be attackers using the Internet itself, much in the way that poisons spread through an organism in its bloodstream. By increasing the power of their users, the tools allow a larger number of individuals, less skilled than the tool creators, to damage information systems. This progression of increasingly sophisticated attacks is illustrated in Table 1.

Benign Causes of Disruption and Lack of Robustness Further Complicate Protection

Excluded from the concept of network abuse are failures that inadvertently result from acts of nature, wear and tear or other usage, approved maintenance and operations status monitoring, and diagnostic activities of network operators. These are considered part of the normal operational environment and part of the terms and con-

TABLE I

The Increasing Sophistication of Computer and Network Attacks

Year	Attack mechanism
1982	Password guessing
1984	Self-replicating code
1985	Password cracking
1986	Exploiting known vulnerabilities
1988	Disabling audit mechanisms
1989	Use of back doors in programs
1990	Hijacking sessions
1991	Sweepers
1992	Packet sniffers
1993	Stealth diagnostics
1994	Packet spoofing
1995	Graphic user interfaces for attack tools
1996	Automated probes and scans
1997	Denial of service
1998	Web attacks
1999	Macro viruses
2000	Distributed attacks

Source: Thomas A. Longstaff, "International Coordination for Cyber Crime and Terrorism in the 21st Century," presentation at the Conference on International Cooperation to Combat Cyber Crime and Terrorism, Hoover Institution, Stanford University, Stanford, California, December 6–7, 1999.

ditions for use of the network that are made explicit in either employment contracts or service agreements. The focus of this discussion is on deliberate acts, not accidents, although the possibility of civil or criminal negligence cannot be excluded.

At the current level of networking technology numerous problems will arise from the inherent lack of robustness of the system and even of incompetence on the part of its users and operators. These unfortunate realities can have consequences as harmful and costly as those caused by deliberate conduct, but they are not addressed.[8]

8. See K. C. Claffy, "Traffic Observation in a Stateless Data Networking Environment," presentation at the Stanford Conference, December 6–7, 1999.

Protecting Individual Computers

As with any form of private property, protecting a single computer is primarily the responsibility of its owner. An owner may seek assistance from appropriate government agencies and jurisdictions, according to the national laws applying to the locations and the activities involved. The broader the impact of such attacks, the greater will be the case for public involvement. Where the information, operation, and impact of an attack involve entities from more than a single sovereign state, which is often the case, the appeal for help may extend to the international community of nations and organizations.

International actions can be as simple as supporting the resolution of civil contract disputes. In other cases they may involve the exchange of information relating to computer crimes, or suspected crimes, or to anomalies in computer operation. It is conceivable that personal information relating to the citizens of one nation might be provided to entities in other countries, such as alerts, warnings, modes of penetration, identities and aliases, and the like. In some cases assistance in the resolution of attacks on individual computers can involve disclosures of personal information that may raise concerns about the requirements of privacy.[9] A balance between property rights and those of personal privacy must be achieved. A possible approach to this problem, involving the use of automated techniques, is discussed later.

Protecting the Global Information Infrastructure

A very different circumstance arises when the information infrastructure itself, in whole or in part, is the target of attack. In this case, the jurisdiction in which such attacks occur is more complicated than for attacks on individual targets, and international agreements become increasingly important. Infrastructure "capabilities" are abstractions, substantially different from their physical manifestations; they depend

9. See Ekaterina A. Drozdova, "Civil Liberties and Security in Cyberspace," Chap. 5 of this volume, for a fuller discussion of privacy rights.

on multiple locations and jurisdictions (including the oceans and space) and, most important, have properties and capabilities that, rather than being simply resident in any of its parts, grow out of their collective existence. Without explicit agreements dealing with the protection of the network, global protective actions may be limited to those common to all jurisdictions taken together. This least common denominator will not, in general, provide the greatest amount, or even adequate amounts, of global protection.

For protection to be adequate, the shared global system should have the capacity to detect and identify violators with sufficient accuracy to deter them through the prospect of being indicted, prosecuted, and punished, or otherwise caused to pay a price for having initiated an attack. To achieve this degree of effectiveness will require creating appropriate tools, procedures, and organizations, not only to satisfy these aims but also to satisfy national authorities that their sovereign rights and the rights of their citizens are protected.

Although in some situations bilateral international interactions may be all that is required to deal with an attack on the Internet itself, in many others multinational action will be required. Certainly a global attack on the entire information system would require a coordinated worldwide response, and such a prospect is properly a subject for political consensus on how best to respond. At a minimum, the governing policies and processes will need to be established in advance.

2. Defending Information Systems Against Cyber Attack

For a realistic assessment of future prospects for the defense of information infrastructures against cyber attack, the current state of practice provides a starting point. In addition to the art and science of system defense, we should examine those areas that security professionals feel could provide the greatest leverage in blunting future attacks.

The View from the Defender: Prepared Defense

In the case of a prepared defense there is a secured network with a perimeter involving, for example, firewalls, virtual private networks, and/or challenge response systems.[10] This perimeter is monitored by an information protection staff using a combination of automated and semiautomated tools. An effective perimeter defense implies that the modes of possible attack are known a priori and that methods are in place to detect the signatures of these attacks. Early warning of an attack might, for example, come from monitoring the TCP, UDP, and ICMP activities occurring on in-bound packets.[11] Early warning could also come from automated searching for key words in the internals of network traffic that would generally indicate an attempt to gain access to systems or privileges not permitted from outside the secured perimeter.[12] This could in addition include the routine scanning of attached files in e-mail, which can contain known viruses or suspicious executable programs.

A potential attack may be indicated to the information protection staff via e-mail, pager, or other means. At this point, the information protection staff must ascertain whether the alert is real or a false alarm. This is done in several ways, and is somewhat dependent on what information is captured or buffered at the firewall. Essentially, the team must look manually at the information collected by the automated monitoring system in order to make an initial assessment. Adequate evidence may or may not be available, but in either case, in

10. See Steven D. Rizzi, "Is Technology the Answer to Infrastructure Protection?" presentation at the Stanford Conference, December 6–7, 1999.

11. For a discussion of TCP, UDP, ICMP, and other protocols, see Douglas Comer, 1 *Internetworking with TCP/IP* (Upper Saddle River, N.J.: Prentice-Hall, 1995).

12. "Internals" refers to the content of networked information. This could be the actual text of an e-mail, the graphics in a computer file, the audio or video of a teleconference, or the audio of a telephone call routed over a computer network. By contrast, "externals" refers to the routing information that is contained in the message that identifies the source and destination without providing detailed information of the message content.

order to support both evidence collection and better situation assessment, the security staff will increase the amount of auditing and data collection being done at the perimeter.

If the increased monitoring and auditing process confirms a suspected attack on the network, rapid engagement of additional processes is necessary. Engagement typically will require disaster preparation and warning, contingency plan execution, system isolation, and ultimately denial of access to the attacker. The security staff must move quickly to determine the nature of the intrusion, as well as to intervene to deny access to the attacker. During this period of the engagement, security personnel will trace the origin of the attack. In most cases, a serious attack will not have originated from the source that has been monitored; the real attacker will be located one or more "hops" away. That means that the defenders must attempt to contact security personnel at the apparent attack source to see if the attack is originating from that location or from some other "hop." This tracing period may take time, and prove difficult, since the only contact information that is usually available is from the personnel at the point of initial contact and the attack may not occur during business hours.

For these reasons, it is usually difficult for security staffs to trace a multiple "hop" attack, and the urge to deny the attacker access, either through the operating system or the firewall/router, is hard to resist. Having an automated way of tracing such attacks would be of great use, for it would increase the number of successful traces and would thus enhance deterrence.

Denial of access to attackers results in the immediate ending of any intrusion, but attackers frequently eliminate the evidence of their activities on some number of the intervening "hops," or they may place confusing or contradictory evidence in log files that would suggest to investigators that the attack came from somewhere other than the true origin. Sometimes the various "hops" along the way are outside the country boundaries of the computers under attack, creating the further difficulty of additional barriers such as different laws, languages, and time zones.

For most practical purposes, the average security staff that is well prepared for an attack of this nature will be in the position to detect, investigate, and terminate the intrusion, yet because of the "network of networks" nature of the Internet, detailed investigation leading to the location of an attacker is not likely to take place without the involvement and cooperation of law enforcement, Internet Service Providers (ISPs), and telecommunications providers. Unfortunately, this seldom occurs simply because the amount of work necessary to coordinate and carry out an investigation outweighs the value of finding the attacker—or at least it would require the group attacked to admit publicly that it had been attacked. These issues could be practically solved if we had an automated method for tracing attacks, particularly one that would protect the identity of the institution under attack.

Hasty Defense Is More Difficult

In many cases, the attack as launched has not been prepared for, and so the defenders must mount a hasty defense—not an easy task. Though the defenders know that something has happened, they may not be sure what, how, when, who, or why, but in all likelihood, speed is of the essence because evidence may be lost at any time. Usually the first step in such situations is to analyze what systems and/or networks may have been affected so that computer backups for those systems can be immediately secured and duplicated. A team may set to work analyzing the data contained on those backups, looking for clues to how the attack occurred. Additionally, the security staff may make duplicates of audit and transactions logs, as well as network traffic and/or firewall logs. At this point, the security staff will increase the level of auditing and monitoring conducted on the network, in order to collect improved evidence in the event of further attack. This may best be done with computers that are dedicated to "sniffing" packets off the network and storing the packets on removable media. Unfortunately, in the case of the hasty defense, it may or may not be clear whether the attack occurred from outside or inside—that is, the attacker may possibly be an authorized user, operating inside the network.

In the process of analyzing the attack, defenders may discover some unique aspect that is characteristic to the attack—for example, certain accounts are used, a particular time of day, and so on. That may be difficult, however, since many computer networks are complicated interconnections of heterogeneous equipment with numerous ways in which they can be accessed. In addition, it is necessary to characterize the attack, and this characterization will form the basis by which investigators will review data, looking for possible intrusions or unauthorized accesses. The process of analyzing the network topology (how computers interact or interconnect with others on the network) may also be of assistance.

This correlation must lead to the development of a profile for the intruder that can be used to search through the large volumes of historical as well as current data, looking for further evidence of intrusion. Ultimately, the endgame in the hasty defense is locating the attacker through a more and more detailed approximation of the "attack signature." Continued refinement of this signature through the collection of a significant number of intrusions helps to identify the attacker, even when normal means to gain access to the computer systems in question are used—such as signing into the system using a stolen user name and password. Once a sufficiently discriminating signature has been developed, the hasty defense takes on the nature of the prepared defense, and defenders can continue to investigate and/or terminate the attacker's access.

Automated search tools are important to detect intrusions in the large volumes of data involved in normal network operation. Since this produces a number of sessions that contain possible events that must be reviewed individually by investigators, review at this level requires the detailed reading of interactions between users, computers, and other users. Most of these sessions, as one would expect, are those of legitimate users so technology could be of enormous value here, if it could provide a means to detect and track unauthorized users without requiring investigators to read message internals. The response process, as seen by the defender, is shown in Figure 2.

Tracking Packets

One mechanism to identify tracks through the network could be facilitated by routers and the Internet service providers who operate them.[13] As indicated in Figure 2, if every time a packet left a router, the packet contents were fingerprinted, for example, by a checksumming or other mechanism implemented in hardware, one network could verify with its neighboring network that a packet with a specific fingerprint passed through the network at a given time.[14] This fingerprint could also be passed to the next network or destination system, which could then use the fingerprint to identify a specific packet, and each network on a hypothetical reverse path could then be queried to determine if it carried that particular packet. This, of course, could generate a very large amount of auxiliary data, which would, depending on how long it would be retained, have to be logged and stored, either by the routers or in repositories associated with them. (See Figure 3.)

A variant on this approach would keep statistical track of packet fingerprints over designated time frames, for example, over ten-minute periods, so that, with relatively much less storage, it could be determined with certainty that a given packet fingerprint did not pass through that network during that time frame. Although such a system would not be able to determine whether a given packet actually did pass through a network, it could be used to establish the negative.

If it were established that a given packet fingerprint was seen by

13. See Kahn and Lukasik, "Fighting Cyber Crime and Terrorism."

14. Such a fingerprint, also called a "Message Digest" by Rizzi ("Is Technology the Answer?") could be a cryptographic operation that takes an arbitrarily large input string and produces a relatively unique numeric representation. In other words, content information, that is, internals, are reduced to a number. The algorithm would be chosen so that it would be difficult to infer the input string from the fingerprint.

```
                    ╭─────────────╮
                    │   Target    │
                    ╰─────────────╯

Detect anomaly in system operation
First question: malfunction?
If no, declare an intrusion; activate internal CERT
Next question: Insider?
If "no," then

                          ↓

              ┌─────────────────────────┐
              │   Solicit Outside Help   │
              └─────────────────────────┘

Voluntary cooperation from other Sys Ads, CERTS
Track back along ISP-Host chain
Establish international crossings
Issue: when to bring in law enforcement?
When "now," then

                          ↓

            ┌───────────────────────────────┐
            │   Work Under Legal Procedures  │
            └───────────────────────────────┘

Limited by legal processes and rights of the innocent
Approved procedures for data collection
Trained and certified collectors
Probable cause for warrants for search and seizure?
Is this a national security attack?
```

yes	no
↓	↓

```
┌─────────────────────┐        ┌─────────────────────┐
│  Transistion to DoD │        │  Prosecute Attacker │
└─────────────────────┘        └─────────────────────┘

   Determination of             Chain of custody of evidence
   national response            Apprehension, indictment,
                                    extradition, trial
```

Fig. 2.   The viewpoint from the defender's position.

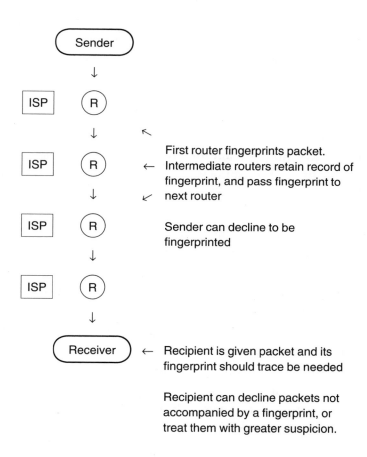

Fig. 3. Recovering the track of a packet.

N networks en route from host A to host B at a given time, that might be sufficient evidence to require disclosure of service-level information retained by host B that is correlated with the specific packet fingerprint, assuming it still existed. This information could then be used to correlate with the corresponding information in host A, which never had access to the packet fingerprint in the first place and therefore could not have initiated the inquiry. However, host A could initiate a reverse query based on received packets from host B, whose packet fingerprint host B was not privy to. This would let host A take the lead in identifying the reverse channel, and let host B take the lead in identifying the forward channel. If executed effectively, this would have an impact similar to the impact that accessing billing records has in tracing use of the telephone system and would be a useful tool for enabling cyber attackers to be identified and located.

A similar suggestion is made by Stephen Rizzi, who notes that technology for privacy-protecting packet tracing would also be desirable.[15] All too often an intrusion event is not investigated extensively because current manual methods do not allow for timely or privacy-protected tracing of multihop attacks. Technology is needed to support near-realtime automated tracing of multihop attacks. Such technology should protect the identity of the institution requesting the trace, to avoid undesired publicity, and in addition, the tracing algorithm should not directly use internals of the message to trace the origin. Such an architecture could be accomplished by the installation of a "trace server" on each registered domain subnet.

With time, such a server could be as important as a firewall. To be useful, all networks willing to support a trace capability would have such a server. The trace server would keep track of all incoming and outgoing traffic, and reduce those exchanges to time-stamped records with origin, destination, and a message digest, such as the fingerprint mentioned above. All this information would be encrypted using the

15. Ibid.

public key of a clearinghouse.[16] A tracing request would originate from a subscriber to the clearinghouse, again, encrypted using the public key of the clearinghouse with a query stating the perceived origin of the attack, the date/time range, and a message digest of suspect communications. The automated system at the clearinghouse would then begin a series of queries to trace servers of networks implicated in the attack. The automated clearinghouse matches up the outgoing traffic of one network with incoming traffic of another, tracing the communications until the point of origin is reached.

The communication channels and information resources used for coordinating investigation of attacks must be separate from the information resources that are the targets of attack, and they must receive special protection. This can be accomplished through an overlay on the network, but its functionality and points of origin must be limited to avoid compromise of the overlay itself. Clearly, the design and operation of such channels is a matter for international cooperation. As noted earlier, a need exists for anonymous communications between incident responders under some conditions, which suggests that care be taken in implementing such "back-channel" facilities.

Integration of Defensive Technologies

Current defenses against a cyber attack include prevention mechanisms such as firewalls, intrusion detection and response components, and security management applications, but a lack of communication and coordination between vendors' security components limits their effectiveness in large heterogeneous environments. Key technical and organizational issues limiting coordinated cyber defense across administrative and national boundaries can be identified, and challenges

---

16. A clearinghouse is an objective third-party organization that is considered a trusted recipient of information from member parties. A clearinghouse makes relevant information available to all parties without divulging source information that could violate the privacy of participating members.

in achieving agreements between international organizations on how these technologies can be integrated are substantial.

Automated response to intrusions is a major need for defending critical systems. Vendors have developed products that support intrusion response.[17] These products use proprietary protocols and are limited by an architecture that requires all response decisions to be made at a central controller. Because an adversary can take actions at computer speeds, systems must react at comparable speeds, implying the absence of human intervention.

Current tracking mechanisms have significant limitations, especially when applied to large heterogeneous environments such as the information infrastructure.[18] First, intrusion detection systems detect local intrusion symptoms and can only react locally, for example, by reconfiguring local boundary controllers and hosts. Because an attacker may cross many network boundaries, a local response by the target cannot identify or mitigate the true source of the attack. Second, even if intrusion detection systems were capable of communicating with boundary controllers near the attacker, there is no common language for remotely instructing them to handle selected traffic. It is also unlikely that intrusion detection systems would know enough about all such devices to be able to reconfigure them remotely using low-level, device-specific commands. Nor is it likely that the owners of such devices would allow it. Third, if intrusion "symptoms" are detected in different areas of an internetworked environment by different intrusion detection systems, current technology lacks the infrastructure and protocols for pooling this information to allow intrusion correlation and to develop and promulgate a coordinated response.

Current research is providing a framework that allows the inte-

17. See: Network Associates, "Active Security," available at ⟨*http://www.nai. com/asp_set/products/tns/activesecurity/acts_intro.asp/*⟩; Internet Security Systems, "RealSecure," available at ⟨*http://www.iss.net/prod/*⟩; AXENT Technologies, "Intruder Alert," available at ⟨*http://www.axent.com/product/smsbu/ITA/*⟩.

18. See Randall Smith, "Coordinated Cyber Defense," presentation at the Stanford Conference, December 6–7, 1999.

gration of detection and response components, thereby enabling experimentation with automated response strategies.[19] The Intruder Detection and Isolation Protocol (IDIP) has been shown to be capable of providing cooperative tracing of intrusions across network boundaries, blocking intrusions at boundary controllers near attack sources, using device-independent tracing and blocking directives, and centralizing reporting and coordination of intrusion responses.

Figure 4 shows system architecture that incorporates the IDIP. Each network in an administrative domain—for example, a company intranet—has an intrusion detector. Networks are connected through boundary controllers. In the example shown, an attacker, having legitimate access to his own network, intrudes upon two more remote networks where he is noted as an intruder. Intrusion reports are forwarded to a central discovery coordinator who is able to discern the attack path. The discovery coordinator issues a response instruction to the boundary controller closest to the attacker. The attacker is thereby identified and either an automated or a manual response can be initiated. Software components that have been successfully integrated using the IDIP are shown in Table 2.

To support communication between the varied IDIP components requires a flexible and extensible language. IDIP uses the Common Intrusion Specification Language (CISL) developed using the Common Intrusion Detection Framework (CIDF) as the language for describing attacks and responses.[20] This language includes terms for describing the blocking actions used in the current IDIP implementation, and it can be extended to support additional responses as they are developed. Currently, IDIP uses only two actions: block and allow. These can be

19. See *Protocol Definition Intruder Detection and Isolation Protocol Definition,* Interim Technical Report (CDRL A005), Boeing Document No. D658-10732-1, January 1997; *Dynamic Cooperating Boundary Controllers,* Final Technical Report (CDRL A003), Boeing Document No. D658-10822-1, February 1998; *Adaptive System Security Policies Preliminary Assessment* (CDRL A005), Boeing Document No. D658-10821-1, February 1998.

20. See Rich Feiertag et al., "A Common Intrusion Specification Language," June 1999, available at ⟨*http://www.gidos.org/*⟩.

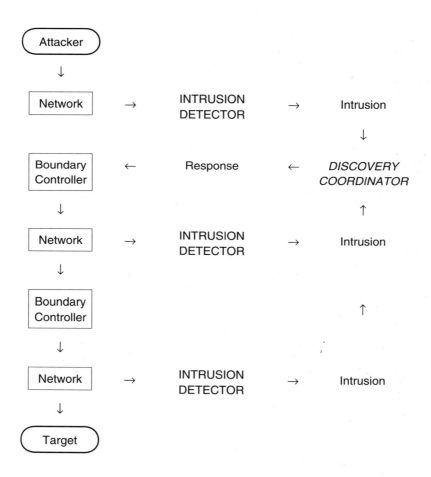

Fig. 4. Intrusion Detection and Isolation Protocol (IDIP) system architecture.

used with various objects (for example, users, processes, messages, or connections) to cause a number of different responses. A "block user" message, for example, is interpreted as a request to stop that user from doing anything; a "block user and connection" message is interpreted as a request that the user be prevented from using the specified connection. Connection information includes protocol, source address, source port, destination address, and destination port. Response messages can also include a specification of when to start and stop such actions.

An IETF working group is currently investigating standards for communications between intrusion detection components. One of the proposed standards is CIDF. The major modifications needed are a limitation of the type of information communicated, definition of data formats and exchange procedures for sharing information of interest with intrusion detection and response systems and the management systems that may need to interact with them, and the integration of the protocol into the TCP/IP suite of protocols. The requirements specification is currently an Internet Draft and has been forwarded to the IESG for publication. Other documents to be produced relate directly to the protocol: a definition of the data items desired in the messages to be exchanged; a definition of the message format; and a protocol for communicating the messages.

Coordinated Response to an Attack

Responses should be in proportion either to the damage already done or to the potential for future damage. Thus damages need to be assessed. When the attacker is inside, no external aid need be solicited, unless domestic law enforcement or other investigatory organizations are brought in. If the attacker is outside, the first question is whether he is located in the target's country; for if the attack is from or through another country, international cooperation will be needed. Furthermore, if the foreign country is the point of origin of the attack rather than a pass-through country, response will be different, because the

TABLE 2

Software Components That Have Been Integrated Through
the Intruder Detection and Isolation Protocol (IDIP)

Boundary controllers	Intrusion detection systems	Host-based responders
NAI Gauntlet™ Internet Firewall [a]	Net Squared Network Radar [b]	NAI Labs Generic Software Wrappers Prototype [c]
Secure Computing Corporation Sidewinder™ Firewall [d]	SRI EMERALD BSM and EMERALD FTP Monitors Prototype [e]	TCP Wrappers [f]
Linux Router [g]	UC Davis Graphical Intrusion Detection System (GRIDS) Prototype [h]	IP Filter [i]

[a] See ⟨*http://www.nai.com/asp_set/products/tns/intro.asp*⟩.

[b] See ⟨*http://www.NetSQ.com/Radar/*⟩.

[c] See T. Fraser et al., "Hardening COTS Software with Generic Software Wrappers," *Proceedings of the 1999 IEEE Symposium on Security and Privacy*, Oakland, Calif., May 1999.

[d] See ⟨*http://www.securecomputing.com/*⟩.

[e] See Ulf Lundqvist and Phillip A. Porras, "Detecting Computer and Network Misuse Through the Production-Based Expert System Toolset (P-BEST)," *Proceedings of the 1999 IEEE Symposium on Security and Privacy*, Oakland, Calif., May 1999.

[f] See ⟨*http://www.nai.com/asp_set/products/tns/intro.asp*⟩.

[g] See ⟨*http://www.linux.org/*⟩.

[h] See S. Saniford-Chen et al., "GRIDs—A Graph-Based Intrusion Detection System for Large Networks," *Proceedings of the 19th National Information Systems Security Conference*, October 1996.

[i] See ⟨*http://coombs.anu.edu.au/~avalon/ip-filter.html*⟩.

required investigation can impinge on its sovereignty. Greater cooperation can be expected if the foreign state is itself a victim or is an uninvolved transit country.

Need for a Global Incident Response Capability

Clearly, information exchange and interaction among many parties is necessary for producing comprehensive approaches and solutions to

TABLE 2
(*continued*)

Boundary controllers	Intrusion detection systems	Host-based responders
NAI Labs ARGuE Prototype [j]	Oregon Graduate Institute StackGuard [k]	
NAI Labs Multiprotocol Object Gateway Prototype [l]	Odyssey Research Associates CORBA Immune System Prototype [m] NAI CyberCop™ Server and CyberCop Monitor [n] Internet Security Systems RealSecure™ [o]	

[j] J. Epstein, "Architecture and Concepts of the ARGuE Guard," Proceedings of the 15th Annual Computer Security Applications Conference, Phoenix, Ariz., December 1999.

[k] C. Cowan et al., "StackGuard: Automatic Adaptive Detection and Prevention of Buffer-Overflow Attacks," Proceedings of the 7th USENIX Security Conference, San Antonio, Tex., January 1998.

[l] See G. Lamperillo, "Architecture and Concepts of the MPOG," NAI Labs reference no. 0768, June 1999.

[m] See "Computational Immunology for Distributed Large Scale Systems," available at ⟨http://www.oracorp.com/Projects/Current/CompImm.htm⟩.

[n] See ⟨http://www.nai.com/asp_set/products/tns/intro.asp⟩.

[o] See ⟨http://www.iss.net./prod/⟩.

system intrusions. The need is to support a global incident response effort and thereby to reduce the number and extent of computer security incidents. The Computer Emergency Response Team Coordination Center (CERT/CC) at Carnegie-Mellon University provides one basis for such a capability.[21] This Center, established by the U.S. Department of Defense in the late 1980s, has extensive practical experience in the conduct of violations of computer security. Incident response and computer security teams consist of practitioners and technologists who have operational experience but may lack authority to make policy and security decisions for their organizations. A re-

21. See Longstaff, "International Coordination for Cyber Crime and Terrorism."

sponse team may not have sufficient staff to respond effectively to all security incidents. At this time there is no infrastructure to support a coordinated global incident response effort, although there are some components that could form the basis of such an infrastructure.

A variety of issues must be addressed when considering how to promote an effective global incident response infrastructure. These include which organizations will coordinate and participate in the development effort, how current groups and forums can fit their missions and objectives into an agenda to create a global infrastructure, and what possible structures and mechanisms might be required in the future.

The 1999 Melissa virus attack underscores the lack of such a global response structure for incident response. Because individual teams focused on individual or national response needs, there was no operational global response effort. Although the Forum of Incident Response and Security Teams (FIRST) played an essential role in the early identification of the problem through reports shared among its member teams and was therefore able to notify others, it lacks the operational mission and funding necessary to facilitate further responses; almost four days elapsed from the initial activity report to solicitation and receipt of status reports and generation of the global activity summary. Even so, the resulting summary provided the needed global perspective on impacts and spread of remedial activity.

A global response capability can be achieved by building on existing incident response and security teams. Successful resolution of international incidents has been possible when the following elements were in place:

- A common terminology between parties involved in the incident to include identification of the intruder's modus operandi, the technical attack details, and the identification of the targets

- Knowledge of the technical skills of all parties involved in resolving the incident

- Existing agreements on how incidents of a variety of types will be handled

- An understanding of the common and conflicting societal issues surrounding the incidents

Such an approach is not necessarily dependent on international agreements or treaties between governments, but government-to-government agreements can significantly improve the effectiveness with which incidents are resolved.

FIRST is a possible basis for such an expanded international technical cooperation. Organized in the early 1990's, FIRST consists of more than eighty incident response and security teams from nineteen countries. It provides a closed forum for these teams to share experiences, exchange information related to incidents, and promote preventive activities. Although other teams exist that are not yet FIRST members, and new teams are constantly being established, the labor-intensive nature of incident response and the growing number of incidents leave the world with a dearth of capability. FIRST is a voluntary organization that provides an introduction service and meeting place for teams to establish trusted interactions, but since it lacks operational elements it cannot provide the necessary coordinated global effort or meet other needs, such as a more open flow of sensitive information and close collaboration to respond to widespread events. Overcoming these shortcomings will require appropriate policies and procedures, formal contractual agreements among its member organizations, and documented procedures to serve as guidance for new entrants.

Beyond formal structure, what is needed is a way to build on personal trust relationships to achieve organizational trust. Gaining entry to the incident response community can be a difficult and lengthy process; the community is ready to embrace new members, but it is wary of interacting with new teams until an existing member of the trusted community can vouch for them. A global incident response capability is difficult to build rapidly, but national boundaries, which provide a demarcation for policies, procedures, and jurisdiction for information exchange, are a natural starting point. Response teams that cross national boundaries, such as incident response teams for multinational corporations, are another useful basis for international cooperation. Above all, there must be participation and cooperation among governments, law enforcement agencies, commercial organizations, the research community, and practitioners who have experience in responding to computer security incidents.

Different Viewpoints of Victims and Law Enforcers

Rapid collection of forensic evidence is needed by both victims and police.[22] Police seek to identify the attacker; the victim has the task of cleaning the attacked hosts and getting them back into operation. With limited technical resources, the defender's efforts must be divided among learning the extent of the invasion, reconfiguring hosts to be resistant to future attacks, getting the hosts back on-line, and helping law enforcement agents track down the attackers. Even though the evidence gathered at these first steps is often too vague to prove a defendant's guilt, it can provide probable cause for further investigation. Rarely does an attacker explicitly give away his or her identity. Either the "smoking gun" evidence is found on the attacker's own computer, or is observed through interception of a data stream while a crime is being committed.

Once law enforcement agencies have collected evidence from the scene of the crime, the evidence must then be combined with the evidence collected by the defender. This should show that the evidence collected from the crime scene is directly tied to evidence collected from the intrusion site. Items found at the scene such as lists of usernames and passwords, computer and network addresses, help screens from attacked applications, and so on, can be correlated with evidence stored by the defender that documents the intrusions. To be usable in

---

22. See William Cheswick, "Internet Forensics and Cyber Crime in Court," prepared for the Stanford Conference, December 6–7, 1999.

court, evidence collected by the defender must be properly collected and stored.

Usually law enforcement and the victim will keep a write-locked copy of each disk image dump. A growing number of tools are available for examining and processing image dumps. Speed is essential because ISPs generally keep their logs for only a few days. In the U.S., ISPs generally require a subpoena before supplying log data to law enforcement agencies. But they will preserve log data, which may normally be kept for only two or three days, in anticipation of a subpoena. Evidence collected at the scene of the crime will provide additional clues for what to look for in the defender's historical data, so that eventually, a comprehensive profile can be developed to re-analyze the data, documenting information to support prosecution.

Computer Forensic Issues in Law Enforcement

Log-keeping is an important part of dealing with the Internet. Logs help identify usage patterns, administrative and configuration errors, misuse, and attacks. Mailers keep logs to help identify sources of spam mail. Firewalls log rejected packets. Authentication servers record account usage, and DHCP servers record caller ID information, accounts, and IP addresses assigned. ISP records of this sort are particularly important in tracing attacks back to their source. Such logs, kept in the ordinary course of business, are admissible in court. However, since nearly all computer forensic evidence is machine-readable, it is subject to easy and undetectable editing. Governments have to deal with this obvious possibility.

Providing access to logs is a source of tension for ISPs, particularly those who do not wish to become involved in legal actions. If logs are discarded routinely, without backup, the investigatory process will have less information to utilize. Logs to handle routine problems such as mailing errors are seldom needed for more than a week. On the other hand, firewall logs of suspicious activity are preserved on a WORM drive, where they remain available indefinitely.

Bulk backups and disk image copies may provide usable and admissible evidence if the chain of evidence is preserved. CD-ROMs are useful for preserving evidence, though they lack the capacity to deal with current online storage technology. Newer technology such as write-once DVD disks should help. Image backup tapes need a write-protect switch to prevent inadvertent overwrites that can be sealed at the time of the dump. Although a switch can be defeated with a modified tape reader, there are cryptographic solutions to this problem as well, since cryptographic checksums verify that data have not been tampered with. There are also time-stamping services that can verifiably time-stamp a checksum without revealing the actual data.[23]

Possession of username and password files is illegal in the U.S.[24] Password files are access devices, and the mere presence of several of these files on a defendant's computer is illegal, even if there is no evidence that they have been cracked. However, the use of a username/password pair is not proof that the owner is at fault, since accounts are easy to steal and many sites offer free e-mail accounts with user-selectable account names. Nor is possession of code evidence that it has been used. Although idiosyncrasies of code may be suspicious, it has been difficult for law enforcement agencies to prove that particular code was actually used. This has been a crucial problem in prosecutions. Code idiosyncrasies may strengthen a case, but software is often widely known. Further complicating prosecution is the fact that cyber crime usually involves innocent third parties.

Issues Surrounding ISPs

Internet Service Providers are the entry point to cyberspace. On one side of the ISP is the "user," the arena of private property, civil rights against unreasonable search and seizure, rights to privacy, and due process. The other side of the ISP can be characterized as "commons,"

---

23. See S. Haber and W. S. Stornetta, "How to Time-Stamp a Digital Document," *Journal of Cryptology* 3 (1990/91): 99–112.
24. 18 U.S.C. § 1029.

something shared, and hence something where the rights of various entities are not absolute but must be balanced against the common good. Damage to the commons affects all who use it. This balancing of rights and responsibilities is a matter of process, which can be voluntary or may be subject to various domestic and international laws and agreements.

Law enforcement agencies need help from ISPs, regardless of their location. They will want real-time access to packet streams and authentication to tap specific sessions, giving stronger links between the user and criminal activities. Some ISPs assist in these matters when they can, but it is a difficult job. The growth of the Internet leaves hardware running at full speed, with few spare facilities for this activity. For a busy router, some kind of hardware assist will be necessary, and this can only be provided by the router manufacturers, and only in response to ISP or legal requirements. Since this would increase the costs of the router, it may take legislation similar to the CALEA requirements for the telephone system.[25] Such requirements would have to be international to be effective, and in the long run they will probably not work, for the ubiquitous encryption that is coming will frustrate many of these efforts. The new generation of CPUs, driven by such needs as voice recognition and game graphics, have adequate power to apply strong encryption to network traffic streams, and there is little hope that even a government will have the resources to penetrate these sessions directly. Even weakened or broken cryptography presents a large economic obstacle to real-time wiretaps; 40-bit encryption is considered weak, but it is not easily amenable to real-time cracking. High-performance hardware is required to extract even plaintext packets from packet streams.

The Fifth Amendment to the U.S. Constitution complicates the question of whether a defendant can be forced to reveal passwords and unlock cryptographic keys. Other complications arise when an

---

25. See Commission on Accreditation for Law Enforcement Agencies 〈*http:// www.calea.org*〉.

ISP is itself under investigation. Specific circuit identifications can be obtained from telephone companies to determine connectivity, but the extent to which one can trust the logs of an ISP that may itself be compromised, possibly inadvertently, is unclear. Given an IP address, there are still questions about the actual location of the computer at the time of the alleged crime, and the identity of the actual user.

The Wide Range of Responsibilities of ISPs

From the standpoint of the ISP, it must, as a first priority, protect its own hardware, software, and databases from compromise, meet contractual commitments to its customers, maintain the continuity of its business, and guard against liabilities arising from allegations of negligence.[26] Attacking routers and switches can compromise the entire network infrastructure, and such attacks are heavily defended against, though how effectively remains to be established.[27] In addition, ISPs must help protect their customers from accidental and malicious actions on the Internet. Finally, they may be seen to have some sort of responsibility, at least implied, to the global community to protect it from the accidental or malicious actions of their customers. These responsibilities are difficult to fulfill in the face of rapidly changing technologies—which imply frequent upgrades in systems; rapidly growing market demands that require frequent upgrades in capacity, rapid changes in the ability of hackers and criminals to compromise networks and computers, and rapid changes in security technology that must be assessed and in which investments must be made.

ISPs cannot ignore security issues, but selecting and implementing appropriate security measures in a timely manner while maintaining high traffic throughput to the Internet nevertheless requires a high degree of cooperation among ISPs and communication providers. The

26. See Barry R. Greene, "ISP Security Issues in Today's Internet," presentation at the Stanford Conference, December 6–7, 1999.

27. See "Improving Security on Cisco Routers," available at ⟨*http:// www.cisco.com/warp/public/707/21.html*⟩.

open management environment in which the Internet operates and the dedication of its vendors and operators to meeting the needs of its users requires the balancing of these opposing tendencies of cooperation in protecting the commons and in competition among themselves. The maintenance of this environment is under severe pressure, however, as the Internet and the number of its users expands. A central consideration, as we move to protect the Internet and its users, is that while doing good, we should also do nothing that will limit its potential for continued growth.

A Proactive Program for Internet Security

Given these considerations, a statement of best common practices for ISPs is needed.[28] Such a document, or family of documents addressing recommended practices to various degrees of depth, should be prepared and updated to reflect current business and technical trends. This is the proper task of an industry or trade association. Adherence would be voluntary, although in view of the tradition of service to Internet users, one might expect it to be adopted for reasons of efficiency and economy. Should risk management through insurance become widespread, such best common practices could naturally assume the role of minimum standards for insurability and protection against allegations of negligence.

Security research and product development is undertaken by ISP hardware and software vendors and this can be expected to increase the level of protection in deployed information networks. A desirable result would be for differences in security to become a market differentiator for ISPs, much as price, quality and reliability of service, and ease of use are today. There are a number of vendor roles including close interaction of router vendors' operations staff with those of ISPs; providing personnel for product support emergency reaction teams; having product development staff working with customers on new

---

28. See "BCPs for ISPs—Essential IOS Features Every ISP Should Consider," available at ⟨*http://www.cisco.com/public/cons/isp/documents/*⟩.

features; providing security consultants for assistance with countering attacks, undertaking audits, and prosecuting intruders; and staff who track hacker communities.[29]

3. Automation of Computer and Network Protection

Labor-intensive approaches to computer and network security can use automated tools and techniques to improve their speed and efficiency. Timeliness will minimize losses due to attacks; efficiency will enable more protection to be provided for a given level of resources applied; scaling to accommodate the growing number of attacks can, in principle, be achieved; and privacy for innocent users can be enhanced to a degree through automated rather than manual screening of traffic. All too frequently, the requirement for privacy conflicts with the need for protection; once people have exhausted their ability to protect themselves, they must appeal for assistance, and this inevitably involves some sacrifice of privacy. Nevertheless, it is reasonable for victims of cyber intrusion to expect their protectors to tread as softly as possible, and that those seeking protection have options as to how much protection they will receive and what price, in terms of loss of privacy, they are willing to pay.

Tools to Automate Protection

Automated tools can improve protection in various ways. For example, if information is only accessible by reference to its unique identifier or handle, the ability to collect and analyze data on system use can be greatly augmented. At a minimum, the ability to establish the presence of a user at a given place in the global information system will be critical for evidentiary purposes, recognizing also that the ability to

---

29. See "Product Security Incident Response Teams (PSIRT)," ⟨*http://www. cisco.com/warp/public/707/sec_incident_response.shtml*⟩.

challenge such evidence and contest differing points of view or interpretations will also be needed.[30]

One class of tools, noted earlier, are those that detect intrusion and other unauthorized uses of network and computer systems and high-level services. These will range from the more obvious tasks of checking log-ins to be sure they match authorized users, to running software agents on the machine to detect other software agents that may arrive without authorization. Agents that are able to detect the presence of, and oppose, other agents may be a possible countermeasure.

Another class of tools for protection would monitor current usage of all relevant machine resources and look for unusual patterns. Periodic checks of user identity might be warranted. Compared with traditional password protection schemes, cryptographic log-in systems provide considerable increases in protection against unauthorized access. Unlike the traditional password systems, cryptographic log-ins are not vulnerable to playback attacks and other attacks that involve stealing passwords. Alternate systems based on public key encryption can be used to authenticate users.

Automation of protection could be implemented in the network, tracking patterns of usage in real-time and alerting system operators to unusual conditions for manual or semiautomated review. Another automated approach to preserving privacy would be to package suspected sessions and e-mail them to the user to verify that it was indeed that user who was actually at the keyboard for that session.

Timely Tracking

Pursuing an attacker can reduce future exploitation of system vulnerabilities. Rapid response will minimize compromise and contain damage that may have occurred. This would require the cooperation of

30. See Joseph Betser. "Tracking Cyber Attacks," presentation at the Stanford Conference, December 6–7, 1999. See also the contributions by Rizzi and by Kahn and Lukasik.

automated software modules en route from and at the attack source. It would also require trust among the cooperating organizations and technical activities that are in place to facilitate such automated communication among software modules.[31]

There are several meanings of "timely." One is "session time," the time during which the intruder is logged-in. Information collected during this time will enable tracking most easily since all the links in the attacker's path are open, but this sort of tracking requires not only an unusual degree of readiness but also technical capability. Once the intruder is no longer on-line, traces of the surreptitious activity, other than any changes made or code purposely left behind, are—if the intruder is skilled—likely to have been erased.

A second time period of importance is the transaction clearing time, that is, the time between the on-line action by the intruder and when the intruder's desired goal is achieved. This will depend on such things as the organizations and business processes involved, the calendar date, and the objectives of the attack. In some cases, the intruder can achieve the goal while still on-line; in others, actions will be required by other organizations to bring the act to fruition.

Another time period is the "revisit" interval of the attacker. From penetration experiments, we recognize that attacks are not single isolated events but frequently consist of multiple intrusions to collect information about the system, to undertake various test and practice actions, or to exploit a vulnerability repeatedly.[32] For the intruder,

31. See M. Wood, "Intrusion Detection Message Exchange," IETF Draft, October 1999; D. Schnackenberg, K. Djahandari, and D. Sterne, "Infrastructure for Intrusion Detection and Response" (forthcoming: DARPA Information Survivability Conference and Exposition (DISCEX), Hilton Head Island, S.C., 2000); R. Smith et al., "Multi Community Cyber Defense," DARPA Information Assurance and Survivability Principal Investigator Meeting, Phoenix, Ariz., August 1999; Smith, "Coordinated Cyber Defense."

32. See Raymond Parks, G. Schudel, and Bradley Wood, "Modeling Behavior of the Cyber-Terrorist," presentation at the Stanford Conference, December 6–7, 1999; B. Wood and G. Schudel, "Red Team Experiments 9901 and 9907," DARPA Information Assurance and Survivability Principal Investigator Meeting, Phoenix, Ariz., August 1999.

success means achieving the objectives of the attack and remaining undetected. Though one may have multiple opportunities to detect an intruder, one may have to sustain repeated successful intrusions before succeeding in plugging the hole.

A fourth measure is the time needed by the attacker to evade pursuit, such as to shift from one location or jurisdiction to another. There might also be an explicit threat time, such as occurs with an announced deadline.

Next Generation IP Protocols

The output of the IETF working groups in the security area may have positive effects on protecting information systems.[33] A major development that will help is the implementation of IPv6, the next generation of the Internet Protocol.[34] IPv6 addresses several issues that can have a significant impact on network security. First, IPv6 expands the address space for network device addresses from 32 bits to 128 bits. A problem with the depletion of addresses in IPv4, the current version of IP, is that in order to support new network hosts, various workarounds have been required, resulting in a situation where not all hosts have unique IP addresses.

IPv6 has another feature likely to prove powerful in tracing the origin of a message: the "hop-by-hop" header, which allows each of the routers along the delivery path to exercise certain options. An obvious option that would enhance tracing activities is to have each router that has forwarded the message record its address in the message header. The problem with using "hop-by-hop" in this manner is that each packet will be modified by a number of devices enroute, with the distinct possibility that one of those devices, for example, controlled by an attacker, could change the routing history.

Another approach that could be used is controlling the intercon-

---

33. See Erlinger, "Internet Protocols for Protection Against Cyber Crime."
34. See S. Deering and R. Hinden, "Internet Protocol, Version 6 (IPv6 Specification)," RFC 2460, available at ⟨http://www.ietf.org/rfc/rfc2460.txt⟩.

nection of routers to the point where routers will only accept traffic from certain other "trusted" routers or users. Although this changes the way routing is currently done, it could provide enhanced security over the current practice.

Encryption is another method of securing network activities from cyber crime. In an environment where each transaction between hosts is encrypted, there is a guarantee that the source and destination are known. This allows traceback, but only if we are willing to support strong encryption and incur the overhead of encryption on network interactions.

Facilities for Internet Monitoring

There is also a need to enhance security by monitoring for persistent but marginal internal network problems from locations outside the network. For example, a network that consistently loses one percent of all packets sent over it may appear to be working well, but the small loss can be important. The loss may be due to a failing component in the network, but it could also be caused by an insider who has altered the network without authorization. Collectively, other networks connected to such a network could federate to detect and report the problem if they had access to all its inputs and outputs, or the network itself could detect the problem if it insisted on the equivalent of double-entry bookkeeping. Some of these problems can be alleviated with more effective cooperation among ISPs, as is happening within the Internet operators (IOPS) organization.[35] IOPS consists of many of the largest national and international ISPs who collaborate to prevent or alleviate problems in the Internet and routinely share information on a confidential basis. In addition, they seek to improve performance and efficiency where such improvements require collaboration.

Whether part of tagging and tracking or as passive observation in a statistical sense, monitoring Internet traffic statistically will require

35. See ⟨*http://www.iops.org*⟩.

an embedded data collection infrastructure that does not currently exist.[36] Modification of router and switch hardware and software is technically possible, although it is unclear whether vendors would be interested. Because of concerns over privacy, it will be even more difficult to secure user buy-in. Regulation is one way of addressing user reluctance; market incentives, such as insurance, are another.

Even granted that Internet monitoring is politically and economically feasible, much detailed technical work must be undertaken. Requirements must be defined, monitoring facilities must be designed and deployed, and an organized data collection operation must be managed.[37]

Scaling and the Need to Provide Information to Aid in Establishing Priorities

Providing international assistance involves more than a potential incursion on a nation's sovereignty and on its citizens' privacy. It will require human and technical resources that are often in short supply. If cyber attacks continue to increase, and if the number of affected countries increases, and as all equip themselves with intrusion detectors, the number of requests for assistance will grow substantially. Furthermore, owing to the presumed time urgency of the requests, responding to such requests will have disruptive effects on the nations involved.

Consider, for example, data reported in recent U.S. GAO reports.[38]

36. Claffy, "Traffic Observation in a Stateless Data Networking Environment."
37. See "High Performance Networks: Measurement and Analysis Collaborations," Workshop, June 29–30, 1999, and "Challenges and Opportunities for Measurement and Analysis in a High Performance Computing Environment," Workshop, July 1, 1999. Both workshops were sponsored by the National Science Foundation and hosted by the San Diego Supercomputer Center, San Diego, Calif. See also ⟨http://www.caida.org⟩ and ⟨http://www.nlanr.net⟩.
38. See *Information Security Computer Attacks at Department of Defense Pose Increasing Risks*, GAO/AIMD-96-84, May 22, 1996; *Information Security Opportunities for Improved OMB Oversight of Agency Practices*, GAO/AIMD-96-110, September 24, 1996.

It is believed that in 1995 there were roughly 250,000 penetrations of computer systems owned by the U.S. federal government alone. Based on controlled penetration testing, it is estimated that 64 percent (160,000) of these were successful. The GAO also estimated that only 1–4 percent of these attacks were detected, and only a quarter of those detected were reported. Based on a database of 30,000 incidents, Thomas Longstaff notes that 40 percent have a foreign component.[39] This would suggest that 600 attacks per year might qualify for requests for foreign assistance in tracking intruders. If, as estimated by the GAO, the number of such attacks is doubling annually, that many more of those detected could be reported, that many more penetrations could be detected with the deployment of new intrusion detection technology, and that these numbers only cover the intrusions into U.S. government computers, the obvious conclusion is that the number of requests in the future for assistance from other countries could easily exceed the ability of those called upon to respond. Therefore nations will need some kind of criteria for assessing the impact of attacks in order to evaluate the seriousness of intrusion events in the light of available investigatory resources.

Reconciling the positions of those who see governments as part of the solution and those who see governments as part of the problem will not be easy. Making Internet protection architectures and operations public will reduce the anxiety of some, but possibly at a certain cost in the effectiveness of the protection offered, and it may complicate the collection of forensic evidence. Since much of the burden will fall on ISPs, we have to evaluate both the economic cost-benefits and the social cost-benefits in deciding how best to strengthen the protection of the commons.

---

39. See Longstaff, "International Coordination for Cyber Crime and Terrorism."

4. The Need for Cooperative Action

The common situation, where the victim and the attacker are in different sovereign jurisdictions, or where the attacker has transited other sovereign jurisdictions, will require agreements on a variety of subjects. In light of the speed with which computer-mediated events unfold, the processes employed by those seeking to understand the nature and source of the attack will require prior agreements if the operation of systems is to be restored in a timely manner and damage minimized.

An International Forum in Which Diverse Stakeholders Can Interact

Since, unlike jurisdictions based on national boundaries, the digital information infrastructure does not have a central location in the physical world, responding to attacks not only is difficult technically, it also limits the use of accepted methods for practicing law enforcement. Recent G-8 and OECD activities are examples of increasing recognition of this international problem. Improving critical information infrastructures requires involvement of diverse parties, including governments, policy- and lawmakers, law enforcement, software vendors, the research community, and practitioners, such as FIRST members, who have experience responding to computer security incidents.[40] Attempting to address the problems in one group without input and feedback from the others can result in incomplete solutions. For example, recent U.S. legislation, the Digital Millennium Copyright Act, resulting from the World Intellectual Property Organization (WIPO) treaty, generated concern within the Internet security community. Practitioners, researchers, software vendors, and incident response teams noted the legislation could limit some aspects of their efforts to address security flaws and reduce risk to critical infrastructures. Though this was clearly not the drafters' intent, it is an example

40. Ibid.

of the need for ongoing communication among policymakers, technologists, and others to ensure that future policies and agreements on national and international scales are practical and effective.

Frequently, information is reported to incident response teams that does not involve a specific victim or computer security incident but does indicate that some activity may be ongoing in some part of the community. Currently, there is no standard way of sharing that information, although sometimes this information is posted to a shared list of FIRST members. The sharing of information relating to emerging technical threats is increasing and this trend is to be encouraged. The technical forums that FIRST sponsors on a periodic basis to discuss recent developments in technical threats and vulnerabilities have been effective for the incident response community, but they are not open to other international experts to relate the technical trends to broader international concerns.

The tracking of sources of even small amounts of traffic is likely to be important in locating perpetrators of crimes. Hints of activity in the form of programs left behind, usernames assumed, methods of operation, and so on are all likely to be of significance in determining identities and locations of attackers. Systematically checking for such information, as well as other best practices is required. Exploiting these understandings of attacker behavior can assist in defending against them, a technique Raymond Parks refers to as "dynamic defense."[41] Therefore it is important to exchange both general and specific information on attacker modus operandi to provide the greatest degree of protection for the greatest part of the global information infrastructure.

A best-practices document prepared by an international group of experts and updated periodically would assist in establishing de facto standards. Conforming to best practices should be a part of justifying international cooperation in obtaining redress.

A database of attacks and known viruses has been compiled by

41. Parks, Schudel, and Wood, "Modeling Behavior of the Cyber Terrorist."

organizations such as the CERT/CC at Carnegie-Mellon University's Software Engineering Institute. It would be helpful to restructure this information so that it can be used directly by automated tools to detect patterns of criminal activity.

Prioritizing Requests for Assistance

Not every case of cyber crime will require international cooperation, nor will every case be equally deserving of such cooperation; it will be necessary, as Kahn and Lukasik have suggested, to establish priorities, with each request that is made being subject to some form of evaluation.[42] As a minimum, and assuming assistance is merited on the basis of the magnitude of the attack or the extent of the loss, the following questions are likely to be raised:

1. Due Diligence. Has the requesting organization conformed to best practices as formulated for its industry?

2. Rapid Response. Has the requesting organization implemented near real-time monitoring and auditing of its information systems?

3. Potential Impact. Has the potential impact of the intrusion been evaluated and ranked in terms of importance to enable an assessment of the degree of international cooperation that is justified?

4. Probable Cause. How has the requesting organization established that the intruder used the facilities of the country whose assistance is sought?

Although all signatories to an international agreement will have a right to assistance under its terms, there are practical limits on what can be reasonably provided. If information systems continue to remain poorly protected and if their vulnerabilities are increasingly exploited,

---

42. Kahn and Lukasik, "Fighting Cyber Crime and Terrorism."

the need for assistance will greatly exceed what can be made available, and the necessary expertise will become a rate-limiting factor in the resolution of intrusions. In such a case, some form of rationing or prioritizing of assistance can be expected. It will be useful to factor such prioritizing criteria into an agreement to encourage improving the state of self-protection throughout the world. Thus, apart from the direct assistance that can arise from an international agreement, the long-term systemic improvement that can be thereby facilitated is an important goal.

Internationally Agreed-Upon Means to Validate Information

Certificates can be used to authenticate information as well as users. A piece of information in digital form can be cryptographically "fingerprinted" and the result attached to the information or stored separately from it. The certificates can be used to verify packet fingerprints, which in turn will verify the underlying information.

Another method of validation could rely on encrypted archived "snapshots" of critical information provided by or taken from key locations in the net or even from user systems. The archive could be run by a trusted third party, who would warehouse the information for whatever period was deemed appropriate. This information could be retrieved and decoded after the fact to provide insight into problems and to corroborate other evidence.

Automated Cooperation Beyond
Local Administrative Domains

Global cyber defense will involve the sharing of cross-organizational intrusion information and arriving at cooperative responses. The mechanisms for doing this must be capable of being tailored to protect sensitive information and must allow organizations to manage their trust relationships. An essential part of such cooperation is the ability to recognize when multiple parts of the global infrastructure are simultaneously under attack.

The Defense Advanced Research Projects Agency (DARPA) program in Multi-Community Cyber Defense (MCCD) is directed to identifying the primary barriers that limit effective sharing of attack-related information with neighboring organizations and mounting a coordinated defense against detected attacks. This work seeks to extend the IDIP by focusing on three key areas: (1) providing local administrative control over the release of their internal attack-related information, including sanitizing data prior to release; (2) establishing and maintaining trust relationships between organizations; and (3) developing higher-level capabilities for conducting attack analyses and data fusion.[43] These capabilities will be integrated into the IDIP framework by adding additional functionality to the IDIP components and by extending the message language used to communicate between components.

To provide strategic defense of critical infrastructure requires that organizations that do not normally share information are able to cooperate in responding to attacks. In the DoD, problems arise when communication occurs between classification domains or across coalition force domains. In the commercial arena, organizations are mutually suspicious. Even when organizations work together as partners, they must protect various types of proprietary information. In either case, there are problems in both releasing data to, and accepting response directives from, remote domains.

In a cooperative environment, the following potential types of information could be sent between administrative domains to improve intrusion detection, correlation, and response:

(a) Near real-time information and requests, including (1) attack notification, and (2) response recommendation

(b) Slower, but still immediate information and requests, includ-

43. Smith, "Coordinated Cyber Defense."

ing (1) correlation results concerning an immediate problem, and (2) discovery coordinator requests for immediate action

(c) Human-speed information and requests, including (1) policy information, (2) correlation results, and (3) other information to be used by higher-level correlators, and alerts from higher-level strategic warning systems

All but the human-speed actions are intended to be sent automatically between administrative domains. The last type would instead be handled by a "trusted" third party that would provide a global situation awareness and response capabilities. In addition to enhancing the IDIP framework to include this type of message, each domain must have the ability to establish a policy for information sharing and for verifying that the policy is implemented.

The likelihood that remote organizations will not completely trust each other, or will not be able to share information fully because of policy, requires more constrained information flows at organizational boundaries—such as, for example, the IDIP requests for severity and certainty fields. The severity field indicates the degree of potential damage the requester might suffer if the attack continues, the certainty field indicates the degree of confidence the requester has that its detection mechanisms have detected a bona fide attack. Together, these fields may reveal the power of the domain's detection mechanisms and the extent to which it can protect itself against various kinds of attacks. That information may need to be sanitized at a domain boundary. Because the remote domain may have fewer safeguards than the local domain, releasing this information can result in giving attackers additional data to be used in an attack. Executing remotely generated response directives requires trusting the originator, or at least establishing controls that limit the damage from untrusted originators. For example, one might take action only if attack information can be corroborated locally.

Blind trust in the results of intrusion-detection algorithms could enable a serious attacker to cause the detection and response system to misbehave by first penetrating the detection component. Unquestioned erroneous reports from a penetrated detection component could have a number of effects, including shutdown of critical subsystems in response to nonexistent attacks, claims that other detectors have been penetrated and therefore should be ignored, or changes to the state of other detectors, causing them to reduce their warning levels. These issues are being addressed by investigating mechanisms for determining: (1) the current trust in a remote domain, (2) changes in detection and response policy based on the current trust relationships between domains, (3) changes in trustworthiness, and (4) the point when trustworthiness has been reinstated.

Research on cryptographic trust models and fault-tolerant systems can be applied to this area. Results from the cryptographic trust model community can be applied to establishing authenticated identity, but the trust computed for what appears to be authentic data must be modified based on intrusion-related data from other sources. Techniques used in fault-tolerant systems for voting, diagnosing components, and redundancy are directly applicable.

The MCCD architecture, based on an enhanced IDIP framework and integrated with high-level analysis and correlation techniques, should provide the capabilities necessary to enable organizations to implement cooperative agreements on sharing attack-related information, analyzing and identifying serious threats, and executing coordinated responses to detected attacks against global information systems.

Cooperative International R&D to Meet Evolving Threats

The global research and development community must be heavily involved in efforts aimed at protecting information systems and their users from cyber attack. As information technology rapidly evolves, threats, vulnerabilities, and protective measures are also changing. Hence continuing R&D activities are required in order to be able to meet the still evolving threats.

In addition to currently available technology, a number of areas of industrial and academic research that might yield novel paradigms for addressing the rising challenges of information assurance and survivability have been noted:[44]

- Economic, financial, and market-based paradigms. Tapping the checks-and-balances, which are used by the financial community in order to reduce unauthorized activities, and using market incentives to promote proper use of cyberspace.

- Biological immunology paradigms. Adopting some of the paradigms that make the human body successful in identifying and fighting invading bodies, in spite of the complex nature of the biological systems involved.

- Public health paradigms. Computer viruses, and perhaps even the computer-based attack, can be considered an invading disease in the multinational body of the Internet. In public health practice, nations participate collaboratively in the exchange of infectious disease information, and concepts such as quarantine, immunization, and treatment may apply.

- Reliability paradigms. Using experience gained in complex process systems, such as chemical and nuclear plants, should be considered. The large number of dynamic variables and the delicate interplay among them might provide insight for dealing with complex cyber scenarios.

- Correlation paradigms. The defense against coordinated attacks that use large enterprises to execute multiphase complex attacks requires correlation of different attack components in order to detect and defend successfully. The development of fast correlation algorithms and their implementation in systems will be important.

- Expert systems paradigms. Learning algorithms are very useful

44. Betser, "Tracking Cyber Attacks."

in studying the normal behavior of a system and achieving the ability to detect abnormal and anomalous behavior that can occur during a cyber attack.

- Data mining paradigms. Obtaining useful information from voluminous audit logs and event records requires expertise in data mining.

- Control science paradigms. The ability to generate an effective adaptive response to combat the attack in progress. Feedback to the response policy could stabilize and move the system to a healthier state.

A distributed international facility for experiments, tests, and demonstrations of security products and services could speed the transfer of R&D advances. The IDIP technology developed to date can be inserted in a number of commercial off-the-shelf (COTS) components, including intrusion-detection products, firewalls and filtering routers, security management components, and clients and servers. The IDIP software was designed for portability and is currently executing on Solaris, BSDI, Linux, and Windows NT platforms. Operating system dependencies were minimized during the development and have been encapsulated. This design provides an easy, low-cost integration path into COTS products, enabling vendors to adopt the technology with minimal investment. Both widespread integration and acceptance of this framework, and agreements on the international use of this technology, are needed to protect global information systems.

Facilitating Trust

Agreements are on paper, and they are necessary for the reasons suggested. But agreements are implemented by people and people tend not to accept matters at face value; they do not trust people with whom they have not previously interacted with satisfactory outcomes. Thus agreements, while necessary, are not sufficient. Trust is another necessary dimension. One can expect that self-protection technologies, agreements, and trust together will provide both necessary and sufficient conditions for global security. Ultimately, some trust must be placed in parts of the system—for example in the authentication systems or encryption systems. But because, as with any human system, even those parts could be compromised, we shall still need trust at the individual level as well as at the organizational level. An international treaty, by facilitating increased interactions among all stakeholders can be expected to help in this process.

Clearinghouses, or other impartial third-party nongovernmental organizations, will be important as security risks become more pervasive and more complex. Having a mechanism whereby anonymous interactions and cooperation can take place through a trusted third party would help in these circumstances. This trusted-third-party construct would be part of a larger "trust network" in which communications can be passed without conveying identity. Institution of a "hot line" concept for computer attack might also reduce risk. Such a secure and redundant system could provide signatory nations in a multinational regime with the means to communicate assessments of the intent of detected activities. It could also provide states the confidence needed to collaborate against a common threat.

Reducing "Safe Harbors" for Criminals Through Adherence to International Agreements

Those nations that do not recognize the realities of cyber vulnerabilities—or wish to exploit them—will ultimately become safe harbors for criminals and cyber terrorists. The international community should seek incentives for all nations to participate in international conventions to combat these threats. Such a convention should put "teeth" into what is expected of signatory nations: signatory nations would put pressure on other nations to meet minimum standards for the deterrence of cyber crime and for investigation, prosecution, and extradition, so that, ultimately, nations that refuse to sign the convention could face sanctions, possibly extending to "disconnection" from international networks—a sort of cyber isolation. The international convention proposed in this volume would satisfy these requirements.

Implementing Cooperative Actions

Most of the above suggestions, such as exchanging intrusion data and attack profiles, undertaking cooperative R&D, and establishing clearinghouses for anonymous communication, do not require broad international agreements; specific actions could be implemented on bilateral or multilateral bases. But if global changes in the security of information infrastructures are to be achieved, some larger international framework can assist in facilitating cooperation. Elements of such a framework for international cooperation, drawn from various international contexts, are:

- Broad membership, consisting of both the world's most technologically advanced nations as well as developing nations, all of whom share the benefits and the risks of global information architectures

- A voluntary and noncoercive environment based on concepts of consensus and practical experience

- Open technical standards that prevent the manipulation of information technology for unilateral gain

- An open organizational structure that provides opportunities for all constituencies to express their concerns

- A mechanism for providing continuous monitoring of actions that can adversely impact privacy

- Mechanisms for reviewing the state of information technology and its practical implementations to enable the international framework to remain relevant in the light of changing capabilities and requirements

- Mechanisms that can assist in building trust relationships globally

- Funding arrangements that can assist less developed nations in meeting their responsibilities to protect the information commons

A specific proposal that incorporates such features is discussed in Chapter 6 of this volume.

5. Looking Ahead

The problems addressed here derive from a confluence of factors: an increasing social dependence on information-based infrastructures, an increasing complexity of those infrastructures that makes it difficult to anticipate all their failure modes, a growing number of people versed in information technology who can harm information systems, and tools readily available to assist in carrying out malicious acts. These have resulted in alarming rates of growth of system malfunction and system intrusion.

Conclusions

1. The Internet operates by means of a voluntary but structured process that provides the capability, in principle, to respond to changing technology and user needs, including enhanced security. But since the process is driven by its developers and users, the incorporation of security features in the Internet is not assured, however valuable that may be from a public policy standpoint.

2. There are a number of existing techniques computer and information system owners and operators can utilize for their protection. These include firewalls, virus protection software, one-time passwords, encryption, and virtual private networks. They also include instituting and enforcing security policies, real-time and off-line auditing of system operation and use, penetration testing, and implementing data and system backup practices at all levels. But enhanced security brings associated financial and operational costs that can result in lesser levels of security than are technically feasible.

3. Intrusion detection systems are available today and are increasingly being deployed, but at the same time the number of system attacks, already large, continues to grow. Furthermore, tracking intruders is difficult, slow, and uncertain. Hence the current state of affairs, where attack is relatively easy and defense is difficult or absent, leaves the balance very much on the side of the attacker.

4. Ongoing security R&D is pointing to ways of protecting information systems such that detecting, tracking, and identifying intruders will be possible with greater ease and certainty through collective actions by users and service providers. These include deploying new Internet protocols, level-of-service agreements making security a contractual requirement, the automation of advanced intrusion-detection systems for warning and tracking, the integration of security tools to provide more complete capabilities to meet wider ranges of needs, the creation of global incident response capabilities, third-party clearinghouses for secure and anonymous communications among incident responders, the use of digital objects to better define ownership of and appropriate uses of information, and increased capabilities for network traffic analysis.

5. Advances in intruder detection and tracking will aid in deterring attacks by increasing the risk of being caught. They can also be expected to reduce intrusions on user privacy implicit in current tracking techniques.

6. International agreements, both informal and formal, will be needed if information infrastructure users are to receive greater protection than they can reasonably provide for themselves. These include extending intrusion detection to operate across larger domains, development of new Internet protocols, coordinating international responses to global incidents, shared R&D to keep pace with evolving international threats, and collecting and providing attack information to users in a timely manner to allow them to provide for adaptive defenses. The Draft Convention presented in this volume illustrates the kinds of steps that can assist in achieving these capabilities.

7. National policies that encourage the introduction of informa-

tion technology into critical infrastructures, thereby allowing systems of unlimited degrees of complexity and vulnerability to be constructed without corresponding increases in system security, should be examined. It is possible that nations can encourage the evolution of their infrastructure systems in ways that will make them more robust as well as more capable.

8. Today's information infrastructure, which has provided such dramatic improvements in access to information, can usefully be re-examined from the point of view of system architecture. What is needed is to overlay on the current information transfer network an assurance network that makes possible the definition and enforcement of standards of behavior among its users. This assurance network will involve both technical facilities to assist in protecting user rights as well as provisions for allowing operators of the assurance network to establish and maintain concomitant trust relationships that will be necessary for international cooperation.

Short-Term Prospects for Enhanced Security Are Encouraging

Protective actions will take time to implement. A central question then becomes one of relative rates. Since available defensive technologies have not been universally deployed, users can do a great deal in the short term to reduce their vulnerabilities. The pace at which short-term enhancements in system security can be made will depend on several elements: the acceptance by users and system operators that increased spending on security is needed, the deployment of available technologies by both individuals and organizations, improvements in current security products to make them easier to integrate, and the availability of new and more powerful security products and services. Looked at from this perspective, the picture over the next several years merits some degree of optimism because there is so much "low-hanging fruit." The combination of defensive technology and operational process redesign can accomplish a great deal in comparatively short times.

Long-Term Prospects Are Less Certain

More difficult to assess is how much society as a whole is willing to change in more fundamental ways. Will infrastructure operators realize that their rush to adopt information technology risks system failures that can only be addressed at the level of system architecture? Will utility regulators recognize that security must be on their agenda and that, without private sector initiatives, a more aggressive public posture may be called for? Will we recognize that deregulation without consideration of the architectural issues can have severe unintended consequences? Will law enforcement agencies increase their levels of investigatory and enforcement capabilities, and will legislators appropriate the required resources? And will the nations of the world agree that the protection of the information commons is a shared responsibility?

The highly dynamic nature of information technology is a further complication in the long-term outlook for protection of infrastructures. New technology creates new vulnerabilities, and it increases the power of attackers as well as that of defenders. System and network security is not a problem that can be solved once and for all; it has the measure-countermeasure and offense-defense nature of military competition. From this perspective there is less reason to be sanguine.

A threshold issue for considering fundamental long-term changes in information systems will be that of weighing the cost of ignoring cyber attacks against the cost of actions to reduce the frequency and severity of their failures. There is no simple or obvious answer to this question. Because no fatal infrastructure failures have so far been induced by cyber attack, our only evidence of catastrophic failure is indirect. The rates of attack, and computer crime of many forms, are increasing, in some cases doubling annually. Such strong exponential increases can rapidly dominate the balance. Unless it can be shown that these exponential growth rates will saturate at some comfortably low level, policymakers in both public and private sectors would be well advised to adopt conservative positions. It would seem prudent to invest now to hedge future downside risks.

CHAPTER 5

Civil Liberties and Security in Cyberspace

Ekaterina A. Drozdova

Measures to protect information systems against cyber attacks are receiving increasing attention as the threat of attacks grows and the nature of that threat is better understood. Among these measures are sophisticated technologies for monitoring computer networks and users, detecting intrusion, identifying and tracing intruders, and preserving and analyzing evidence, all discussed in the previous chapter. What legal standards should govern the use of these measures? What non-technical constraints are likely to be placed, or ought to be placed, on them? What importance should be assigned to these constraints in designing and implementing technologically robust solutions, as well as international agreements to facilitate law enforcement?

Specific answers to these questions will ultimately be determined by evaluating the specific measures or agreements proposed. But certain legal principles are broadly applicable, including the right to privacy, the protections against self-incrimination and unwarranted searches and seizures, and the right to due process of law. These civil liberties are supported in international law and guaranteed in varying forms by the national laws and institutions of many countries. An international regime against cyber crime and terrorism must operate within the constraints of these principles, as defined by the legal frameworks of its States Parties.

There is often a tension between protecting civil liberties and enforcing laws to maintain public safety and order. States resolve this tension differently. Agreeing upon a common global level of protection of citizens' rights is problematic owing to international variance in normative standards, legal practices, and political objectives. An international common denominator could reduce the level of protections currently afforded in some states to the level of authoritarian states. In the interest of promoting international cooperation and a timely response to the growing threat of cyber attacks, seeking measures other than agreement on a specific level of protection is more likely to succeed.

However, the differences in domestic values and rules may allow misuse of systems set up for preventing, tracking, or punishing cyber crime. The diversion of technologies for illegitimate purposes—such as unwarranted surveillance—is a real threat, especially in countries that give little weight to civil liberty principles constraining such activities. Countries may be tempted to circumvent legal constraints, moreover, when faced with a national security threat. Systems set up for international cooperation would also introduce new cyber vulnerabilities, since they may be "hacked" or "cracked" and misused by criminals or unauthorized persons. States should address these dangers in the course of developing forms of international cooperation that extend to sharing information and coordinating technology.

This chapter considers the basic protective and reactive approaches to security in cyberspace in section 1 and the legal principles that apply to security measures in sections 2 and 3. Issues concerning search, seizure, and due process of law apply primarily to criminal law enforcement. Threats to privacy, however, extend beyond law enforcement into commercial and all other spheres of social life; privacy is discussed in section 2 in this broader context, and in section 3 the discussion turns to criminal law and constraints on police behavior in the course of investigations. Applicable aspects of the right to freedom of expression are addressed throughout.[1]

1. Protective and Reactive Approaches to Security in Cyberspace

The world's use of and dependence on international computer networks fosters transnational computer crime. Sophisticated criminals are able to operate from a distance and cover up or confuse the origins of their attacks. To respond to attacks in a timely and effective manner, system operators need to monitor user behavior and detect intrusions in real time. To identify suspects and launch investigations once a crime is detected, large-scale screening, tracing, and analysis of electronic evidence may be required.

Such methods demand substantial commitments of technological, economic, and human resources. States, as well as commercial and other public and private entities, face difficult trade-offs in allocating resources to fight cyber crime. Increased network security and investigative measures may come at the expense of network performance, privacy, and users' desire for anonymity. States may also find their domestic laws, national security objectives, and political or economic priorities at odds with the conditions required for effective international cooperation. Restrictions on cross-border flows of information imposed for policing purposes may impede electronic commerce and other transactions.

There are two basic approaches to security in cyberspace: a pro-

1. On freedom of expression in cyberspace, see also *Reno v. American Civil Liberties Union*, 521 U.S. 844 (1997).

tective one and a reactive one.[2] Each is constrained in different ways. The protective approach aims to deter criminals through measures that deny access or make a potential target less vulnerable to an attack. This approach is focused on defense. It involves designing more secure Internet protocols, introducing trusted routers and virtual private networks, and utilizing firewalls, encryption, automated intrusion-detection systems, and other security measures. The reactive approach seeks to deter the threat through effective investigation, prosecution, and punishment.[3] Both approaches involve monitoring and diagnosing abnormal and unauthorized activity. The protective approach favors automation as well as oversight and decisionmaking by computer security experts. The reactive one depends more heavily on the participation of law enforcement and requires end user–oriented (rather than anonymous) traffic analysis, which may be as intrusive as scanning of attached files, keyword searches, and content filtering for signs of potential breaches of criminal law. Real-time investigative capabilities may extend to creating embedded data collection infrastructures and modifying hardware and/or software to provide for confidential law enforcement access to business, governmental, and private computer networks.[4]

The two approaches can be complementary. Their relative weights depend on the preferences and capabilities of implementing parties. Although there are significant obstacles to achieving high levels of cyber security,[5] the protective approach is likely to facilitate greater

2. As discussed at the Conference on International Cooperation to Combat Cyber Crime and Terrorism, Hoover Institution, Stanford University, December 6–7, 1999. Neither exhaustive nor mutually exclusive, the two approaches provide a useful framework for evaluating with respect to civil liberties the technical and legal measures against cyber crime.

3. Whitfield Diffie, presentation at the Stanford Conference, December 6–7, 1999.

4. Forms of this are being implemented by the Russian and U.S. governments, as discussed in the privacy section below.

5. These obstacles include budget constraints, technical complexity, unclear responsibilities, security weaknesses in products, lack of awareness, lack of good security tools, lack of competent information security personnel, privacy and ethics issues, and

security with less intrusion. The reactive approach may be more effective in cases of inadequate defense and in safeguarding users who are unable to afford, or unwilling to implement, sufficient protective measures. However, the reactive approach is inherently more intrusive and more threatening to civil liberties.

2. Privacy and Data Protection

Among the issues considered in this chapter, privacy in cyberspace is the most controversial and publicly debated. Privacy concerns not only the context of law enforcement but also day-to-day business practices and an individual's ability to control the treatment of personal data made available in electronic format or accumulated during Internet use. Commercial exploitation of personal data without consent is already leading to enhanced legal protections for privacy. The enforcement of such protections will raise the issue of the desirability of using protective versus reactive methods, leading to discussions of what can be done to ensure that any method used will protect privacy interests against unwanted intrusion.

The Value, Law, and Status of Privacy Protection

Privacy is not an absolute, well-defined, or uniformly protected value. Individuals, organizations, and societies have traditionally sacrificed some privacy in exchange for greater security, economic gain, or convenience. Trade-offs between privacy and intrusion (by government, industry, etc.) reflect the different historical and social contexts in which they were made. The norm of privacy is linked to an individual's independence, dignity, and integrity.

---

legal or regulatory issues. Yet computer security requires a comprehensive and integrated approach, which extends throughout the entire information life cycle and recognizes the interdependencies of information security with such factors as system management, organizational management, legal issues, and physical and personnel security. See Dorothy E. Denning, *Information Warfare and Security* (Reading, Mass.: ACM Press and Addison-Wesley Longman, 1999), pp. 396, 397–400.

Protection of privacy has evolved historically through international and domestic law. Privacy is a fundamental human right recognized by the 1948 Universal Declaration of Human Rights and many other international and regional instruments and treaties.[6] The Universal Declaration proclaims that "no one shall be subjected to arbitrary interference with his privacy, family, home or correspondence, nor to attacks upon his honour and reputation," and "everyone has the right to the protection of the law against such interference or attacks."[7] It also states that "everyone has the right to freedom of opinion and expression; this right includes freedom to hold opinions without interference and to seek, receive and impart information and ideas through any media and regardless of frontiers."[8] These provisions create the basic international law framework for the right to privacy, which extends to cyberspace.[9]

On the national level, privacy is protected through a combination of constitutional and legislative instruments and self-regulation. Nearly every country in the world recognizes a constitutional right to privacy, including at least the rights to inviolability of home and secrecy of communications. Some recently written constitutions, such as those of South Africa and Hungary, contain rights to access and control of one's personal information. In countries where the right to

6. The Universal Declaration of Human Rights, UN GA Res. 217A (III) (1948) and the International Covenant on Civil and Political Rights, UN GA Res. 2200A (XXI) (1966, entry into force 1976), oblige state signatories to adopt legislative and other measures to protect against unlawful and arbitrary interference with and attacks on privacy by state authorities or natural or legal persons. The 1950 European Convention on Human Rights (Council of Europe, European Treaties, ETS No. 5) is a binding treaty that obligates its signatories to protect privacy interests, such as the right to private and family life, home, and correspondence, and enforces this obligation through the European Court of Human Rights. A state, person, nongovernmental organization or group of individuals claiming to be a victim of a violation by a contracting party may apply to the court for redress.

7. Universal Declaration of Human Rights, art. 12.

8. Ibid., art. 19.

9. Stein Schjolberg, Chief Judge, Moss Byrett City, Norway, "Legal Mechanisms for International Cooperation—Protecting Privacy and Other Rights," presentation at the Stanford Conference, December 6–7, 1999.

privacy is not explicitly guaranteed by the constitution—the United States, Ireland, and India, for example—this right has been established through other legal provisions or judicial rulings.[10]

The advent of information technology provided a new context in which to consider privacy and a new legal impetus for the protection of personal data. The first modern legislation on collecting and handling personal data emerged in the early 1970s in Sweden (1973) and the United States (1974).[11] The Organization for Economic Cooperation and Development (OECD) was the first international organization to issue a policy, "Guidelines on the Protection of Privacy and Transborder Flows of Personal Data," adopted in 1980 (see Figure 1). The OECD's policy applies to personal data, whether in the public or private sectors, that pose a danger to privacy and individual liberties because of their nature or the manner in which they are processed and used.[12]

Development of international standards continued in the 1980s and 1990s. The Council of Europe (COE) adopted a "Convention for the Protection of Individuals with regard to the Automatic Processing of Personal Data" (1981) and "Guidelines on the Use of Computerized

10. The 1995 U.S. Department of State review on human rights practices reported that 110 countries guaranteed the right to privacy in their constitutions. See David Banisar, "U.S. State Department Reports Worldwide Privacy Abuses," excerpts from "U.S. Department of State Country Reports on Human Rights Practices for 1995," Privacy International, available at ⟨www.privacy.org/pi/reports/1995_hranalysis.html⟩. The 1999 survey by the Electronic Privacy Information Center (EPIC) ("Privacy and Human Rights: An International Survey of Privacy Laws and Developments") updated this count to nearly every country and reported that at least 55 countries do not have constitutional provisions on privacy but establish protections through other legal means. For a discussion of privacy law in the U.S., see Robert Gellman, "Does Privacy Law Work?" in Philip E. Agre and Marc Rotenberg, eds., *Technology and Privacy: The New Landscape* (Cambridge, Mass.: MIT Press, 1998), pp. 193–218.

11. Ulrich Sieber, "Legal Aspects of Computer-Related Crime in the Information Society—COMCRIME-Study—prepared for the European Commission," Version 1.0 (January 1, 1998), Section I.B.2.a, "Protection of Privacy," pp. 62–64.

12. "Implementing the OECD Privacy Guidelines in the Electronic Environment: Focus on the Internet," Group of Experts on Information Security and Privacy, OECD, DSTI/ICCP/REG(97)6/FINAL, pp. 6–10.

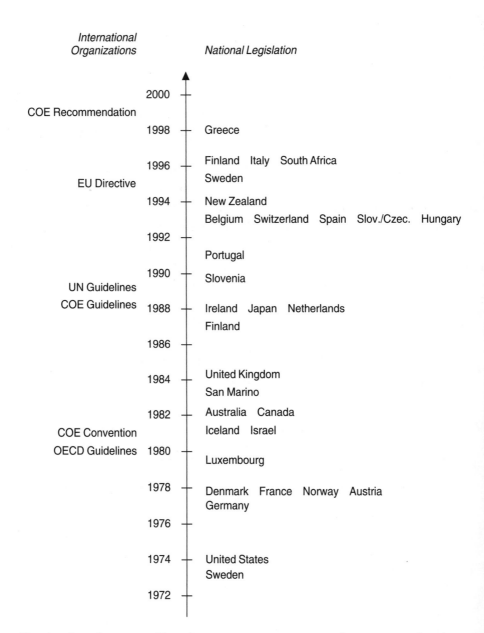

Fig. 1.   Development of law for privacy protection in cyberspace. Updated from Ulrich Sieber, "Legal Aspects of Computer-Related Crime in Information Society" (1998).

Personal Data Flow" (1989).[13] The United Nations (UN) produced "Guidelines for the Regulation of Computerized Personal Data Files" (1989).[14] These documents establish principles of minimum privacy guarantees for personal information at all stages of its collection, storage, and dissemination by other parties. They also create new rights for "data subjects"—those whose data are collected and manipulated by government agencies, businesses, and so on—requiring that accurate and up-to-date personal information must be obtained fairly and lawfully, used only for the original, intended purpose, and destroyed after the purpose is achieved. Data subjects are granted the right to access and amend information about them.

The 1995 European Union (EU) Data Protection Directive established a regulatory framework for free movement of personal data, while allowing individual EU countries to exercise their unique approaches to implementation. "Data subjects" are guaranteed the right to know where the data originated, the right to have inaccurate data corrected, the right of appeal in the case of unlawful processing, and the right to deny permission to use data under certain circumstances.[15] The 1999 COE Recommendation provides guidelines for the protection of privacy on the Internet.[16] Whereas the COE and UN guidelines

13. The Convention (ETS no. 108, January 28, 1981, Entry into force: October 1, 1985) has since become law in over twenty countries. See "Privacy and Human Rights: An International Survey of Privacy Laws and Developments," Electronic Privacy Information Center (EPIC) in association with Privacy International (1999), p. 10.

14. UN GA Res. 44/132, 44 UN GAOR Supp. (No. 49) at 211, UN Doc. A/44/49 (1989).

15. Directive 95/46/EC of the European Parliament and of the Council "On the protection of individuals with regard to the processing of personal data and on the free movement of such data." "Council Definitively Adopts Directive on Protection of Personal Data," European Commission Press Release: IP/95/822, July 25, 1995.

16. Recommendation no. R(99)5 of the Committee of Ministers to Member States for the "Protection of Privacy on the Internet: Guidelines for the protection of individuals with regard to the collection and processing of personal data on information highways," adopted by the Committee of Ministers at the 660th meeting of the Ministers' Deputies, February 23, 1999. The text of the Recommendation can be viewed at ⟨http://www.coe.fr/cm/ta/rec/1999/99r5.htm⟩.

are recommendations, the EU Directives are binding: member states must adopt them into their domestic law.

Currently, nearly fifty countries and jurisdictions have enacted or are in the process of enacting privacy laws, designed to ensure compatibility with international standards, to address past government abuses, and/or to promote electronic commerce.[17]

Threats to Privacy in Cyberspace

Privacy in cyberspace is threatened by businesses and other entities that collect and manipulate personal data, by criminals who steal such data or stalk people over the Internet, and by governments that pursue surveillance or allow intrusive law enforcement practices. Sophisticated electronic capabilities to collect, analyze, manipulate, and disseminate information, as well as to enable tracking, surveillance, and interference with communications, create unprecedented challenges to privacy. Such technologies are becoming more effective, available, and affordable internationally. At the same time, globalization and growing dependence on information technology in all spheres of society have led to a dramatic increase in the level of electronically compiled and transmitted personal data. The differences in domestic legal standards and practices also endanger private data transmitted over international networks. Even if one state has robust privacy laws, it cannot currently guarantee equivalent levels of protection once the data flow beyond its borders. Gaps in protection will be created to the extent that market forces undervalue privacy, laws and law enforcement fail to keep up with technological capabilities, and international discrepancies undermine domestic levels of protection.

17. Electronic Privacy Information Center (EPIC) Privacy Survey (1999), p. v. For specific information on laws and instruments for the protection of privacy and personal data in various countries, see "Inventory of Instruments and Mechanisms Contributing to the Implementation and Enforcement of the OECD Privacy Guidelines on Global Networks," OECD, DSTI/ICCP/REG(98)12/FINAL; and "Excerpts on Privacy from U.S. State Department Human Rights Guides," prepared by Global Internet Liberty Campaign, available at ⟨http://www.gilc.org/privacy/⟩.

The U.S. Federal Trade Commission found that privacy policies, posted on many commercial websites, did not provide sufficient protection for on-line consumers.[18] Businesses track on-line behavior, sell personal information, and misuse personal profiles built on the basis of financial, medical, and other sensitive information.[19] Employers' intrusion into electronic communications of employees in the workplace is another area of concern. Privacy protection is often subordinated to property rights of employers as the providers of their employees' electronic communication services. In the United States, for example, legislation prohibits employers from eavesdropping on the private telephone conversations of their employees at work, but no similar protection extends to electronic mail communications.[20]

Criminals take advantage of deficiencies in the protection of sensitive information transmitted and accumulated in electronic form. Identity theft is among the fastest-growing cyber crimes; in the U.S. alone, it has increased more than 300 percent, from 7,868 cases in 1997 to 30,115 in 1999. Pedophiles entice victims in Internet chat rooms and use electronic communications to arrange actual meetings. Spurned suitors forge vindictive e-mails inviting rape.[21] Stalkers identify victims on the Internet and threaten them physically.[22]

The spread and growing severity of cyber crime require greater security and better law enforcement.[23] Where security and policing methods are intrusive, achieving these objectives may demand some

18. Schjolberg, "Legal Mechanisms for International Cooperation."

19. See Jeffrey Rosen, "The Eroded Self," *New York Times Magazine*, April 30, 2000, pp. 46–53.

20. See Ann Beeson, "Privacy in Cyberspace: Is Your E-mail Safe from the Boss, the SysOp, the Hackers, and the Cops?" American Civil Liberties Union, *Cyber-Liberties* (1996), available at ⟨*http://www.aclu.org/issues/cyber/priv/privpap.html*⟩.

21. See Stephen J. Lukasik, "Combating Cyber Crime and Terrorism," presentation at the Technical Seminar, Center for International Security and Cooperation, Stanford University, May 2, 2000; Lukasik cites identity theft figures reported by the Social Security Administration.

22. Sam Howe Verhovek, "Creators of Anti-Abortion Web Site Told to Pay Millions," *New York Times*, February 3, 1999, p. A11.

23. Chap. 1 of this volume.

limitations of privacy. Should governments treat Internet communications like a phone call, paper correspondence, or a discussion in a public place? Responses to this question determine the extent of permissible infringements, as well as the specific rules governing law enforcement functions, and responses vary among states. Even the relatively strong European Convention on Human Rights makes exceptions to the exercise of the right to privacy "in accordance with the law," when it is "necessary in a democratic society in the interests of national security, public safety or the economic well-being of the country, for the prevention of disorder or crime, for the protection of health or morals, or for the protection of the rights and freedoms of others."[24] Although the burden of proof to establish the need for this exception rests with the potential intruder, the scope of the exception is very broad. Many national laws have similar provisions. Such breadth can lead to abuse if police attempt to assume excessive powers or governments pursue unlawful surveillance.

Caspar Bowden of the United Kingdom's Foundation for Information Policy Research has warned about the implications of improving detection, prosecution, and prevention of cyber crime at the expense of privacy:

> There are now traffic-analysis tools commercially available to law enforcement which can take telephone number logs in machine-readable form and draw "friendship trees," which show the grouping and relationships between parties calling each other in time, and can match patterns of association automatically using sophisticated artificial intelligence programming.
>
> There is enormous potential for law enforcement in increased use of traffic analysis, but there are a number of fundamental distinctions between traffic analysis of telephony, and Internet traffic—especially in a fully wired Information Society. The Internet Protocol ("IP") abolishes any meaningful distinction between domestic and foreign communications intelligence. A well-funded national communications intelligence agency, which already captures large quantities of

24. European Convention on Human Rights, art. 8.

both traffic and content data and has the organization to process it and integrate it effectively with other forms of intelligence gathering, presents an enormous temptation to government simply to leverage that capability for wider domestic coverage.

Intelligence-integrated traffic analysis is phenomenally corrosive of civil liberties. If government was in a position to know which websites you visit, what you buy online, the e-mail addresses of those who e-mail you and those you have e-mailed, and analyze and archive that information without hindrance, there is potential for an unprecedentedly serious abuse of power.[25]

The threat of systematic government intrusion into electronic communications has already received attention around the world. Russia's Federal Security Bureau (FSB) is implementing an Internet surveillance system that requires all Internet service providers (ISPs) to enable routine FSB monitoring of communications.[26] Russian human rights advocates report that many of the country's 350 ISPs have already been forced to comply, endangering secrecy of communications and other civil liberties of users and persons whose sensitive information may be transmitted over the Internet.[27] The U.S. Federal Bureau of

25. Caspar Bowden, "Unprecedented Safeguards for Unprecedented Capabilities," Foundation for Information Policy Research (FIPR), United Kingdom, presentation at the Stanford Conference, December 6–7, 1999.

26. This System to Conduct Investigations and Field Operations in Russia is known as SORM, which stands for *Sistema Operativno-Rozysknykh Meropriiatii.* In an open letter to the Russian government, representatives of the Russian Internet community and organized Internet societies stated that "particular danger nests in the Technical Requirements for SORM. Today's version of legislation puts the control for the presence of a jury or prosecutor's warrant in the hands of the same authority that is doing wiretapping. This approach cannot guarantee in practice to Internet users their constitutional rights." The letter can be viewed in Russian and downloaded in English at ⟨http://www.libertarium.ru/eng/⟩. See also Moscow Libertarium, ⟨http://www.libertarium.ru/⟩, for a discussion and background documents on SORM.

27. "Russia's Security Agency Spies on Internet," Features and Commentary, *HPCwire*, February 25, 2000. Article 23 of the Constitution of the Russian Federation (1993) guarantees the right to privacy of correspondence, telephone communications, mail, cables, and other communications. Article 24 forbids gathering, storing, using, and disseminating information on the private life of any person without his or her consent, and obligates state and local authorities to provide to each citizen access to any materials directly affecting his rights and liberties unless otherwise stipulated by

Investigation (FBI) is using a similar wiretapping system with special-ized software that can scan millions of e-mails a second. When de-ployed, the system must be connected directly into ISPs' computer networks, thus giving the government potential access to all customers' digital communications. Typical Internet wiretaps last about forty-five days, after which the FBI removes the equipment. Critics contend that the system is open to abuse, raising dire privacy and security con-cerns.[28]

Threatening surveillance has also taken place on the international scale. The United States, the United Kingdom, Canada, Australia, and New Zealand allegedly engage in selective multinational screening of telephone, fax, satellite, and Internet communications for foreign in-telligence purposes. This system, known as Echelon, supposedly links computers around the world to capture large volumes of information, and to sort and analyze it through sophisticated keyword searches and artificial intelligence aids. The information collected is compiled and routed according to requests of the participating parties.[29] Allegations of unlawful surveillance and violation of privacy, in the United States and abroad, have been raised in regard to this system.[30]

---

law. The Law on Operational Investigative Activity permits FSB, the Tax Police, and the Ministry of Interior to monitor telephone and other types of communication pursuant to a court order. *Zakon Operativno-Rozisknoi Deiatelnosti* (The Law on Operational Investigative Activity), no. 144-FZ, (8/12/1995). See also Catherine New-combe, "Russian Federation," in Craig M. Bradley, ed., *Criminal Procedure: A World-wide Study* (Durham, N.C.: Carolina Academic Press, 1999), pp. 294–95.

28. Neil King Jr. and Ted Bridis, "FBI's System to Covertly Search E-mail Raises Privacy, Legal Issues," *Wall Street Journal*, July 11, 2000. See also testimony of James X. Dempsey, Senior Staff Counsel, Center for Democracy and Technology, on "In-ternet Security and Privacy," before the United States Senate Judiciary Committee, May 25, 2000.

29. See *Echelon Watch*, ⟨*http://www.aclu.org/echelonwatch/*⟩, administered by the American Civil Liberties Union in conjunction with the Free Congress Foundation, the Electronic Privacy Information Center, Cyber-Rights and Cyber-Liberties (UK), and the Omega Foundation. "An Appraisal of Technologies of Political Control," European Parliament, Scientific and Technological Options Assessment, Working Document (January 6, 1998), Luxembourg, available at ⟨*http://cryptome.org/stoa-atpc.htm*⟩.

30. See: "Memo on International Electronic Surveillance Concerns" addressed to

There are inherent dangers in a system for advanced monitoring, searching, tracking, and analyzing of communications. Though it could be very helpful against cyber crime and terrorism, it would also provide participating governments, especially authoritarian governments or agencies with little accountability, tools to violate civil liberties domestically and abroad. Correspondence of innocent people could be intercepted and people could be repressed as a result. Systems set up for international policing of cyberspace could also be hacked or misused by an insider to undermine a participating government or to damage the interests of a state. The technology and know-how, which will be developed and provided to less technologically advanced countries in the course of international cooperation, could be used to enhance domestic surveillance and suppression by governments that disregard human rights.

These threats exist now and they are likely to expand in the future as advanced computer networking becomes pervasive in public and private lives and methods for intercepting and analyzing information become more sophisticated, widespread, and affordable. Integrating attributed personal data from different systems could make comprehensive, detailed profiles available for retrieval, manipulation, and abuse. Abuses by the private sector may range from inundation with unsolicited targeted advertisements to various forms of covert discrimination, such as denial of employment on the basis of prior knowledge of health conditions, or denial of medical services on the basis of financial debts. Such conglomerations of data would be vulnerable to

---

the United States Congress by the American Civil Liberties Union, Center for Democracy and Technology, Eagle Forum, Electronic Frontier Foundation, Electronic Privacy Information Center, and Free Congress Foundation, January 7, 1999, available at ⟨http://www.aclu.org/congress/l060899a.html⟩; "Lawsuit Seeks Memos on Surveillance of Americans; EPIC Launches Study of NSA Interception Activities," Electronic Privacy Information Center Press Release, December 3, 1999, available at ⟨http://www.epic.org/open_gov/foia/nsa_suit_12_99.html⟩; "French Prosecutor Starts Probe of U.S. Spy System," *Reuters*, July 4, 2000, reported at ⟨http://news.excite.com/news/r/000704/08/news-france-usa-dc⟩.

identity theft and other cyber crimes. As for possible government abuses, the totalitarian regimes of the twentieth century—with ubiquitous informers, government controls over all spheres of society, and egregious violations of human rights—should serve as a reminder and a warning.

Privacy Protection Modes and Constraints on Measures Against Cyber Crime

Several models of data protection have emerged—public enforcement, sector-specific regulation, and self-regulation—reflecting different legal approaches to privacy. Methods are also used in combination. The EU, Australia, Hong Kong, New Zealand, Canada, and many countries of Central and Eastern Europe have adopted the first model, in which a public official (a commissioner, ombudsman, or registrar) enforces a comprehensive data protection law. This official monitors compliance, conducts investigations into alleged violations, and requests legal action in case of a breach. The official is also usually responsible for public education and international interaction with respect to data protection and transfer. Alternatively, the United States has adopted sector-specific rules (covering video rental records or financial privacy, for example) rather than comprehensive laws. Singapore, Australia, and the United States also promote a form of self-regulation, whereby companies and industries establish codes of practice. Enforcement in these cases typically proceeds through private, as opposed to government, actions.[31]

Industry self-regulation will be insufficient, however, as long as market forces undervalue privacy in cyberspace. Sector-specific rules may be sufficient, but protection may also fail if data are transferred

31. Global Internet Liberty Campaign (GILC) Privacy Survey 1997, Models of Privacy Protection. See also David Flaherty, "Controlling Surveillance: Can Privacy Protection Be Made Effective?" in Agre and Rotenberg, eds., *Technology and Privacy*, pp. 167–92. Flaherty is the Information and Privacy Commissioner for British Columbia, Canada.

or sold to entities in sectors with lower standards. Public enforcement has provided higher levels of privacy protection, but it is vulnerable to the same problem: transmittal of sensitive data beyond the networks of the country with strong legal enforcement of privacy is likely to result in decreased levels of protection.

The countries of the European Union protect personal data more rigorously than the United States, and this discrepancy has fueled an international controversy. The 1995 EU Data Protection Directive requires that personal data may be collected only for specific, explicit, and legitimate purposes. Only relevant, accurate, and up-to-date data may be held. Member states of the EU are obliged to maintain these standards when exporting or processing information pertaining to EU citizens abroad, or they must halt the movement of data in the absence of "adequate" (equivalent) protections. The United States has no similar statute, and the EU considers the U.S. industry's self-regulating approach inadequate.[32] To mitigate the ensuing limitations on transborder data flow, a "safe harbor" agreement was recently reached that will enable some U.S. companies to collect data about EU citizens, if the companies demonstrate safeguards that meet European approval. These companies will be required to give notice to European citizens about how their information is to be gathered and used, allow them to withhold data, and offer them reasonable access to their own records.[33] Such partial resolution toward greater privacy standards is encouraging. Nonetheless, the dispute is alarming. If the most advanced democracies disagree on adequate protection of privacy, agreement and observance of this norm can hardly be expected in a global setting that includes less democratic and less accountable governments.

32. Hearing: "The European Union and Data Protection," European Parliament, Committee on Citizens' Freedoms and Rights, Justice and Home Affairs, the Committee on Legal Affairs and the Internal Market, February 22–23, 2000. The hearing program, statements, and background documents can be viewed at ⟨www.europarl. eu.int/dg2/hearings/20000222/libe/agenda/en/default.htm⟩.

33. Robert O'Harrow Jr., "U.S., EU Agree on Privacy Standard," *Washington Post*, June 1, 2000, p. E01.

From the standpoint of security against cyber crime, the 1995 EU Data Protection Directive does not necessarily impede law enforcement activities and international cooperation in cyberspace. The directive fully applies to the first two Pillars of the Treaty of the European Union: (I) the European Community, which covers democratization of the institutions, citizenship, and economic and monetary union, and (II) the common foreign and security policy. It is the third Pillar (III), however, that addresses the issues of justice and home affairs, including police and judicial cooperation to combat drug trafficking, international fraud, and other crimes.[34] The scope of the directive does not cover law enforcement procedures. This means that there are opportunities for international cooperation against cyber crime and also threats to privacy in the course of such cooperation. Privacy-related law enforcement practices are being examined by the European Commission and may be subject to more intense scrutiny in the near future.[35]

To compensate for the uneven or insufficient privacy protections in commercial and public settings, and to reduce their vulnerability to cyber crime, public and private organizations and individuals can adopt existing protective measures. Encryption, anonymous remailers, proxy servers, and other technologies, described in the preceding chapter, are commercially available.[36] Many of these technologies offer protection against cyber crime coupled with enhancement of privacy. These include more secure network protocols and routers, encryption, firewalls, virtual private networks, secure anonymous communications, challenge response systems, and security management applications. IP version 6 (IPv6), the next generation of Internet Protocols, allows routers along delivery paths to record addresses of previous

---

34. The Maastricht Treaty that established the European Union and the three Pillars can be viewed at ⟨*www.felixent.force9.co.uk/europe/eu.html*⟩.

35. See Hearing, European Parliament.

36. Stephen J. Lukasik, "Current and Future Technical Capabilities," Chap. 4 of this volume, in particular, section 2, "Defending Information Systems Against Cyber Attack," and the conclusion to the chapter.

destinations in the header of the message. This feature would enable the searching and tracing of suspect messages without prior disclosure of their content or author, thus protecting the identity of the sender and the secrecy of communications.[37]

Information exchanges among computer security staff regarding modes of penetration and attack, suspected crimes, early warnings, and anomalies in computer operation can facilitate prevention and timely incident response. Incentives for greater protection can be created by placing more legal or financial responsibility on the owners and principal operators of computers and networks—be they businesses, organizations, or individuals. Stronger cyber security would deter some cyber crimes, but not all. Moreover, technologically and economically advanced nations can enhance cyber security and privacy by making protective technologies available and affordable on the market, but citizens of less advanced countries may not be able to afford these alternatives.

The United States has proposed creating an international cyber police.[38] Such a system would need to be worldwide in both coverage and participation, and would enable police to conduct rapid investigations over global communication networks. Although it is unclear

---

37. Dynamically allocated IP addresses may still present a tracking problem. Moreover, IPv6 allows for the allocation of unique addresses for each network node (addresses in the current IP version 4 have been depleted). This will enable greater clarity and reliability in determining originators and recipients of suspect messages. See ibid., "Next Generation IP Protocols," in section 3, and Lee Garber, "Steve Deering on IP Next Generation," *Computer*, April 1999, pp. 11–13. If the non-disclosure feature is not used, however, privacy may be compromised.

38. José Luis Barbería, "Los países europeos del G-8 rechazan el plan de EE UU de crear una 'ciberpolicía' mundial," *El País Digital*, May 16, 2000, reported at ⟨www.elpais.es/p/d/20000516/sociedad/ciberpol.htm⟩; "Rich Nations to Work Together Against Cyber Crime" (Reuters), *New York Times on the Web*, May 15, 2000, reported at ⟨www.nytimes.com/reuters/international/international-crime-c.html⟩. Joelle Diderich, "G8 to Work Together Against Cyber Crime" *Reuters*, May 14, 2000, which was reported at ⟨http://www.zdnet.com/zdnn/stories/news/0,4586, 2569402,00.html⟩. See also Anne Swardson, "International Officials Admit Internet Security Holes," *Washington Post on Line*, May 16, 2000, available at ⟨washington-post.com/wp-dyn/articles/A12013-2000May16.html⟩.

what the United States intends beyond voluntary coordination, the European Union reacted unfavorably, citing privacy implications.[39] A full-fledged international police force would exemplify an extreme of the reactive approach; its mere existence would pose concerns about the security and integrity of information it acquires, the reliability of its operators and users, the trustworthiness of international participants, and the possibility of its use for unlawful purposes (by member states, police officials, or criminals and terrorists).

Some forms of international cooperation will nonetheless be required to combat transnational cyber crime. The draft "International Convention to Enhance Protection from Cyber Crime and Terrorism," presented following Chapter 6, combines protective and reactive measures with provisions for protecting privacy and other civil liberties. This draft calls upon States Parties to establish cyber offenses as crimes under domestic law. Thereafter, investigations, extraditions, prosecutions, mutual legal assistance, and judicial proceedings are to be carried out in accordance with the laws of the States Parties.[40] Intrusive international law enforcement procedures may be allowed, but only in accordance with domestic legal standards and mutual legal assistance treaties. The proposed convention explicitly states that it shall not be construed to require an infringement of the privacy or other human rights of any person as defined by the laws of the requested state. To ensure systematic monitoring and implementation of this provision, the draft proposes to create a group of experts dedicated to the protection of privacy and other human rights.[41]

In some cases, especially those involving international exchanges of sensitive information and monitoring of networks by law enforcement, special procedural safeguards for privacy may also be necessary. Domestic and international exchanges among technology and law enforcement experts of data regarding past and suspected computer

39. Diderich and Reuters, May 14, 2000.
40. Draft "International Convention to Enhance Protection from Cyber Crime and Terrorism," arts. 2–8.
41. Ibid., art. 13.

crimes, anomalies in computer operation, network vulnerabilities, modes of penetration, alerts, and warnings, fall into this category. Such data—no doubt relevant and probably crucial for effective response to cyber crime—are likely to contain sensitive security and personal information, including aliases, identities, and passwords. Information about the citizens of one country may be provided to entities in other countries, whose privacy laws may not afford the same level of protection. An agreed-upon privacy policy—whether deference to domestic practices or a reasonable minimum level of protection—acceptable to parties in the international exchange, would help guard privacy during such information exchanges.

Businesses, such as information infrastructure or service providers, may also be called upon to reveal sensitive information concerning attacks, vulnerabilities, and personnel as part of investigative or preventive measures. Even though the support of commercial entities is often required, they are reluctant to share sensitive security-related information with the government.[42] Disclosure and attribution of such information may have the consequences of disrupting business objectives, causing economic losses, triggering unwelcome legal proceedings, and threatening individual employees. Employees are in many cases subject to loss of their jobs for unauthorized revelation of suspected criminal activity; and businesses should be concerned about the personal safety and privacy of employees when dealing with a suspected crime or perpetrator, or they should be compelled to have such concern by legislation or economic incentives. Preserving the identity of institutions and their employees in tracking, tracing, and investigating crime against them may be a crucial vehicle for building the necessary public–private sector cooperation in this area.

Automation is particularly important to enhance both security and

---

42. See Donn B. Parker, "Sharing Infrastructures' Cyber Crime Intelligence," SRI Consulting, unpublished paper, December 1999, pp. 16–17; and David J. Thelander, presentation at the Stanford Conference, December 6–7, 1999; testimony of Bruce J. Heinman, executive director, Americans for Computer Privacy, on "Internet Security and Privacy," before the United States Senate Judiciary Committee, May 25, 2000.

privacy. The use of automated and semiautomated tools facilitates near-real-time detection of security breaches, tracing to origin of attack, scalability of action (detecting intrusions among large volumes of data involved in normal network operations and responding to intrusions that may hop across international networks), and ultimately increased efficiency and effectiveness. Automation in searching, tracing, and tracking preserves the anonymity and privacy of innocent individuals whose messages may be subjected to search in the course of an investigation. The protection of privacy ultimately relies on a combination of automated and other protective technologies as well as laws that constrain law enforcement. Where law enforcement methods are intrusive and automation is not available or fully reliable, legal constraints are especially necessary.

3. Criminal Law and Constraints on Police Behavior

Constraints on police behavior in cyberspace have received far less public attention than privacy problems. This is partly because they are narrowly focused on criminal investigation—whereas privacy interests span personal, commercial, and government realms—and partly because what is necessary and legally permissible in cyber-related investigation and prosecution procedures is still being determined.

The protections against self-incrimination and unwarranted searches and seizures and the rights to due process of law apply in cyberspace as anywhere else, yet technological realities can complicate the observance of these rights. The pursuit of crimes committed over international computer networks is also complicated by the differences in domestic procedures and the absence of a system of international criminal law.

Search and Seizure

In most legal systems, the main sources of law that govern searches, seizures, and other modes of police behavior are constitutions, legislation, and case law. Investigation and seizure of evidence in democratic states are governed by laws that protect citizens vis-à-vis the state and its law enforcement powers. In many states, searches and seizures must not only be legally authorized, they must also be carried out with due respect for civil liberties.[43] In the United States, for example, these principles are protected by the Fourth Amendment to the Constitution, which states that "the right of the people to be secure in their persons, houses, papers, and effects, against unreasonable searches and seizures, shall not be violated, and no warrants shall issue, but upon probable cause, supported by oath or affirmation, and particularly describing the place to be searched, and the persons or things to be seized."

The concept of "search" can be defined broadly to include not only the search of a place or person but also other invasions of privacy such as wiretapping. Searches may be held upon consent of the individual to be searched, as long as specific consent criteria are satisfied. Many national legal systems prohibit the admission in criminal prosecutions of evidence obtained unlawfully; the rationale for and the extent of exclusion vary.[44]

Such differences make it difficult for states to agree on a common international standard of police behavior. Sovereignty issues, ad-

43. In most countries, the competent authority to issue a search warrant is a judge or a magistrate. In China, Italy, and South Africa, however, this authority can be vested in a member of the prosecution service or the police. See Johannes Lensing, "General Comments," in Bradley, ed., *Criminal Procedure*, p. 427.

44. U.S. courts exclude evidence obtained as a result of unlawful police conduct. Argentina, Canada, England, France, Germany, Russia, South Africa, and the U.K. determine the admissibility of evidence depending on the fairness of the proceedings. Courts in France and Germany enjoy some discretion depending on the rules violated in obtaining the evidence. China and Israel consider only the reliability of evidence. See ibid., pp. 427–29.

dressed by Drew Arena of the U.S. Department of Justice, complicate
international investigations:

> [T]he basic problem is presented by a nation's perception of its na-
> tional sovereignty. To what extent must it assert its sovereignty to
> protect its citizens and enforce its criminal law? To what degree is it
> prepared to compromise that sovereignty for the sake of (reciprocal)
> international cooperation? For example, could the U.S. enter into an
> agreement which provided that foreign officials, armed with legal
> process in their country, would be searching data bases in the U.S.
> from abroad, unless we were satisfied that the Fourth Amendment's
> probable cause requirements had been met? How would we reconcile
> such an agreement with the rigorous standards to be met for domestic
> law enforcement to obtain access and disclosure of electronically
> stored data in our criminal law (Title 18 Section 2703)? How would
> we avoid treating it as an unauthorized access under Title 18 Section
> 1030? On a practical level, how would we know that a foreign law
> enforcement access to a data base was not a hacker's attack?[45]

These challenges do not preclude international cooperation. For
example, the convention proposed in this volume explicitly recognizes
the priority of national laws. It also helps clarify which rules should
apply in transnational investigations, extraditions, and judicial proceedings by establishing priority in jurisdiction and venues for cooperation and mutual legal assistance. When a requested state is asked
to assist—in identifying and tracing cyber attacks, executing searches
and seizures, locating or identifying persons, examining objects and
sites, securing and exchanging information and evidentiary items, and
so on, by electronic and other means—rules of this requested state will
apply.[46] Moreover, the proposed convention requires that requests be
made upon a reasonable belief that an offense has occurred and that
evidence is contained in cyber systems within the territory of a requested state. The requested state will then undertake the preservation

45. Drew C. Arena, "Obstacles to Consensus in Multilateral Responses to Cyber
Crime," Presentation at the Stanford Conference, December 6–7, 1999, pp. 5–6.

46. Draft "International Convention to Enhance Protection from Cyber Crime
and Terrorism," arts. 5, 6, and 11.

of such data, but it will not be compelled to release the data unless presented by the requesting state with adequate cause for release.[47]

The technology of searching and seizing electronic evidence presents challenges of a different nature.[48] Computer hardware and disks may need to be obtained as evidence. Surveillance of network and user behavior may also be necessary, along with searches and forensic investigation of e-mail messages, user files, customer or employee records, and encryption keys. Surveillance may be needed before, during, and after an incident to determine whether a crime has occurred and how to respond. Available methods range from wiretaps on phone calls and Internet communications to various tagging and tracing techniques (user, chip or software ID, network IP address, location detector, etc.), room bugs, and cameras (possibly tied into face-recognition systems). Suspect computers can be remotely monitored by capturing keystrokes, passwords, e-mail messages, attachments, and desktop files. Police may also monitor the "computer underground"—skilled but not directly suspected hacker communities—to gain insights into the nature of the attack and possible attackers.[49]

National laws often contain exceptions to balance protective civil liberty principles with the need to maintain public safety and order. These exceptions can help guide the police to determine the legal boundaries in computer searches and seizures in the absence, or in early stages of development, of cyber laws. Exceptions can also create opportunities for abuse of law enforcement powers. Many countries still lack specific computer-related laws and procedures, so they refer to general criminal laws in cyber cases. Alternatively, the U.S. Department of Justice has published, and regularly updates, specific "Federal Guidelines for Searching and Seizing Computers." The guidelines address the Supreme Court's strong preference for warrants in searches

47. Ibid., art. 9.

48. As discussed by Dorothy E. Denning, "Constraints to Technical Cooperation," presentation at the Stanford Conference, December 6–7, 1999.

49. For more on this, see Whitfield Diffie and Susan Landau, *Privacy on the Line: The Politics of Wiretapping and Encryption* (Cambridge, Mass.: MIT Press, 1998).

and seizures, as well as the limited exceptions to Fourth Amendment requirements. As such, the guidelines provide a suitable background for the discussion of the exceptions, drawing upon technical and international realities to evaluate their application in cyberspace. The exceptions to the warrant requirement include:[50]

(a) *Lack of reasonable expectation of privacy.* The Supreme Court defines a "search" as an intrusion by police into an area where individuals have a "reasonable expectation of privacy."[51] Generally, no one has an expectation of privacy as to something that can be observed by the public.[52]

Whether the Internet is a public space or a private space, where search warrants are usually required, is still legally unsettled.[53] Determinations have been made in specific cases, depending on the type of electronic transmission sent and the recipient of the transmission.[54] For example, real-time, Internet conversations observed by an agent in a chat room lacked Fourth Amendment protection, because the defendant did not have a reasonable expectation of privacy vis-à-vis

50. "Federal Guidelines for Searching and Seizing Computers," available at ⟨*http://www.usdoj.gov/criminal/cybercrime/search_docs/toc.htm*⟩, additional documents available at ⟨*http://www.usdoj.gov/criminal/cybercrime/searching.html*⟩. See also Craig M. Bradley, "United States," in Bradley, ed., *Criminal Procedures*, pp. 395–424. Specific cases establishing the principles are noted.

51. *Katz v. United States*, 389 U.S. 507 (1967).

52. For example, flying over a suspect's land in a helicopter to verify the growing of marijuana (*Florida v. Riley*, 488 U.S. 445 (1989)), searching trash bins left at the curb of the house for pickup (*California v. Greenwood*, 486 U.S. 35 (1999)), and using an electronic beeper to track a car's location on the highway (*United States v. Knotts*, 460 U.S. 276 (1983)) are not considered to be "searches." However, placing an electronic beeper in a container of chemicals in order to determine whether the container remained inside the suspect's house was considered a "search" subject to Fourth Amendment requirements (*United States v. Karo*, 468 U.S. 705 (1984)).

53. See Bradley, "United States," p. 403 for a discussion and references on searches in private versus public spaces, such as in structures versus outdoors. See also Noah D. Zatz, "Sidewalks in Cyberspace: Making Space for Public Forums in the Electronic Environment," *Harvard Journal of Law and Technology* 12 (Fall 1998): 149.

54. Supplement to Federal Guidelines for Searching and Seizing Computers (1999), available at ⟨*http://www.usdoj.gov/criminal/cybercrime/supplement/s&sup pii.htm#IIF*⟩.

other participants in chat room discussions.[55] However, a determination regarding the public or private nature of the Internet cannot be made categorically, because the Internet can be used in different ways, with more or less reasonable or justifiable expectations of privacy.

(b) Informants and undercover agents. The use of informants or undercover agents to aid investigation is generally permitted by law.

In accessing electronic bulletin boards and chat rooms undercover agents are not required to identify themselves as such, but must confine their activities to those authorized for other users.[56] The sender of an e-mail message, like the sender of a letter, runs the risk that he is sending that message to an undercover agent. A government informant or undercover agent may capture and record the contents of electronic conversations to which he is a party, just as an agent may record a conversation in which he is a participant.[57] However, the inexperience of police in Internet-related cases may lead them to draw erroneous conclusions about apparently incriminating information. If an agent is to exercise law enforcement powers as a result of undercover activities, he must still demonstrate probable cause and fulfill other requirements.[58]

(c) Plain view doctrine. Evidence of a crime may be seized without a warrant, if a police officer is in a lawful position to observe such evidence and its incriminating character is immediately apparent. This applies to situations where police enhance their ability to observe by commonly used means, such as binoculars or a flashlight. In such cases, there is no reasonable expectation of privacy, and police observation is not considered a search. However, creating plain view by means of

---

55. *United States v. Charbonneau*, 979 F. Supp. 1177 (S.D. Ohio 1997).

56. *United States v. Aquilar*, 883 F. 2d 662, 705 (9th Cir. 1989), *cert. denied*, 498 U.S. 1046 (1991); *Pleasant v. Lovell*, 876 F. 2d 787, 803 (10th Cir. 1989).

57. Supplement to Federal Guidelines.

58. See *Steve Jackson Games, Inc. v. United States Secret Service*, 816 F. Supp. 432 (W.D. Tex. 1993), *aff'd*, 36 F. 3d 457 (5th Cir. 1994). The court ruled that, even though the agent believed the probable cause in good faith, his lack of due diligence in learning about the suspect and his seizing of materials, which were intended for publication but were not recognized as such by the agent, were unlawful.

"moving" or "disturbing" items, or using sophisticated electronic devices, must be justified by probable cause.[59]

If agents with a warrant to search a computer for evidence of narcotics trafficking observe a list of passwords taped to the computer monitor, the list may also be seized.[60] The application of enhanced plain view to cyberspace is less clear. Some applications may depend on what is considered public or private space on the Internet, because government investigators can lawfully be in a public space without a warrant and they may observe illegal activity in plain view.[61] Discretion in using this exception is necessary because computer and multimedia communications technologies advance very rapidly, making it difficult to distinguish what electronic devices are sophisticated and uncommon enough to require probable cause.

(d) Wiretaps. Wiretaps may be performed by federal agents only for certain specific crimes, upon application to a judge through high-level officials at the Department of Justice. State agents must gain approval of high-level state law enforcement officials. Approval may be waived in case of emergencies that involve "conspiratorial activities threatening to national security," "conspiratorial activities characteristic of organized crime," and "immediate danger of death or serious bodily injury to any person."[62]

It may be difficult to detect and determine, in a timely manner, whether an Internet surfer is engaged in conspiratorial activity rather than electronic commerce or mere chatting. To assist such detection and determination, Bowden proposed the use of "trawling warrants."

59. Creating plain view by moving or disturbing items was ruled unlawful in *Arizona v. Hicks*, 480 U.S. 321 (1987). In *United States v. Place*, 462 U.S. 696 (1983), the Supreme Court concluded that the limited and "low tech" nature of enhanced plain view intrusion did not require probable cause. However, the use of sophisticated devices to enhance plain view would intrude upon a citizen's reasonable expectation of privacy and does require probable cause. See Bradley, "United States," pp. 403–4.
60. Supplement to Federal Guidelines.
61. See Zatz, "Sidewalks in Cyberspace." See also Larry Downes, "Electronic Communications and the Plain View Exception: More 'Bad Physics,'" *Harvard Journal of Law and Technology* 7 (Spring 1994): 239.
62. 18 U.S.C. §§ 2510-2518.

A required "trawling warrant" would specify a logical circuit or domain of capture, rather than allowing the capture of all messages on a topic or from or to a person. Signals from this specified domain would be automatically selected by computer against a "certificate" issued by a Secretary of State (or similar authority) that contains the description of the target subject matter suitable for machine searching. To limit abuse, the issuer would need to guarantee that uncertified intercepted material would not be looked at, read, or listened to by any person. Exemptions for extended interceptions for national security reasons could be given on a case-by-case basis only.[63] However, one must be warned that facing the difficulty of such narrow, targeted wiretapping of speedy and possibly disguised electronic communications, law enforcement may be—and has been—tempted to utilize large-scale, indiscriminate, and intrusive surveillance instead.[64]

(e) *Exigent circumstances.* "When destruction of evidence is imminent, a warrantless seizure of that evidence is justified if there is probable cause to believe that the item seized constitutes evidence of criminal activity."[65] Investigators must consider the degree of urgency, the time necessary to obtain a warrant, whether the evidence is about to be removed or destroyed, the destructibility of evidence, the possibility of danger, and whether suspects are aware that they are being observed or followed. This exception also justifies warrantless searches if the circumstances would cause a reasonable person to believe that an immediate search is necessary. Such circumstances involve the need for immediate aid,[66] escape of a suspect, or another emergency or

63. Bowden, "Unprecedented Safeguards for Unprecedented Capabilities."

64. According to Mark Rasch, a former federal computer-crime prosecutor, the wiretapping system used by the FBI is "the electronic equivalent of listening to everybody's phone calls to see if it's the phone call you should be monitoring." See King and Bridis, "FBI's System."

65. *United States v. David*, 756 F. Supp. 1385, 1392 (D. Nev. 1991). For a discussion of exigent circumstances in computer searches and seizures, see Federal Guidelines.

66. *Mincey v. Arizona*, 437 U.S. 385, 392–93 (1978).

frustration of legitimate law enforcement objectives.[67] A warrantless seizure under exigent circumstances does not automatically justify a warrantless search.[68]

If police lawfully observe a suspect's computer screen displaying evidence of crime, and then see the suspect modifying or deleting files containing such evidence, police may justifiably download them or seize the computer. However, the application of exigent circumstances to searching and seizing data from two or more computers on a wide-area network, used by individuals other than suspects, is less clear and should be determined upon a careful examination of each situation.[69] Electronic data are generally perishable. Integrity of data can be compromised by humidity, temperature, vibrations, physical mutilation, strong magnetic fields, computer commands to erase or re-format, and so on. This condition may strengthen the grounds for this exception, but only in the presence of probable cause.

(f) Consent search. Neither probable cause nor a warrant is required if a police officer obtains a suspect's consent for a search. The police are not required to inform the suspect of his right to withhold consent.[70] The only criterion that must be satisfied is "voluntariness," defined in terms of whether a reasonable "person would feel free to decline the officers' requests or otherwise terminate the encounter."[71] The burden is on the government to prove that the criterion is met.

Defining the scope of consented search on a networked computer can be problematic when consent to search one computer does not necessarily extend to other computers or equipment that may be physically or virtually connected to it. Encryption creates another challenge. An encrypted computer file can be analogous to a locked file cabinet (because the owner is attempting to preserve secrecy) or to a

---

67. *United States v. Arias*, 923 F.2d 1387 (9th Cir.), *cert. denied*, 112 S. Ct. 130 (1991).
68. *United States v. David*, 756 F. Supp. 1385, (D. Nev. 1991).
69. Federal Guidelines.
70. *Schneckloth v. Bustamonte*, 412 U.S. 218 (1973).
71. *Florida v. Bostick*, 501 U.S. 429 (1991).

document written in a language foreign to the reader. A warranted search would authorize searching for and seizing encrypted information, as well as requesting authority to decrypt (to "break the lock" on the cabinet or to "translate" the document). If, however, the search is based on consent, a court may find that a target who encrypted his data and did not disclose the necessary decryption key has tacitly limited the scope of his consent. If police do not ask explicitly for consent to search the encrypted material, or such consent is refused, a warrant may be required for the encrypted data.[72]

(g) Border search. As a condition of crossing the border or its "functional equivalent," officials can search people and property without a warrant and without probable cause.[73] Incoming baggage, persons, mail, as well as diskettes, tapes, computer hard drives, and other media, fall under this exception.[74]

This exception highlights the quintessential law enforcement problem created by cyberspace. On the one hand, cyberspace is tied to physical locations of ISPs and Internet users within some sovereign territory. On the other hand, sending an e-mail message is categorically different from crossing a national border in person or sending a paper letter. Regular mail travels intact and enters its international destination through an established border post. E-mail travels in the form of several packets of coded information that may separate enroute and pass through servers located in various countries. The border search exception does not readily apply to data transmitted electronically because its justification, based on the sovereign's power to exclude illegal articles from the country, no longer applies once such articles have come into the country undetected.[75]

Network monitoring, as a protective measure conducted by computer security specialists (without involvement of law enforcement)

72. *United States v. David*, 756 F. Supp. 1385 (D. Nev. 1991); Federal Guidelines.
73. *United States v. Ramsey*, 431 U.S. 606 (1977), *cert. denied*, 434 U.S. 1062 (1978).
74. Federal Guidelines.
75. Ibid.

for the purposes of optimizing network performance and ensuring security, generally will not face constraints of criminal law. Cooperation among ISPs and computer security professionals could be summoned to protect hardware, software, and databases. This would serve not only the goal of combating cyber crime (which may have a lower priority in nongovernmental, for-profit organizations), but also immediate goals of meeting contractual commitments to customers, maintaining continuity of business, and guarding against liabilities that may arise from allegations of negligence. More effective computer security and timely detection of and response to unauthorized access or use of cyber systems would help reduce both cyber crime and intrusive law enforcement.

Should police investigation become necessary, the use of automated near-real-time intrusion detection, tracking, containment, response, and reporting capabilities would more readily satisfy the legal constraints imposed on this activity. Automation may not solve all problems, but where available and appropriate, it could provide grounds for probable cause, identify suspects, and collect a certain amount of evidence, while preserving the anonymity of uninvolved network users. Some automated methods may be limited in scope to local orientation and reaction, which is ineffective in the internetworked global environment. A global response to cyber crime demands capabilities to correlate intrusion/attack symptoms occurring seemingly independently in different parts of the network. Reaction must be coordinated and uniform. Constraints on search, seizure, and due process of law under these circumstances are necessarily more important.

Due Process of Law

International human rights agreements and many national constitutions guarantee equal and proper treatment of individuals before the law. This guarantee entitles individuals to protection against self-incrimination and arbitrary arrest, detention, or exile. If arrested, one must be informed at the time of arrest of the reasons for the arrest and the charges made. The Universal Declaration of Human Rights and the International Covenant of Civil and Political Rights entitle every person to a fair and public hearing by a competent, independent, and impartial tribunal, in the determination of the person's rights and obligations and of any criminal charge. Moreover, everyone charged with a penal offense has the right to be presumed innocent until proved guilty according to law in a public trial, and the right to call and confront witnesses and to introduce evidence. No one may be found guilty of any penal offense that did not constitute a penal offense under national or international law at the time it was committed, nor may a heavier penalty be imposed than the one applicable at the time the penal offense was committed.[76]

States implement such provisions through national criminal justice systems. Suspects typically have the right to silence, although the levels of protection differ.[77] Due process of law is generally interpreted to require a trial or other legal proceedings, which provide fair procedures under accepted standards of national law and international norms. The right to qualified counsel is fairly common, but it differs in scope.[78]

---

76. Universal Declaration of Human Rights, arts. 6–11; International Covenant of Civil and Political Rights, arts. 9 and 14. The binding European Convention on Human Rights embodies these principles in the "right to liberty and security," the "right to fair trial," and the prohibition of "punishment without law," arts. 5, 6, and 7, respectively.

77. In the U.S., the Fifth Amendment to the Constitution provides that no person "shall be compelled in any criminal case to be a witness against himself, nor be deprived of life, liberty, or property, without due process of law." In Israel, a suspect under arrest must be informed that anything he says might incriminate him. The suspect has the right to silence, but refusal to answer questions could strengthen evidence against him. See Boaz Guttman, "The Right of Non-Self-Incrimination in Israeli Law in the Context of Computer Crimes" (April 20, 2000); Israeli Criminal Procedure Order (Testimony), 1927, ¶ 2(2); Israeli Evidence Order (new version), 1971, ¶ 47(a); Israeli Criminal Procedures Order (combined version), 1982, ¶ 152(b) Criminal Procedures Law (Enforcement—Arrest), 1996, ¶ 28(a). China, by contrast, recognizes no right to silence, see Liling Yue, "China," in Bradley, ed., *Criminal Procedure*, p. 86. The European Convention on Human Rights has no explicit provision against self-incrimination.

78. South Africa, the United Kingdom, Italy, and Germany are among the strong-

Regardless of the existing domestic and international legal safe-guards, violations of due process principles persist around the world. The U.S. State Department reports widespread denials of basic legal protections and due process to criminal defendants, detentions without trial or charge, prolonged pretrial detentions and trial delays, illegal searches, and infringements on citizens' privacy rights.[79]

Requirements for due process of law and accountability apply fully to computer-related cases. They also augment technological, legal, and organizational challenges involved in combating cyber crime. Effective and timely information exchanges among ISPs, technical experts, and law enforcement can improve investigative functions. A global incident response capability may require teams of technical, legal, and police experts, linked to their respective organizations, to track trends and activities of known and potential cyber criminals and terrorists. Accomplishing such cooperation among individuals and organizations with different goals, cultures, and procedures is likely to be difficult from the operational standpoint. The legitimacy of specific methods used to accomplish such goals will be judged according to specific situations.

General warnings are also appropriate. Proposals have been made to assign a presumption of guilt to suspects who withhold decryption keys, unless the defense could somehow prove nonpossession.[80] Reversing burdens of proof in this manner may deprive an accused of the right to a fair trial. Extensive profiling of individual behaviors on the Internet may lead to self-incrimination. Once an infrastructure for

---

est protectors of this right from the perspective of the accused. See Lensing, in Bradley, ed., *Criminal Procedure*, pp. 427–28. Russian citizens have a constitutional right to qualified legal counsel, but the law permits both licensed attorneys and nonlawyers (members of a social organizations or close family) to act as defense counsel in criminal proceedings. See Newcombe, ibid., p. 290. In China, judges appoint legal counsel to criminal defendants if they consider it necessary. See Liling Yue, ibid., p. 88.

79. See, e.g., "1999 Country Reports on Human Rights Practices," Bureau of Democracy, Human Rights, and Labor, U.S. Department of State, February 25, 2000, available at ⟨*http://www.state.gov/www/global/human_rights/99hrp_index.html*⟩.

80. Bowden, "Unprecedented Safeguards."

policing of international networks is in place, it could be used to the detriment of private citizens. The extent of intrusion justified in a targeted and warranted police investigation is unacceptable in the general societal context.[81]

Concern over due process of law in the course of international cooperation against cyber crime and terrorism has led to a number of provisions in the proposed Draft Convention. As a minimum level of protection, it allows States Parties to insist on the preservation of national norms. It entitles any person detained by a State Party to rights extended under national law to: communicate without unnecessary delay with the appropriate representative of the detained person's state or authority entitled to protect his or her rights; be visited by a representative of that state; have this representative physically present to observe any legal proceedings that may result in punishment; and be informed of these entitlements promptly after detention. The Draft Convention prohibits any denial or impairment of these entitlements.[82]

The proposed convention also prohibits extradition or legal assistance if there are grounds to believe that a suspect will be prosecuted or punished on account of political offense, or on account of that person's race, religion, nationality, ethnic origin, or political belief.[83] Although strong differences exist among states concerning restrictions on expression and political activity, this provision allows states to prevent or hinder politically motivated or unfair prosecutions by refusing or ceasing cooperation with the prosecuting state. In case of a serious and unresolvable situation of abuse of the international regime of technical and legal cooperation, effective economic and political sanctions may be imposed on the offending state.[84] The sanctions may

81. This view was also argued by Barry Steinhardt, presentation at the Stanford Conference, December 6–7, 1999.
82. Draft "International Convention to Enhance Protection from Cyber Crime and Terrorism," art. 10.
83. Ibid., art. 19.
84. See ibid., arts. 12, 13, and 21 for the sanctions afforded by the proposed convention.

extend to denial of technological and economic assistance under the regime, expulsion from the regime, and measures to limit the ability of the offending government to benefit from participating in the international information infrastructure.

4. Conclusion

The extent to which the rights to privacy, the protections against unwarranted searches and seizures, and the rights to due process of law constrain an international regime against cyber crime and terrorism depends on the regime and the domestic laws of participating states. National laws often contain exceptions or special privileges for law enforcement to pursue criminal investigations. These privileges may also threaten the protection of human rights. States have different attitudes toward privacy, law enforcement powers, and due process. However, unilateral responses to cyber crime are not likely to be effective. Confronted with the need for international cooperation, states will look for ways to reconcile these differences or attempt to justify some inappropriate behavior. Greater emphasis on protective technological and legal measures, and respect for civil liberties in the course of cooperation, will help reduce the latter outcome.

Overall, protective measures, which aim to reduce cyber vulnerabilities and rely on computer security staff for initial reaction to incidents, are less intrusive than measures designed to allow extensive law enforcement presence in cyberspace. The protective approach can be implemented through encryption, automation, and anonymous tagging and tracking—recording fields in packet header information, for example, which does not intrude on the content of messages, or router-assisted fingerprinting of packets without disclosure of their originator unless sufficient evidence of crime emerges. Although better measures will need to be designed and updated continuously to keep up with offenses, this approach can afford greater protection against both cyber crime and intrusive law enforcement.

The reactive approach necessarily involves the participation of law enforcement officials, who will likely scan files, review content, and engage in other surveillance of communications to collect evidence and to identify perpetrators. Engaging in such activities on a wide "preventive" scale, rather than in specific cases with established probable cause of crime, would raise legal and moral concerns of unduly intrusive policing. Furthermore, even in specific cases of suspected crime, limiting the scope of targeted surveillance may be technologically and operationally difficult. This approach places communications of innocent people and their private information at risk. The reactive approach requires greater scrutiny.

While clearly threatening to civil liberties, reactive measures would not necessarily result in fewer crimes and better law enforcement. Even in most technologically and economically developed countries today, police lack equipment and training to meet the growing challenge of the electronic dimensions of crime. Technical experts agree that greater automation is crucial for a timely, scalable, and less intrusive response to international cyber crime. This offers hope that, in the name of both efficiency and civil liberties, relatively nonintrusive technological measures will be developed and implemented in the near future. Such solutions should provide a more suitable balance among security, law enforcement, and civil liberties in cyberspace. Reactive measures will also be enhanced, however, and will need to be fashioned and monitored so as to ensure adequate protection of human rights.

The technologies of crime and punishment are undergoing a rapid and profound evolution. But though such technologies constitute a moving target for evaluation, the legal and normative principles discussed here will endure, because they are independent of specific technological means. As such, they can provide a framework for building a global infrastructure and policy environment that balances the needs for crime-free business, government, and personal communications, with the protection of property, privacy, and civil liberties.

Tensions between security and civil liberties may emerge. These tensions should be carefully examined with the awareness of threats and social implications of measures against cyber crime and terrorism.

Ensuring the protection of fundamental rights to privacy, protection against self-incrimination and unwarranted searches and seizures, and due process of law is critical. Such protections should be prominent among the design criteria for technological, policy, and legal measures, and should be enforced by law and strong economic and political incentives.

Governments value liberty, privacy, and security differently. National rules concerning the intrusiveness of law enforcement, protection of citizen's rights, and international cooperation, reflect the country's normative choices about the roles of the state, market, and individual. Constituting the basis of domestic law, these norms affect the international behavior of nation-states. An international regime can help influence these norms over time. Today, when an international regime to combat cyber crime and terrorism is becoming a reality, there is a special opportunity to promote greater respect for human rights. At the very least, methods for international technological and legal cooperation against cyber crime and terrorism should not be permitted to become a vehicle for governments to oppress society.

CHAPTER 6

Toward an International Convention on Cyber Security

Abraham D. Sofaer

The case for international cooperation in dealing with cyber crime is overwhelming. The presentations and discussion at the Stanford Conference, distilled in this volume, demonstrate the growing threat and cost of such crime, as well as its transnational nature. The debate currently under way is over the form and scope such cooperation should take, and the extent to which the United States and other technologically advanced states should rely upon multilateral efforts to enhance cyber security.

Proposals for voluntary international cooperation have been advanced and are being implemented.[1] The principal elements of these proposals—to train law enforcement officials to understand and cope with cyber crimes, and to establish round-the-clock emergency response teams—are widely supported. In addition, the Group of Eight (G-8) and private groups such as the Internet Alliance have issued guidelines aimed at making voluntary cooperation more effective.[2] Although these groups recognize that international cooperation is essential, they have yet to accept the idea that an international treaty should be negotiated establishing legally mandated standards and obligations.

Support for voluntary, as opposed to legally mandated, international measures rests upon several arguments. Most cyber crime, it is argued, is conventional crime (fraud, drug dealing, money laundering, sexual exploitation of minors), in which cyber technology happens to be used. Existing treaties and international arrangements, including those providing for extradition and legal assistance, are potentially applicable in these cases. Securing international agreement on the wording of new cyber crimes will be difficult, moreover, and vast differences exist among states regarding appropriate regulation of content, the proper scope of transnational investigation, and the bases

1. See, e.g., Remarks of Attorney General Janet Reno to the National Association of Attorneys General, January 10, 2000, available at ⟨*http://www.usdoj.gov/ag/ speeches/*⟩; U.S. Department of Justice Computer Crime and Intellectual Property Section (CCIPS) materials, including "The Electronic Frontier: The Challenge of Unlawful Conduct Involving the Use of the Internet: A Report of the President's Working Group on Unlawful Conduct on the Internet," March 2000, available at ⟨*http:// www.usdoj.gov/criminal/cybercrime/*⟩.

2. See, e.g., "Ministerial Conference of the G-8 Countries on Combating Transnational Organized Crime," Moscow, October 19–20, 1999, Communiqué, available at ⟨*http://www.library.utoronto.ca/g7/adhoc/crime99.htm*⟩. See also Tom Heneghan, "G8 Nations Meet to Discuss Cybercrime," May 15, 2000, reported at ⟨*http:// dailynews.yahoo.com/h/nm/20000515/ts/crime cyberspace 2.html*⟩. For details on Internet Alliance, see the materials posted at ⟨*http://www.Internetalliance.org/policy/ index.html*⟩, as well as "Testimony of Jeff B. Richards, Executive Director of the Internet Alliance, Before the U.S. Senate Committee on Appropriations, Subcommittee on Commerce, Justice, State, and Judiciary," *Hearing on Cybercrime*, February 16, 2000, available at ⟨*http://www.senate.gov/~appropriations/commerce/richards 00. html*⟩.

upon which tracking information and messages should be subject to seizure and scrutiny. Furthermore, a great disparity exists among states—even technologically advanced ones—as to the scope of privacy and other rights possessed by individuals under national laws that would either operate to limit an international agreement or be compromised by one. Finally, the Internet, many believe, has been a powerful vehicle for economic growth and enhanced communication in large part because it is controlled by the private sector rather than by governments, and this growth and creativity may be adversely affected by international legal requirements and regulation.

For these reasons, Drew C. Arena, then senior counsel to the assistant attorney general, U.S. Department of Justice, commented at the Stanford Conference that achieving consensus on "the specific steps" to be taken in negotiating a multilateral treaty would be "too hard" at the present time to warrant the effort.[3] University of Chicago School of Law Professor Jack L. Goldsmith has argued that, in the absence of a suitable international regime, the United States should rely on unilateral measures in fighting transnational cyber crime.[4] However, he does, in principle, favor the pursuit of such a regime.

These arguments against the creation of an international legal regime to deal with cyber security are cogent, but they are based on difficulties and dangers that are avoidable. Not only is the case for a multilateral agreement to combat cyber crime and terrorism strong, the need to undertake the effort of negotiating one is becoming clearer with the increasing costs of such activity. Though it may indeed be true that most crimes in which computers and networks are involved are conventional and potentially covered by international agreements, these are not the crimes against which a new treaty is needed. Existing

3. Drew C. Arena, "Obstacles to Consensus in Multilateral Responses to Cyber Crime," presentation at the Conference on International Cooperation to Combat Cyber Crime and Terrorism, Hoover Institution, Stanford University, Stanford, California, December 6–7, 1999, p. 3.

4. Jack L. Goldsmith, "Cybercrime and Jurisdiction," presentation at the Stanford Conference, December 6–7, 1999, p. 9.

international agreements provide no help in dealing with crimes related directly to the information infrastructure, including attacks utilizing viruses (such as "Melissa" and "I Love You"), denials of service, and other destructive conduct. Furthermore, the need for an international agreement to deal with cyber crime rests not merely on the fact that such acts include new types of conduct but also on the need for new methods by which cyber crimes will have to be investigated and prosecuted to provide effective protection. Certainly it would be complicated to secure multilateral agreement on the precise wording of cyber crimes, but that effort need not be undertaken: a broad consensus exists with regard to certain conduct involving the information infrastructure that should be made criminal;[5] and a treaty could readily be drafted that describes such conduct and requires all States Parties to make such conduct criminal through any formula they choose to utilize.

The differences that exist among states concerning several key issues in developing a treaty must be taken into account and will limit and shape the arrangements that are currently feasible. But differences concerning such issues as regulation of content, scope of extraterritorial investigation, standards of proof, and protection of privacy and other rights can be resolved, largely through a willingness to begin this effort by focusing on measures likely to secure universal agreement. The sharp differences that exist among states with regard to what can be done unilaterally demonstrate, in fact, the need to attempt to secure agreed, multilateral arrangements, rather than establishing a basis for making no effort to do so.

The notion that the United States should act unilaterally when necessary to protect its interests is in principle sound. As discussed further below, the proposed draft international convention herein (the

5. See Tonya L. Putnam and David D. Elliott, "International Responses to Cyber Crime," Chap. 2 of this volume. The presentations on which this conclusion is based include those by Marc D. Goodman, Dietrich Neumann, and George C. C. Chen at Session Two, "International Response to Cyber Crime," of the Stanford Conference, December 6–7, 1999.

Stanford Draft) explicitly (in Article 20) excludes from its coverage the national security activities of states. Professor Goldsmith seems to recognize, however, that unilateral activities must be legally defensible, and resort to them must be in the nation's best interests. His assumption that it will take many years to negotiate and implement a multilateral convention may turn out to be wrong, in light of the increasingly obvious need and growing momentum for such an arrangement. Furthermore, even before a multilateral treaty is complete, the United States may be able to reach less comprehensive arrangements with other states to enhance legal protections. Unilateral conduct that offends other states, and leads them to reject or delay negotiating a desirable treaty, would harm U.S. interests.

Concerns expressed by the private sector over establishing legally mandated norms and obligations stem from the fear that law enforcement considerations will adversely affect (and greatly burden) Internet businesses and freedom of expression. Government control of the information infrastructure could well have detrimental effects, and international regulation could be especially damaging if political objectives and bureaucratic requirements are allowed to interfere with the present, privately dominated Internet regime.[6] National governments, including the U.S. government, have sought or imposed potentially damaging restrictions on Internet users, including limitations on the use and sale of advanced encryption, demands for the power to intrude upon, hear, and record Internet traffic,[7] and suggestions that private entities assume quasi-prosecutorial responsibilities in criminal investigations. These policies and suggestions have, however, unjustifiably evoked suspicion of all efforts to establish legally mandated

6. See Stephen J. Lukasik, "Current and Future Technical Capabilities," Chap. 4 of this volume, for a description of the present governing structure of the Internet.

7. Consider, for example, the Clinton administration's January 2000 "National Plan for Information Systems Protection," which drew criticism for, among other things, relying too heavily on monitoring and surveillance instead of simply focusing on making systems more secure. See Jennifer Jones, "U.S. Cyberattack Protection Plan Draws Criticism," February 3, 2000, which was reported at ⟨*http://cnn.com/2000/ TEC...cyberprotection.crit.idg/index.html*⟩.

obligations. If, as we believe, voluntary efforts will not provide adequate security, legal obligations to cooperate can be devised that are consistent with continued private creativity and control. An international regime can be fashioned to satisfy the full range of cyber-security needs, in a manner that ensures continued private-sector control of Internet technology and practices. The United States is party to several international regimes encompassing the creation of consensus-based, nonmandatory measures crafted by public and private-sector experts, which a treaty for cyber security could draw on in providing a comprehensive and lasting system for international cooperation.

The strong case for a legally mandated, international regime has led to several significant developments. Treaty provisions are being proposed to close loopholes in existing multilateral commitments in the specific area of civil aviation.[8] This approach may be feasible in other areas, particularly to protect critical infrastructures from criminal and terrorist attacks, and it seems likely to cause little controversy.

The Council of Europe (COE) has taken a more comprehensive approach, publishing and refining a draft treaty on cyber crime.[9] This proposal includes definitions of cyber activities that must be made criminal by all States Parties, as well as other features and forms of cooperation.[10] The COE's draft assumes, correctly, that substantial consensus exists with respect to what cyber activities should be considered criminal, and that substantial benefits can be derived from a multilateral arrangement with common standards, investigative cooperation, and extradition.

---

8. See Mariano-Florentino Cuéllar, "Past as Prologue: International Aviation Security Treaties as Precedents for International Cooperation Against Cyber Terrorism and Cyber Crimes," Chap. 3, III, of this volume.

9. See "Draft Convention on Cyber-Crime (No. 24, Rev. 2)" released for public discussion on November 19, 2000, available at ⟨*http://conventions.coe.int/treaty/en/ projets/cybercrime24.htm*⟩. The COE's Justice Ministers resolved on June 9, 2000, that the Council should speed its work and "conclude an international treaty by the end of the year." See ⟨*http://www.coe.fr/cp/2000/427a(2000).htm*⟩.

10. See, e.g., ibid., Chap. II ("Measures to be taken at the national level"), arts. 2–9; Chap. III ("International Co-operation").

This chapter seeks to demonstrate the advantages and feasibility of an even more comprehensive regime by proposing a draft international convention (the Stanford Draft) and discussing its principal elements. The Stanford Draft differs from the draft COE Convention on Cyber-Crime in several important respects. Most significantly, the Stanford Draft would limit the acts it covers to attacks on the information infrastructure and violations of antiterrorist conventions, whereas the COE Draft includes conventional crimes in which computers are used as well as content-related offenses but does not include violations of antiterrorist conventions. The Stanford Draft also would establish an international agency, modeled along the lines of successful, specialized United Nations agencies, to prepare and promulgate— on the basis of advice from nonpolitical experts—standards and recommended practices (SARPs) to enhance the effectiveness of protective and investigative measures, whereas the COE proposes detailed forms of cooperation without such a process.

I. Covered Conduct

The basis for international cooperation rests, most fundamentally, on the combination of a demonstrable need for international agreement to combat harmful cyber conduct and the existence of an international consensus on what conduct should be considered criminal. A review of existing statutory law and proposed international arrangements reflects widespread consensus on prosecuting as criminal the conduct covered in the Stanford Draft: attacks aimed at disrupting or damaging computer operations, deliberate and unauthorized intrusions, interference with computer-security measures, maliciously altering content, intentionally and materially facilitating the commission of prohibited conduct, using a cyber system in committing violations of any of several widely adopted antiterrorist conventions, and using a cyber system to attack critical infrastructures.

Most of these forms of conduct are covered in the COE's draft proposal, although that draft attempts to classify cyber crimes into a number of specific categories: illegal access, illegal interception, data interference, system interference, and the misuse of "devices" for the purpose of committing acts in the preceding categories.[11] The COE effort to generalize makes the categories of offenses relatively easy to comprehend, but may have created coverage on some issues that is undesirably broad. The prohibition on illegal access, for example, would prohibit intentional access to any part of a computer system "without right."[12] Acts "without right" may include conduct not deliberately undertaken to violate adequately communicated prohibitions on entry. This vague standard is included in most of the COE's proposed offenses. The draft then continues: "A party may require that the offense be committed either by infringing security measures or with the intent of obtaining computer data or other dishonest intent."[13] To the extent the COE Draft permits members to vary conduct it covers, in this and many other provisions,[14] the treaty's effectiveness will be undermined. Uniformity of commitments is in general of greater importance than any particular form or level of coverage.

The introductory language to Article 3 of the Stanford Draft— specifically the concept of "legally recognized authority"—is intended to incorporate the concept of self-defense. Efforts of governments, companies, and individuals to defend themselves from attacks may sometimes require measures that, if adopted without authorization or justification, would be criminal, such as alterations of code, or interfering with operation of computers being used by attackers. At times, such efforts may affect innocent third parties, but nonetheless may be reasonable. The complex issues that are certain to arise in applying

11. See "Draft Convention on Cyber-Crime," arts. 2–6.
12. See ibid., art. 2.
13. Ibid.
14. For example, Article 3's prohibition of "illegal interception"—one of the COE Draft's most fundamental provisions—provides in part: "A Party may require that the offence be committed with dishonest intent, or in relation to a computer system that is connected to another computer system." These questionable exceptions (and many others) would enable Parties to create significantly disparate coverage, and raise difficult dual-criminality issues.

established principles of law to this new area of technological activity will be resolved over time, on the basis of experience.[15]

The Stanford Draft recognizes and attempts to deal with the fact that states have different standards in statutes that cover the conduct it proscribes. Instead of attempting to list specific, commonly defined "offenses," as in most extradition treaties, the Stanford Draft refers to types of conduct, and secures commitments from all States Parties to enforce any applicable law against every form of covered conduct, or to adopt new laws necessary to create authority to prosecute or extradite for such conduct. This approach overcomes the problem of attempting to develop precise, agreed-upon definitions of offenses, and therefore the requirement that every State Party adopt particular for-mulations as national crimes.

In addition to requiring criminal enforcement against conduct spe-cifically aimed at the information infrastructure, the Stanford Draft requires criminal enforcement against the use of computers in the commission of offenses under certain widely adopted multilateral trea-ties. These include clearly defined crimes against aircraft, ships, and diplomats, and terrorist bombings. Computers can greatly enhance the potential damage caused by crimes, and can make them especially difficult to investigate. Therefore, since most states are parties to these multilateral treaties, they should be prepared to impose more stringent punishment for the use of cyber capacities in committing the targeted offenses. (The COE Draft, No. 24, Rev. 2, does not include such provisions.) Other, widely recognized forms of criminal conduct may also become more aggravated through the use of computers, such as forgery, fraud, theft, and conversion. These crimes are not included in the Stanford Draft, however, since they are in general already encom-passed in extradition treaties, to the extent States Parties want such coverage. The cyber dimension of such activities, moreover, would generally involve conduct covered in the Stanford Draft, irrespective

15. See generally Gregory D. Grove, Seymour E. Goodman, and Stephen J. Lu-kasik, "Cyber-attacks, Counter-attacks, and International Law," *Survival* 42 IISS, London, Autumn 2000.

of the crimes such conduct may have facilitated. (The COE Draft includes coverage of "computer-related" forgery and fraud, but its definitions of these offenses seem likely to cause uncertainties.)[16]

Other types of conduct, when related to the information infrastructure, have been prohibited in some states, including copyright violations and sexual exploitation of minors. Such types of conduct are not covered in the Stanford Draft because their inclusion may prove controversial. These areas are covered by the COE Draft, however, as "Content-related offences."[17] In fact, a sufficient consensus for including some of these offenses—especially the use of computers for sexual exploitation of minors—may exist, and the Stanford Draft's coverage could be expanded to include such offenses. The COE Draft covers offenses related to child pornography, as well as "copyright and related rights," but whether the scope of copyright coverage should be coterminous with treaties in the area, such as the Berne Convention and other copyright treaties administered by the World Intellectual Property Organization, is left unsettled, and Parties are explicitly allowed to "reserve the right not to impose criminal liability" for copyright violations, "provided that other effective remedies are available."[18]

The Stanford Draft includes very limited coverage of "content" offenses, in part to avoid the strong differences that exist among states concerning restrictions on speech and political activity. No type of speech, or publication, is required to be treated as criminal under the Stanford Draft; if, for example, Germany were to decide to ban publication on the Internet of *Mein Kampf*, it would have to do so unilaterally and could not expect to receive enforcement assistance under the Stanford Draft. The single exception to this principle in the Stanford Draft is the narrow coverage of conduct described as the "distri-

16. The definition of forgery, for example, leaves members free to require or dispense with any dishonest intent, and that of fraud requires neither a false representation nor reliance. See "Draft Convention on Cyber-Crime," arts. 7 and 8.

17. Ibid., Tit. 3.

18. See ibid., art. 10.

bution of devices or programs intended for the purpose of committing" other conduct made criminal by the Stanford Draft. The Draft thereby makes criminal the knowing and deliberate effort to cause illegal attacks through such distribution, but not discussions of computer vulnerability intended for evaluating exposure to attacks on the Internet, or other protected speech. States Parties wishing to encourage open discussion of computer attacks and vulnerabilities could designate "safe harbor" sites at which discussion would be considered lawful. (The COE Draft would prohibit the "Misuse of Devices," defined to include the production or transfer, etc. of programs designed primarily to commit other violations, or passwords or other code used for access to computers for that purpose.)[19]

While the Stanford Draft avoids content regulation by focusing on protecting the information infrastructure and computers, the protection proposed is comprehensive. A convention based on such coverage could be used to protect activities that some States Parties may decline to protect as a matter of policy. For example, a company could use code to design protection for information that it could not otherwise protect; a person having the right under the law to obtain such information through lawful means might be prevented from doing so because of the convention's prohibition of efforts to gain access through any proscribed form of conduct. This is a serious concern, since the convention is not intended to enable parties to create a new method for restricting otherwise permissible personal, business, or political activities. It is unclear, however, whether the scope of the Draft's proposed protection could convincingly be restricted in terms that allowed any of the proscribed activities without undermining its credibility. The Draft therefore includes a public-policy exception to its enforcement in Article 13; a similar provision is included in the COE Draft.[20]

---

19. See ibid., art. 6. The COE Draft allows Parties to require that "a number of such items be possessed before criminal liability attaches."

20. Ibid., art. 27(4)(b). A requested Party may refuse assistance if "it considers

A final issue concerning offenses is whether a cyber crime convention should cover only those offenses that provide for penalties exceeding some minimum term of imprisonment. Extradition treaties generally contain such a limitation, usually that the crime for which extradition is sought be punishable by one year of imprisonment or more. This rule is intended to exclude minor offenses from coverage. Given the complications and the effort required to satisfy extradition requests, this consideration is at least as important in a cyber crime convention as in any other. By having such a requirement, moreover, States Parties would in effect be required to cover prohibited conduct with potential penalties of at least one year in prison. The Stanford Draft therefore includes only crimes for which a potential penalty of at least one year's imprisonment is provided. (The COE Draft includes a separate article on this subject, which is designed to ensure serious penal and civil sanctions.[21])

2. Jurisdiction

The Stanford Draft anticipates that the conduct it covers will have effects potentially conferring jurisdiction on multiple States Parties for the same offense. It provides a set of priorities that Parties would agree to follow in performing their duties and pursuing their rights, to the extent practicable, given the difficulty of anticipating all the possible contingencies. A State Party must establish jurisdiction to try offenders who commit offenses in its territory, who are its nationals, or who are stateless residents in its territory and whose extradition from its territory is refused. A State Party may establish jurisdiction to try offenders who attempt to harm it or its nationals, or to compel it to perform or abstain from performing an act, or whose offenses have substantial

---

that execution of the request is likely to prejudice its sovereignty, security, *ordre public* or other essential interests."

21. See ibid., art. 13. The COE Draft provides for "Corporate liability," but in terms that would allow several defenses that uniform treatment of all covered entities would not permit. See ibid., art. 12.

effects within its territory. (The COE Draft provides less comprehensive coverage, and fails to provide any guidance with regard to priorities, requiring only "consultation" aimed at determining the "most appropriate" jurisdiction for prosecution.[22])

The problem of multiple-state jurisdiction over crime is by now commonplace in international law. Transnational fraud, for example, has led to decisions by national courts assuming jurisdiction on the basis of any significant connection to the conduct involved. Among these are the states where a fraud was planned, where an effort to defraud was initiated, where individuals worked at implementing the fraud, where or through which communications were made that were intrinsic to the fraud, where the victims were located, and where the fraud had material and intended effects.[23] The widespread recognition of fraud as criminal activity leads states readily to find jurisdiction over such activity, despite the significant relationship particular frauds may have to other states. They tend to assume that punishing fraud will be supported by other affected states, rather than opposed as violating their sovereignty.

Cyber crime is quintessentially transnational, and will often involve jurisdictional assertions of multiple states. To avoid the conflict such assertions of jurisdiction could cause, enforcement under the Stanford Draft is limited to cyber activities that are universally condemned. The Stanford Draft does not accede to a state's jurisdiction merely because someone within its territory is able to access a website in another state; to confer jurisdiction, someone in control of the

---

22. See ibid., art. 23.

23. See *Libman v. The Queen* [1985] 2 S.C.R. 178, a leading decision of the Canadian Supreme Court providing in-depth description of modern developments with regard to jurisdiction to prosecute conduct involving extraterritorial elements. See also Laurent Belsie, "Cops Narrow Gap on Web Criminals: This Week's Arrest of a Teen Hacker Shows That Law Enforcement Is Getting More Savvy," *Christian Science Monitor*, April 21, 2000, available at 2000 WL 4427576, reporting on the arrest in Montreal after investigations by the Royal Canadian Mounted Police and the FBI of "Mafiaboy" for allegedly sabotaging the CNN.com website in February 2000.

website must deliberately cause one of the covered crimes, with effects in the state seeking to assert jurisdiction. It seems likely, therefore, that states will in general accept all of the reasonably based jurisdictional claims approved in the Draft.

3. Cooperation in Criminal Enforcement

The Stanford Draft includes commitments by States Parties to engage in the full range of cooperative activities found in widely adopted international agreements. Under it, States Parties would agree to extradite or prosecute persons reasonably believed to have engaged in any form of the covered conduct or offenses. Where necessary, and on a proper evidentiary basis, they would arrest and hold alleged offenders for a short period pending an extradition request. They would also agree to cooperate in seizing, preserving, developing, and providing in usable form evidence for the prosecution of offenders in the courts of other States Parties. They would coordinate these activities through designated "Central Authorities," as in Mutual Legal Assistance Treaties, so that each State Party would know whom to address requests to, and would have an identified agency or person responsible for dealing with such requests in a timely and proper manner.

The COE Draft is detailed and comprehensive in the obligations it contains related to (what it terms) "Procedural Measures." It mandates prompt responses to cyber attacks and requests for cooperation, on a twenty-four-hour/seven-days-per-week basis.[24] (The Stanford Draft incorporates a similar commitment.) The COE Draft provides, among other things, for the expedited preservation and disclosure of stored or traffic data; production orders for computer data and subscriber information from service providers; search and seizure of data; real-time collection of data from service providers; and interception of content data.[25] Several of these provisions are controversial. The COE Draft deals with this by requiring that all such measures be

24. See "Draft Convention on Cyber-Crime," art. 35.
25. See ibid., arts. 16–21.

implemented in accordance with the domestic law of the requested Party, with due regard for the protection of human rights; and it also allows Parties to limit to certain cases their obligations to provide real-time collection of traffic data, and interception of content data.[26] Although these rules may prove useful, they have evoked distrust and opposition, and may well become dated or problematic over time, with the availability of new technologies or methods. The Stanford Draft avoids these problems by providing for commitments to cooperate on each of the subjects covered by the COE Draft, but without further specification, leaving it to the Parties to develop on a consensus basis detailed standards and practices with public input.

But if the basic principles of cooperation are clear, when it comes to implementation many problems still exist, and many more are certain to arise, for which answers have not as yet been developed. What, for example, should be the scope of a state's power unilaterally to seek information in a foreign state? A state may not know whether its electronic effort to obtain information about a crime will enter or have any significant effect within another state or states; it could not avoid such uncertainty even if it tried. Some tolerance of extraterritorial effects would, therefore, seem to be imperative in any viable, multilateral cyber-related arrangement. Both the Stanford Draft and the COE Draft call for the widest possible cooperation,[27] and both provide for reasonable unilateral action.[28]

Another area of current uncertainty is what duties an Internet Service Provider (ISP) should have to preserve and provide information of cyber crimes. Should any such duty be enforceable by law, and if so by what means? These are sensitive issues, since states have not yet imposed duties on ISPs and other Internet participants, such as those imposed in analogous contexts. What should states be required to do to enhance the prospects of preserving evidence that could be helpful in investigating an attack; in particular, should a state be required to

26. See ibid., art. 15.
27. See ibid., arts. 24 and 26.
28. Compare Article 6(5) of the Stanford Draft with Article 32 of the COE Draft.

seize such information? As noted, the COE Draft is much more specific on these issues than the Stanford Draft, although the former contains significant room for reservations.

These sorts of issues related to transnational investigation of cyber crime and terrorism raise several common questions. The first concerns technology: What technological measures are possible and/or desirable to assist States Parties in securing cooperation that goes beyond the conventional steps currently undertaken in treaties of extradition and mutual legal assistance? Rapidly changing technological capacities and needs make it fruitless to attempt to deal definitively in a draft convention with this aspect of the cyber crime and terrorism problem.[29] Instead, the Draft proposes general principles supporting certain existing technological objectives, and would establish an international agency (the "Agency for Information Infrastructure Protection" or "AIIP,") through which States Parties would cooperate in considering and proposing the use of particular technological measures to enhance cooperative efforts.

In addition to the technological dimension there are certain questions of principle concerning the right of States Parties to defend against or to investigate cyber crime. May a State Party, for instance, deliberately initiate investigative actions or countermeasures for law enforcement purposes that could involve sending transmissions into cyber systems located in other, sovereign territories? Based on experience to date, fast-spreading computer viruses and other cyber attacks demand prompt efforts to track down attackers, and it is difficult if not impossible to know in advance all the places to or through which any part of any cyber transmission might travel. Therefore, both the Stanford Draft and the COE Draft approve in principle unilateral measures where they are electronic and reasonable. The Stanford Draft provides, moreover, that any law enforcement activity undertaken that knowingly affects another State Party, including any effort to seek

---

29. Drew Arena is correct in making this point, but wrong to assume that any multilateral regime must share this deficiency. See Arena, "Obstacles to Consensus," p. 10.

cooperative measures from an entity located in another State Party, must be made known to the central authority of that state as soon as practicable. In addition, the Stanford Draft would require all entities, including ISPs, to comply with any standard or procedure developed by the AIIP and accepted by the State Party in which they are located, and would mandate that all States Parties enforce all such standards and procedures. Arrangements based on these principles seem likely to garner widespread support, and would be preferable to unilateral actions that some states could find objectionable (or even criminal).

The Stanford Draft includes a provision authorizing the seizure and forfeiture of equipment utilized in the commission of offenses, subject to due process protections. States could use the information contained in such equipment, or dispose of the equipment as they see fit, consistent with national law. Funds derived from forfeitures have provided resources in other areas for use in upgrading law enforcement capabilities.[30] The seizure and/or forfeiture of cyber equipment used in committing covered offenses is consistent with the universally recognized right of governments to seize instruments of crime.

4. Structure for Technological Cooperation

An effective transnational response to cyber crime requires a high level of technological cooperation with regard to virtually every function expected to be performed by the States Parties. Cyber criminals exploit the technological possibilities available, including the ability to mask their identity, to hide the origin of attacks and other actions by conducting them through intermediate sites, and to find and exploit weaknesses throughout the worldwide information infrastructure. The challenges of dealing with these capacities are further exacerbated by dynamic changes in technology, the continuing development of new

30. See, e.g., United Nations Convention Against Illicit Traffic in Narcotic Drugs and Psychotropic Substances, December 20, 1988, T.I.A.S., 20 I.L.M. 493 ("Narcotics Convention" or "Vienna Convention on Narcotics").

methods for committing cyber crimes, the current widespread sharing of information and ideas about cyber system vulnerabilities, and a culture among users of cyberspace that is skeptical of, if not outright hostile to, government involvement.

Given these circumstances, it is unrealistic to expect that cyber crime will be significantly controlled or deterred through unilateral or voluntary or purely defensive measures. Defensive measures always make sense, and will prove effective for some entities, some of the time. But the pressure to operate openly in business, education, research, entertainment, and personal activities leads users to develop or choose accessible (hence more vulnerable) technology. Governments have seemed especially unable to defend their sites and systems, and have been frequent targets of attack.[31] Furthermore, the objectives sought through cooperation, and simply unavailable to states acting unilaterally, require a high level of technological coordination.[32] Take, for example, the need to anticipate, freeze, and trace information packets that are used in cyber crime. Those measures, once devised, will need to be approved and implemented by all participants in the information infrastructure, in a technologically compatible manner, or criminals will find and use gaps in coverage. Similarly, to enable states to conduct searches and seizures, to provide for extradition, and to develop evidence that is usable in the courts of all cooperating states, will require

---

31. Consider, for example, the numerous attacks in January 2000 that paralyzed several Japanese government websites. See Howard W. French, "Internet Raiders in Japan Denounce Rape of Nanjing," *New York Times*, January 31, 2000, available at 2000 WL 12395311, reporting that hackers posted messages on the website of Japan's postal service criticizing Japan's wartime role in China in the 1930s, "as a series of similar attacks" over the previous week "began to look like a daily ritual." See also "Hackers Become an Increasing Threat," *New York Times on the Web/Breaking News from Associated Press*, July 7, 1999, reporting on "high-profile electronic assaults [that] have included [U.S.] government" sites such as the White House, FBI, Senate, and Army Department), reported at ⟨*http://www.nytimes.com/aponline/w/ AP-Hacker-Threat.html*⟩; Daniel Verton, "Cyberattacks Against DOD up 300 Percent This Year," which was reported at *CNN.com*, November 5, 1999.

32. Recall the discussion by Stephen Lukasik in Chap. 4.

adoption of uniform and mutually acceptable standards and techno-logical solutions, on which all states can rely.

The pressures for multilateral solutions to information-infrastruc-ture problems are, indeed, likely to be so great that solutions will be developed without the formal, open, and accountable processes as-sociated with established international institutions. The story of how private and public actors developed and secured U.S. government support for a system of website domain protection illustrates both the need for and inevitability of multilateral solutions to at least some of the key issues, as well as the ad hoc and relatively undemocratic process that may occur in the absence of established, publicly accountable mechanisms.[33]

The process by which effective standards and practices are estab-lished for international cooperation in dealing with cyber crime and terrorism is likely to be the most important aspect of any multilateral agreement. Considerable guidance can be gained in designing a struc-ture for setting such standards from other areas in which transnational standard-setting activities occur, such as airline safety, marine safety, telecommunications, and banking. In general, standard setting and cooperation in such areas is achieved by establishing an international agency assigned clearly articulated and widely shared objectives, with the technical and material resources to achieve those objectives, a professional and nonpolitical staff, substantial reliance on the private sector (especially on highly skilled technical experts), and continuous political involvement and ultimate control by representatives of the participating states.

The history and structure of the International Civil Aviation Or-ganization (ICAO) are instructive in this regard.[34] ICAO is governed

33. For more on this subject, see Yochai Benkler, "Internet Law: A Case Study in the Problem of Unilateralism," *New York University School of Law: Public Law and Legal Theory Working Paper Series* no. 11 (Fall 1999), to be published in *European Journal of International Law*, available at ⟨*http://papers.ssrn.com/paper.taf? abstract id=206828*⟩.

34. ICAO was established under Part II of the Convention on International Civil Aviation, December 7, 1944, 59 Stat. 1693, 84 UNTS 389 ("Chicago Convention").

by an Assembly consisting of representatives from all its States Parties (185), which meets at least once every three years, establishes basic policies consistent with governing treaties, considers and recommends treaty revisions, approves the budget, which it funds through an apportionment among Member States, and elects delegates to the Council for three-year terms. The Council currently has thirty-three members, including representatives from states of chief importance in air transport, from states that make the largest contributions to international aviation, or chosen to ensure that all major geographical areas are represented. The Council implements Assembly decisions, prepares the budget, administers ICAO's finances, appoints the Secretary General and provides a Secretariat, and is empowered to adopt Standards and Recommended Practices (SARPs), which are incorporated into the ICAO Convention through Annexes. The Council acts by majority vote in carrying out its functions, including the adoption of SARPs, which are only adopted after exhaustive development and "technical monitoring, evaluation and backstopping."[35] Though it may delegate authority in any particular matter to a committee of its members, decisions of any such committee may be appealed to the Council by any interested contracting state.

The subjects dealt with in SARPs reflect the Council's authority to adopt measures necessary to maintain the safety and efficiency of international air transport. In performing these functions, the Council is assisted by the Air Navigation Commission, a body of fifteen persons with "suitable qualifications and experience," appointed by the Council from among nominees of Member States. This expert body is responsible for considering and recommending new or amended SARPs, establishing technical subgroups, and ensuring that the Council col-

---

See Mariano-Florentino Cuéllar's evaluation of the utility of international agreements on civil aviation security as precedents for the regulation of cyber activities and his recommendations for specific modifications to existing civil aviation conventions to close certain loopholes.

35. See "ICAO Technical Co-operation," available at ⟨*http://www.icao.int/ icao/en/tcb desc.htm*⟩, and discussed in Chap. 3.

lects and disseminates to all Member States the information necessary and useful for the advancement of air navigation.

Technical assistance is a major aspect of ICAO's work. Member States license pilots in accordance with ICAO standards. Standardization of equipment and procedures is a major aim and activity, on the whole array of technical issues, including navigation, meteorology, charts, measurement, aircraft operation, air traffic services, search and rescue, accident inquiry, and security. Developing countries are actively assisted through a variety of programs, funded by ICAO, the United Nations Development Program (UNDP), and other sources. Some 80 staff members are involved in about 120 assistance projects each year, with an overall budget of $55 million. They provide training, technical advice, and help in purchasing necessary equipment.

A second international agency that performs duties analogous to those relevant to cyber security is the International Telecommunication Union (ITU). The ITU is the oldest intergovernmental organization in existence, having been formed in 1865 to implement the Telegraph Convention. It expanded its activities to radio in 1906, and currently deals with issues related to all forms of "telecommunications," including telephone, television, and telex. It operates along the same lines as ICAO,[36] and relies heavily on private-sector expertise and involvement.[37] In recent statements, the ITU has expressed its

36. The ITU Plenipotentiary Conference (of about 170 members) establishes general policies consistent with governing treaties; proposes revisions to the International Telecommunication Convention when necessary; develops the basis for a budget; and elects an Administrative Council, composed of 43 members chosen with due regard to equitable geographic representation, which meets once each year, supervises the Union's administrative operations, coordinates the activities of its permanent bodies, approves the annual budget, and interacts with other international bodies. Expenses are borne by the Member States, which are divided into several contribution classes based on relevant capacities. The Plenipotentiary also elects a Secretary General, who supervises the operations of the Secretariat, which is responsible for the ITU's administrative and financial affairs. The ITU, like ICAO, has a substantial program of technical assistance and training, especially for needy states, funded in part by the UNDP.

37. Technical activities constitute the bulk of the ITU's activities. It has several boards and committees of politically independent experts who make recommenda-

intent to become more involved with information-infrastructure is-sues.[38]

The ICAO and ITU regimes deal with underlying technological matters that differ from each other, and from Internet communica-tions, in significant ways. But the needs that led to the creation of these, and of other, similar regulatory mechanisms, are largely analogous to those affecting the cyber world. The key factors behind establishment of these multilateral bodies have been safety and efficiency—the same considerations supporting a multilateral solution to the problem of cyber crime and terrorism. In addition, these multilateral entities are designed to: (1) enable all States Parties to learn of and become in-volved in the multilateral solutions of problems related to transna-tional technologies; (2) enable technologically advanced states to pro-tect their interests; (3) ensure that solutions are based on the best possible scientific knowledge, developed with the input of expert ad-vice; and (4) benefit from involvement and expertise of private interests (both commercial and nonprofit).

The Stanford Draft draws on the ICAO and ITU patterns in cre-ating a proposed international institution, the "Agency for Informa-tion Infrastructure Protection" or "AIIP," to implement the objectives of States Parties with regard to protecting the information infrastruc-ture from criminal and terrorist cyber activities. No single set of tech-

---

tions concerning technical and operating issues in different areas of telecommunica-tions, including the International Frequency Registration Board, five radio experts elected by the Plenipotentiary from different regions of the world, which records frequency assignments and advises Member States concerning such issues as interfer-ence. In addition to representatives of Member States, experts from private companies operating telecommunication services routinely participate in the Committees' work.

38. See, e.g., "ITU Efforts to Build a New Global Information Infrastructure," available through ⟨*http://www.itu.int/newsroom/index.html*⟩, stating in part: "While many countries are already beginning to implement their own strategies to put in place new high-speed information infrastructures, there remains a need for a global approach which will foster worldwide compatibility between new technologies. The ITU, with its 188 government members and around 500 members from private in-dustry, represents a global forum through which global standards that reflect the needs of a broad cross section of the infocommunications industry, from operators and governments to service providers and consumers, can be developed."

nical fixes will solve the problems that now exist, let alone those that will develop as the technological possibilities expand. The AIIP is therefore designed to play an ongoing role in formulating and revising standards and in proposing treaty revisions for enhanced safety, efficiency, and effective cooperation in light of continuing technological and political developments. Properly designed and structured, this type of agency should contribute materially to cyber security.

The Stanford Draft would require States Parties to establish the AIIP, with the following key components: an Assembly having functions similar to those exercised by the plenary bodies that operate in ICAO, the ITU, and some other specialized agencies; a Council that implements the policies set by the Assembly, through committees of experts, with heavy private-sector representation; and a Secretary General and Secretariat to implement Assembly and Council instructions and perform administrative tasks. The Council would formulate and the Assembly would adopt recommended standards and practices (SARPs) to advance the purposes of the Stanford Draft, and the AIIP would also propose amendments and additional international agreements to implement solutions to problems that require new authority from states. Some of the UN's specialized agencies have an impressive record for developing and proposing international agreements to deal with important areas not covered by their founding instruments. The International Maritime Organization (IMO), for example, has proposed over twenty treaties to deal with important issues of maritime safety or efficiency, most of which have been widely ratified. In addition, the AIIP Council would be authorized to create and implement, with the Assembly's support, assistance programs to help needy States Parties participate effectively in the activities contemplated in the Stanford Draft.

The standards and recommendations to be developed by the AIIP would be designed to have the same legal force attributed to SARPs developed by ICAO. SARPs adopted by ICAO are not legally binding; they become part of appendices to the ICAO Convention, and States Parties are expected to implement them. States Parties are, however, required to advise other States Parties of their failure to implement SARPs, and the latter would be free to act to protect themselves from the potential consequences of a state's failure to abide by the standard or practice at issue. This type of arrangement has proved universally acceptable in civil aviation and in other areas of transnational regulation, to ensure that standards and practices proposed are thoroughly evaluated, widely supported, and accepted voluntarily on the basis of sovereign self interest and mutuality of obligation.

Authority is provided in Article 12 to the AIIP in the Stanford Draft to enable it to discipline States Parties, or states that are not parties but are participating in the information infrastructure. Where a state acts or allows persons to act in a manner that undermines the objectives of the Draft, the Council is authorized to recommend sanctions, and the Assembly is authorized to impose them on a two-thirds vote, up to and including expulsion from the AIIP, and a recommendation to states of exclusion from the information infrastructure. Although the Draft avoids regulating state conduct, actions that undermine its purposes, such as allowing persons to use a state's territory to launch attacks affecting other states, would allow the AIIP to exclude such states from membership or to recommend punishing persons and/or non–States Parties by excluding them from participation in the international information infrastructure.

5. Protection of Individual Rights

Transnational regulation of the Internet raises several important issues related to privacy and other individual rights.[39] The Stanford Draft ensures that, at a minimum, individual rights afforded by States Parties are not adversely affected. No State Party has any duty under the Stanford Draft to act in any manner that might infringe upon the privacy or other human rights of any individual or entity, as defined

---

39. See Ekaterina A. Drozdova, "Civil Liberties and Security in Cyberspace," Chap. 5 of this volume.

by the law of that state.[40] In addition, the Stanford Draft authorizes States Parties to refuse or cease cooperation in investigations or prosecutions they consider politically motivated or unfair. It would also create a subcommittee of experts as part of the AIIP, assigned the task of following and reporting upon the protection of privacy and human rights. Finally, the Draft provides that certain fundamental protections must be extended to persons detained for violations of any offense covered by its terms, including notice to the representative of the state of which an accused is a national, and the right to such representative's assistance.

Efforts to protect privacy and other human rights will involve complications for States Parties, for private entities, and for the AIIP as an organization. Notions of privacy and the scope of procedural and human rights vary considerably among the states whose participation is needed for a workable international regime. These differences have led the Internet Alliance to conclude that a legally mandatory regime on Internet crime would likely "wreak havoc" on privacy protections.[41] In fact, no such result is necessary to have effective multilateral cooperation. By allowing States Parties to insist on the preservation of national norms as a minimum level of protection, the Stanford Draft would preclude its use to deprive any person of rights granted by any State Party, and the problems anticipated will be analogous to those created under the air transport and other antiterrorism conventions. Just as the United States and USSR were able to live with such differences in those contexts and still benefit from the agreements (for example, by securing extradition and prosecutions of hijackers), the Stanford Draft has been designed to enable states with radically different political values to work together on achieving mutually ben-

---

40. An analogous provision appears in the COE Draft. See "Draft Convention on Cyber-Crime," *supra* n. 10, available at ⟨*http://conventions.coe.int/treaty/en/projets/cybercrime24.htm*⟩, art. 27(4)(b).

41. See "An International Policy Framework for Internet Law Enforcement and Security: An Internet Alliance White Paper," May 2000, available at ⟨*http://www.Internetalliance.org/policy/leswp.html*⟩.

eficial aims without sacrificing those values. If, however, a serious and unresolvable situation emerged in which, for example, the regime of technical and operational cooperation developed under the Draft was abused by a state in some manner, the Assembly is empowered to impose sanctions in Articles 12, 13, and 21, including expulsion from the AIIP or a recommendation against the offending state's participation in the international information infrastructure.

In some situations, the requirement that all actions requested of a State Party must be consistent with its laws may provide less than optimal protection. A State Party could, for example, establish a method for preventing information from reaching its nationals that could be breached only through conduct inconsistent with one or more of the types of activities prohibited by the Stanford Draft. If a U.S. national engaged in a prohibited form of conduct in sending information into such a state he or she would theoretically be subject to extradition or prosecution, since the U.S. Constitution does not guarantee a right to communicate information into another state in a particular manner that is prohibited by treaty. States Parties should be able to determine, in such situations, whether compliance with a demand for cooperation would be manifestly inconsistent with established public policy, and on such a finding to decline cooperation. The Stanford Draft and the COE Draft both contain such provisions (Article 13(1) and Article 27(4)(b), respectively), which are consistent with the power explicit or implicit in all extradition treaties to decline cooperation as a matter of sovereign discretion.

6. National Security

The Stanford Draft makes clear, in a manner similar to other multilateral agreements, that it is inapplicable to state conduct and national security affairs.[42] A multilateral agreement on cyber crime will have

42. Deputy National Security Adviser Richard A. Clarke reportedly, at a June 19, 2000, American Enterprise Institute meeting—"Cyber Attacks and Critical Infrastructure: Where National Security and Business Converge"—declared publicly his oppo-

novel, complex, and important objectives apart from the possible use of cyber systems by states as military or intelligence tools. Efforts to control state conduct related to national security will be unhelpful in advancing the development of a multilateral approach to the problem of cyber crime, and unnecessary as well.[43] ICAO protects civilian aircraft from attack, and the ITU protects radio transmissions from interference. But these treaties do not attempt directly to control states in the conduct of their national security affairs. To the extent use of cyber technology as a weapon is a concern, existing arms control agreements, and treaties incorporating the laws of war, are all potentially applicable, as are the UN Charter provisions concerning the use of force.[44] The Draft does provide sanctions against conduct that undermines its purposes. If further measures need to be considered to limit the use of cyber technologies in areas of national security, they should be taken up separately and not used to hold hostage the development of a multilateral regime to advance the process of dealing with

---

sition to a multilateral treaty regulating cyber crime on the ground that it might foreclose the U.S. option to conduct information warfare. This position is based on an erroneous premise. The Stanford Draft would preclude such limitations even more comprehensively than other existing treaties. See, e.g., Convention for the Suppression of Unlawful Acts Against the Safety of Civil Aviation (Sabotage), September 23, 1971, 24 U.S.T. 564 [Montreal Convention], art. 4(1): "This Convention shall not apply to aircraft used in military, customs or police services." See also International Convention for the Suppression of Terrorist Bombings, December 15, 1997, 37 I.L.M. 249 (Terrorist Bombings Convention), art. 19: "1. Nothing in this Convention shall affect other rights, obligations and responsibilities of states and individuals under international law, in particular the purposes and principles of the Charter of the United Nations and international humanitarian law. 2. The activities of armed forces during an armed conflict, as those terms are understood under international humanitarian law, which are governed by that law, are not governed by this Convention, and the activities undertaken by military forces of a state in the exercise of their official duties, inasmuch as they are governed by other rules of international law, are not governed by this Convention."

43. See "Developments in the Field of Information and Telecommunications in the Context of International Security," UN General Assembly Doc. A/54/213, August 10, 1999, pp. 8–10, in which the Russian Federation comments on UN initiative and warns against the creation of an "information weapon."

44. See Grove, Goodman, and Lukasik, "Cyber-attacks, Counter-attacks, and International Law."

criminal activities harmful to all states, their peoples, and their economies.

7. Dispute Resolution

The Stanford Draft relies initially on consensual resolution of disputes through negotiation and mediation. States Parties unable to resolve their disputes consensually are required to submit to arbitration in any agreed form. The Stanford Draft contemplates that the Council of the AIIP will, after its creation,[45] propose for the Assembly's consideration an arbitration mechanism through which disputes would be resolved by expert panels designated in advance to hear and decide such matters, perhaps in the relatively informal manner preferred by the industry for resolving disputes over website domain names.[46]

8. Amendments

The Stanford Draft contains a standard treaty provision enabling the States Parties to propose and approve amendments as necessary and appropriate.

45. The Stanford Draft makes no effort to deal with the technical measures necessary to create the AIIP, which would presumably be similar to the steps taken when, for example, ICAO was created toward the end of World War II.

46. See, e.g., *Noodle Time, Inc. v. Max Marketing*, DeC AF-0100 (March 9, 2000), reported in *Int'l Law in Brief*, April 1–14, 2000, available at ⟨*http:// www.asil/org/ilibindx.htm*⟩, an example of the procedure set up by Internet users (with U.S. government support) to apply the rules governing website domain names, as established in the Uniform Domain Name Dispute Resolution Policy.

Draft International Convention
To Enhance Protection from
Cyber Crime and Terrorism

Preamble

The States Parties to this Convention,

Acknowledging that developments in science and technology have enabled unprecedented transnational communications through information infrastructures;

Affirming the worldwide benefits enabled by those infrastructures;

Understanding the growing reliance and dependence of persons and governments upon proper operation of information infrastructures and their growing interdependence;

Recognizing the vulnerability of information infrastructures to attacks and improper utilization;

Considering the potentially grave consequences of attacks and improper utilization to persons and governments worldwide, including failures of systems and damage to critical infrastructure, economic losses, and interruption of communications;

Resolving that there is a need to protect transnational information infrastructures from attacks and improper utilization and to deter such conduct by means of appropriate penalties and technology;

Mindful of the limitations of unilateral approaches;

This Draft Convention was prepared by Abraham D. Sofaer, Gregory D. Grove, and George D. Wilson.

Mindful also of the need to ensure appropriate protection of privacy, freedom of communication, and other human rights;

Desiring active international cooperation through voluntary and mandatory measures effectively to investigate and prosecute cyber criminals and terrorists and to develop technological standards and practices to enhance cyber security;

Desiring also the establishment of a specialized agency designed to marshal the expertise to achieve the voluntary and mandatory objectives of this Convention, through a structure based on voluntary, private-sector activities, expertise, and involvement;

Convinced that there is an emerging consensus regarding certain conduct that should be prosecuted as criminal, as well as regarding the need for agreed standards and practices to enhance security; and

Recognizing the need to ensure that all cooperating states should have the technological capacities required for participating in and benefiting from advances in communication, and that all feasible assistance should be provided by technologically advanced states;

Have agreed as follows:

Article 1
Definitions and Use of Terms

For the purposes of this Convention:

1. "cyber crime" means conduct, with respect to cyber systems, that is classified as an offense punishable by this Convention;

2. [Not used]

3. "information infrastructure" and "cyber system" mean any computer or network of computers used to relay, transmit, coordinate, or control communications of data or programs;

4. "data" is information or communications content, including speech, text, photographs, sound, video, control signals, and other formats for information or communications;

5. a "program" is an instruction or set of instructions intended or designed to cause a computer or network of computers to manipulate data, display

data, use data, perform a task, perform a function, or any combination of these;

6. "transnational information infrastructures" means information infrastructures with component parts physically present in the territory of two or more States Parties;

7. "critical infrastructures" are the interconnected networks of physical devices, pathways, people, and computers that provide for timely delivery of government services; medical care; protection of the general population by law enforcement; firefighting; food; water; transportation services, including travel of persons and transport of goods by air, water, rail, or road; supply of energy, including electricity, petroleum, oil and gas products; financial and banking services and transactions; and information and communications services;

8. a "person" may be any of the following: (a) a human being or (b) a corporation or business organization recognized as a legally separate entity under the governing domestic law of a State Party or (c) any other legally recognized entity capable of performing or contributing to the conduct prohibited by this Convention;

9. "legally recognized authority" is authority under a governing State Party's domestic law for persons to enter into private places, to examine private papers, to observe private communications, or to engage in other legally authorized investigative activities;

10. "legally recognized permission" or "legally recognized consent" is permission recognized under a governing State Party's domestic law (when given by a person with a legally recognized interest in a place, tangible property, or intangible property) to enter into private places, to examine private papers, to intercept private communications, or to engage in other legally authorized investigative activities;

11. "misrouting" of communications content or data means intentionally changing or manipulating the ordinary operation of an information infrastructure with the purpose of delaying or diverting the delivery of a protected packet en route to its intended destination, or with knowledge that such delay or diversion will result;

12. a "protected packet" is an assembly of data used to convey communications content through a transnational information infrastructure, conform-

ing to an international standard for transmission of data established by the Internet Engineering Task Force (IETF) or other widely accepted process;

13. a "treaty offense" is conduct prohibited by multilateral treaty, convention, or agreement (other than this Convention) for which an individual may be punished under the governing domestic law implementing the terms of that treaty, convention, or agreement.

Article 2
Enactment of Domestic Laws

Each State Party shall adopt such measures as may be necessary:

1. to establish as criminal offenses under its domestic law the conduct set forth in Articles 3 and 4;

2. to make such conduct punishable by appropriate penalties that take into account its potentially grave consequences, including possible imprisonment for one year or more; and,

3. to consider for prompt implementation through domestic laws all standards and recommended practices proposed by the Agency for Information Infrastructure Protection (AIIP) pursuant to Article 12.

Article 3
Offenses

1. Offenses under this Convention are committed if any person unlawfully and intentionally engages in any of the following conduct without legally recognized authority, permission, or consent:

(a) creates, stores, alters, deletes, transmits, diverts, misroutes, manipulates, or interferes with data or programs in a cyber system with the purpose of causing, or knowing that such activities would cause, said cyber system or another cyber system to cease functioning as intended, or to perform functions or activities not intended by its owner and considered illegal under this Convention;

(b) creates, stores, alters, deletes, transmits, diverts, misroutes, manipulates, or interferes with data in a cyber system for the purpose and with the effect of providing false information in order to cause substantial damage to persons or property;

(c) enters into a cyber system for which access is restricted in a conspicuous and unambiguous manner;

(d) interferes with tamper-detection or authentication mechanisms;

(e) manufactures, sells, uses, posts, or otherwise distributes any device or program intended for the purpose of committing any conduct prohibited by Articles 3 and 4 of this Convention;

(f) uses a cyber system as a material factor in committing an act made unlawful or prohibited by any of the following treaties: (i) Convention on Offenses and Certain Other Acts Committed on Board Aircraft, September 14, 1963, 20 U.S.T. 2941 [Tokyo Convention]; (ii) Convention for the Suppression of Unlawful Seizure of Aircraft (Hijacking), December 16, 1970, 22 U.S.T. 1641 [Hague Convention]; (iii) Convention for the Suppression of Unlawful Acts Against the Safety of Civil Aviation (Sabotage), September 23, 1971, 24 U.S.T. 564 [Montreal Convention]; (iv) International Convention Against the Taking of Hostages, December 17, 1979, T.I.A.S. 11081 [Hostages Convention]; (v) International Convention for the Suppression of Terrorist Bombings, December 15, 1997, 37 I.L.M. 249 [Terrorist Bombings Convention]; (vi) United Nations Convention Against Illicit Traffic in Narcotic Drugs and Psychotropic Substances, December 20, 1988, T.IA.S., 20 I.L.M. 493 [Vienna Convention on Narcotics]; (vii) International Maritime Organization Convention for the Suppression of Unlawful Acts against the Safety of Maritime Navigation [Maritime Terrorism Convention], March 10, 1988, IMO Doc. SUA/CON/15/Rev.1, 1993 Can. T.S. No. 10.

(g) engages in any conduct prohibited under Articles 3 and 4 of this Convention with a purpose of targeting the critical infrastructure of any State Party.

2. Purpose, intent, or knowledge with respect to the crimes set forth in paragraph 1 of this section may be inferred from objective factual circumstances.

Article 4
Attempts, Aiding and Abetting, Conspiracy

An offense under this Convention is committed if any person unlawfully and intentionally:

1. attempts to engage in any conduct prohibited in Article 3;

2. aids or abets others in engaging or attempting to engage in any conduct prohibited in Article 3; or

3. conspires with others to engage in any conduct prohibited in Article 3.

Article 5
Jurisdiction

1. Each State Party to this Convention shall take such measures as may be necessary to establish its jurisdiction over the offenses set forth in Articles 3 and 4 in the following cases:

(a) when the offense is committed in the territory of that State or on board a ship, aircraft, or satellite registered in that State or in any other place under its jurisdiction as recognized by international law;

(b) when the alleged offender is a national of that State;

(c) when the alleged offender is a stateless person whose primary residence is in its territory;

(d) when the alleged offender is present in its territory and it does not extradite such person pursuant to this Convention.

2. Each State Party to this Convention may take such measures as may be necessary to establish its jurisdiction over the offenses set forth in Articles 3 and 4 in the following cases:

(a) when the offense is committed with intent or purpose to harm that State or its nationals or to compel that State to do or abstain from doing any act; or

(b) when the offense has substantial effects in that State.

3. This Convention does not exclude any criminal jurisdiction exercised in accordance with domestic law, including any domestic law giving effect to Articles 3 and 4, or any criminal jurisdiction established pursuant to any other bilateral or multilateral treaty.

4. Each State Party will exercise its rights and fulfill its obligations under this Convention to the extent practicable in accordance with the following priority of jurisdiction: first, the State Party in which the alleged offender was physically present when the alleged offense was committed; second, the State Party in which substantial harm was suffered as a result of the alleged offense; third, the State Party of the alleged offender's dominant nationality; fourth, any

State Party where the alleged offender may be found; and fifth, any other State Party with a reasonable basis for jurisdiction.

Article 6
Mutual Legal Assistance

1. States Parties shall adopt such measures as are necessary to enable themselves to afford one another the widest measure of mutual legal assistance on an expedited and continuous basis (within conditions prescribed by treaties, domestic laws, or regulations concerning such assistance) in investigations, extraditions, prosecutions, and judicial proceedings brought in respect of the offenses set forth in Articles 3 and 4, including assistance for the following purposes:

(a) identifying and tracing attacks upon cyber systems by electronic and other means;

(b) locating or identifying persons;

(c) taking statements from persons;

(d) executing searches and seizures by electronic and other means;

(e) examining objects and sites;

(f) securing and exchanging information and evidentiary items, including documents and records; and,

(g) transferring persons in custody.

2. Requests for assistance will be made in accordance with arrangements under existing agreements between or among the States Parties involved, or through Central Authorities designated by States Parties in ratifying this Convention. Requests made for emergency assistance will be dealt with by response teams that function as necessary on a continuous basis.

3. States Parties shall promote appropriate methods of obtaining information and testimony from persons who are willing to cooperate in the investigation and prosecution of offenses established in Articles 3 and 4 and shall, as appropriate, assist each other in promoting such cooperation. Such methods of cooperation may include, among other things: granting immunity from prosecution to a person who cooperates substantially with law enforcement authorities in investigations, extraditions, prosecutions, and judicial proceedings; considering the provision by an accused person of substantial coopera-

tion as a mitigating factor in determining the person's punishment; and entering into arrangements concerning immunities or nonprosecution or reduced penalties.

4. Any physical property of substantial intrinsic value seized by a State Party that is later delivered pursuant to the request of a prosecuting State Party to facilitate the prosecution of a suspected offense shall, upon request within a reasonable time after final resolution of all proceedings of prosecution and appeal in the courts of the prosecuting State Party, be returned to the State Party that seized the property for disposition according to the domestic laws of that State Party.

5. States Parties shall be free to engage in reasonable, electronic methods of investigation of conduct covered by Articles 3 and 4 of this Convention, over which they have jurisdiction to prosecute under Article 5, even if such conduct results in the transfer of electronic signals into the territory of other States Parties. A State Party aware that its investigative efforts will likely result in such transfers of electronic signals shall as soon as practicable inform all affected States Parties of such efforts.

6. States Parties shall consider for prompt implementation through law all standards and recommended practices adopted and proposed by the AIIP pursuant to Article 12 as methods for enhancing mutual legal assistance provided under this Article 6.

7. States Parties agree to extend on a voluntary basis cooperation in all possible areas of activity bearing upon mutual legal assistance, both individually and through efforts under the auspices of the AIIP or other governmental and nongovernmental entities.

Article 7
Extradition

1. Offenses under the domestic laws of each State Party concerning any conduct set forth in Articles 3 and 4 shall be deemed to be included as extraditable offenses in any extradition treaty existing between or among States Parties. States Parties undertake to include such offenses as extraditable offenses in every extradition treaty subsequently concluded between them; however, failure to include these offenses in such treaties shall not affect the obligations undertaken herein.

2. If a State Party that makes extradition conditional on the existence of a

treaty receives a request for extradition from another State Party with which it has no extradition treaty, it may consider this Convention as the legal basis for extradition in respect of the offenses covering conduct set forth in Articles 3 and 4. Extradition shall remain subject to any other requirement of the law of the requested State.

3. States Parties that do not make extradition conditional on the existence of a treaty shall recognize offenses covering the conduct set forth in Articles 3 and 4 as extraditable offenses as between themselves, subject to any other requirement of the law of the requested State.

4. Offenses covering the conduct set forth under Articles 3 and 4 shall to that extent be treated, for the purpose of extradition between States Parties, as if they had been committed in the place in which they occurred, and also in the territories of the State or States required or authorized to establish their jurisdiction under Article 5.

5. When extradition is requested by more than one requesting State Party, the requested State Party shall respond to such requests in accordance with the priorities for jurisdiction set out in Article 5, paragraph 4.

Article 8
Prosecution

1. The State Party in the territory of which an alleged offender is found shall, if it does not extradite such person, be obliged, without exception and whether or not the offense was committed in its territory, to submit the case without delay to competent authorities for the purpose of prosecution, through proceedings in accordance with the laws of that State. Those authorities shall pursue such prosecutions in the same manner as other serious offenses under the laws of that State. If a State Party is unable or unwilling to prosecute such cases, it must promptly inform the original requesting State Party or States Parties.

2. A requesting State Party may prosecute an alleged offender over whom it secures jurisdiction through extradition only for crimes specified in its extradition request and found legally sufficient by the requested State Party, unless the requested State Party agrees to permit prosecution for additional offenses.

Article 9
Provisional Remedies

1. Upon the request of a State Party based upon its reasonable belief that a named suspected offender engaged in conduct covered by this Convention may be found in the territory of a requested State Party, the requested State Party undertakes to apprehend the named suspected offender if found in its territory and hold the suspected offender for up to a maximum of ten (10) days, during which period the requesting State Party will supply information sufficient to show cause for continued detention pending the resolution of its request for extradition.

2. Upon the request of a State Party based upon its reasonable belief that conduct covered by Articles 3 and 4 of this Convention has occurred, and that evidence of such conduct is present in the stored data contained in cyber systems located within the territory of a requested State Party, the requested State Party will attempt to preserve or to require preservation of the stored data in such cyber systems for a reasonable period to permit the requesting State Party to supply information sufficient to show adequate cause for release of all or part of the preserved stored data to the requesting State Party.

3. States Parties shall consider for prompt implementation through national law all standards and recommended practices adopted and proposed by the AIIP pursuant to Article 12 as methods for enhancing the capacity of States Parties to advance this Convention's purposes through provisional remedies.

Article 10
Entitlements of an Accused Person

1. Any person detained by a State Party pursuant to one or more of Articles 3, 4, 5, 6, 7, 8, or 9 shall be entitled, in addition to rights extended under the national law of such State Party, to:

(a) communicate without unnecessary delay with the nearest appropriate representative of the State of which that person is a national or which is otherwise entitled to protect that person's rights or, if that person is stateless, the State of that person's primary residence;

(b) be visited by a representative of that State;

(c) have a representative of that State physically present to observe any legal proceedings that may result in punishment; and,

(d) be informed promptly after detention of that person's entitlements under subparagraphs (a), (b), and (c) of this Article 10.

2. States Parties shall not deny any person, or impair in any way, the entitlements described in paragraph 1.

Article 11
Cooperation in Law Enforcement

States Parties shall cooperate closely with one another through their law enforcement agencies in preventing any conduct set forth in Articles 3 and 4, by among other things:

1. taking all practicable measures to prevent preparations in their respective territories for the commission of such conduct within or outside their territories;

2. exchanging information and coordinating the taking of administrative and other measures as appropriate to prevent commission of such conduct; and,

3. considering for prompt implementation all standards and recommended practices adopted and proposed by the AIIP pursuant to Article 12 as methods for deterring and preventing the crimes covered by this Convention.

Article 12
Agency for Information Infrastructure Protection (AIIP)

The States Parties hereby establish, and agree to make operational as soon as practicable after the effective date of this Convention, the Agency for Information Infrastructure Protection (AIIP), an international agency composed of all States Parties as Members, and consisting of an Assembly, a Council, a Secretariat managed by a Secretary General, and such committees and other subordinate bodies as are necessary in the judgment of the Assembly or Council to implement this Convention's objectives. The AIIP and all its component entities and functions will be funded by a mandatory assessment imposed biannually upon its Members in accordance with a formula proposed by the Council and approved by the Assembly.

1. *Assembly.* The AIIP Assembly will consist of all States Parties, each of which will be represented by an individual competent in cyber technologies, who will have a single vote on all Assembly activities. The Assembly shall meet at least once every three (3) years and shall make decisions by a majority

of Members voting. The Assembly shall have the following responsibilities and powers:

(a) to adopt objectives and policies authorized by and consistent with this Convention;

(b) to instruct the Council to formulate and/or implement measures to achieve such objectives and policies;

(c) to consider and approve standards and practices proposed by the Council for adoption by States Parties;

(d) to consider and approve the AIIP budget and assessment formula prepared and proposed by the Council;

(e) to recommend to States Parties modifications or supplementary agreements to the present Convention, including the addition of types of conduct to be considered criminal;

(f) to elect no fewer than one-fifth and no more than one-fourth of its Members to the Council, which shall include at least one representative from each of the five Permanent Members of the United Nations Security Council;

(g) to consider and approve proposals by the Council to provide technical and material assistance to deserving States Parties for the purpose of encouraging the safe and widespread use of the international information infrastructure;

(h) to propose to all States Parties as recommendations or as proposed amendments to this Convention, standards, practices, and technological measures approved by the Council;

(i) to consider and approve measures proposed by the Council to prevent any State from being used as a safe haven or otherwise in order to enable persons to secure protection from successful prevention, investigation, or prosecution for conduct set forth in Articles 3 and 4; and,

(j) to adopt regulations for its own governance, which shall include authority to suspend or expel States Parties, and to recommend to States Parties the exclusion of any State from participation in the international information infrastructure, for conduct that undermines the objectives of this Convention, on a vote of at least two-thirds (2/3) of all States Parties voting.

2. *Council.* The AIIP Council will consist of representatives from Member States elected by the Assembly. The Council shall meet at least once every

year and shall decide on all matters by majority vote. The Council shall have the following responsibilities and powers:

(a) to prepare the AIIP budget and assessment formula for consideration and approval by the Assembly;

(b) to appoint and supervise the Secretary General, and to provide for a Secretariat to administer AIIP activities with a staff limited in number and role to the extent that reliance on nonpermanent volunteer and contract personnel is practicable;

(c) to appoint standing and special committees, consisting of persons from the public and private sectors (including volunteers) who are experts in the fields of the committees' activities, which shall meet as necessary to consider and recommend to the Council standards and practices, as well as technological measures to improve the security of information infrastructures, including the capacities of States Parties and law enforcement agencies to detect, prevent, investigate, and successfully prosecute conduct set forth in Articles 3 and 4, and to prevent any State from being used as a safe haven;

(d) to consider, and where the Council sees fit to propose to the Assembly for adoption as recommendations, or as proposed amendments to this Convention, standards, practices, or measures prepared by the AIIP's standing or special committees, taking into account the work of public and private entities, such as the IETF, in order to ensure consistency of standards and practices;

(e) to receive, consider, and report to the Assembly concerning the annual reports filed by States Parties under Article 14;

(f) to consider and to recommend to the Assembly which States Parties should be deemed eligible for technical and financial assistance to enable them to satisfy their obligations under this Convention and to participate to the extent feasible in useful activities associated with cyber systems;

(g) to adopt and implement programs of technical and financial assistance to all States Parties, including training programs for law enforcement and cyber security personnel, with particular attention to reaching States Parties eligible for financial assistance, and to work with other public and private organizations in this regard;

(h) to consider and recommend as appropriate to the Assembly sanctions on States Parties or other States for conduct that undermines the objectives of this Convention; and,

(i) to adopt regulations for its own governance.

3. *Secretariat.* The Secretariat will function as directed by the Secretary General. The Secretariat staff provided for by the Assembly, on recommendation of the Council, will be appointed by the Secretary General.

4. *Public Participation.* Meetings of the Assembly and Council of the AIIP shall be open to the public, with such public participation as is feasible. Meetings of committees, working groups, and other AIIP entities shall also be open to the public, subject to the need for confidential consideration of sensitive information.

Article 13
Protection of Privacy and Other Human Rights

1. This Convention shall not be construed to require an infringement of the privacy or other human rights of any person as defined by the laws of the State Party requested to perform any duty agreed to under this Convention. A State Party may decline to perform any duty agreed to under this Convention if it determines that doing so would be manifestly inconsistent with its established public policy.

2. As part of the obligation to establish systematic monitoring of implementation of this Convention under Article 14, a permanent subcommittee of experts shall be established by the Council to evaluate and comment upon the manner in which the Convention is being implemented with regard to the protection of privacy and other human rights, and to recommend appropriate measures to the Council and Assembly for the purpose of protecting such rights.

Article 14
Annual Reports of States Parties

1. Each State Party shall on or before the end of each calendar year commencing with the year of its accession to this Convention provide to the AIIP any relevant information concerning:

(a) the legislative and administrative measures taken by it to implement this Convention.

(b) any change in its domestic laws and regulations affecting the implementation of this Convention;

(c) the circumstances of any offense over which it has established its jurisdiction pursuant to Article 5;

(d) the measures taken by it in relation to each alleged offender who was detained for any period of time under the Convention or under its domestic law implementing all or any part of the Convention, and, in particular, the results of any extradition or other legal proceedings; and

(e) any decision not to implement a standard or recommended practice approved by the AIIP Assembly.

2. The AIIP Secretariat shall annually collate and transmit to all States Parties the information collected from them under this Article 14.

Article 15
Signature, Ratification, Acceptance, Approval, Accession, and Reservations

1. This Convention shall be open for signature by any State after _____ [DATE] at _____ [LOCATION IN DEPOSITARY STATE], in the State of _____, which shall act as Depositary.

2. This Convention is subject to ratification, acceptance, approval, or accession. The instruments of ratification, acceptance, approval, or accession shall be deposited with the Depositary State.

Article 16
Entry into Force

1. This Convention shall enter into force on the thirtieth (30th) day following the date of the deposit of the _____ [ORDINAL NUMBER] instrument of ratification, acceptance, approval, or accession with the Depositary State.

2. For each State ratifying, accepting, approving, or acceding to the Convention after the deposit of the _____ [ORDINAL NUMBER] instrument of ratification, acceptance, approval, or accession, the Convention shall enter into force on the thirtieth (30th) day after deposit by such State of its instrument of ratification, acceptance, approval, or accession with the Depositary State.

Article 17
Amendments

1. A State Party or the AIIP may propose an amendment to this Convention and file it with the Depositary State. The Depositary State shall communicate each proposed amendment to the States Parties. If, within four (4) months from the date of such communication, at least a _____ [FRACTION] majority of States Parties vote for approval of the amendment the Depositary State shall so inform all States Parties, who will thereafter communicate any ratification of such proposed amendments. Proposed amendments will become effective upon their ratification by a _____ [FRACTION] majority of States Parties.

2. When an amendment enters into force, it shall be binding on those States Parties that have ratified it. Other States Parties will remain bound by the provisions of the present Convention and any earlier amendments that they have ratified.

Article 18
Denunciation

A State Party may denounce this Convention by written notification to the Depositary State. The Depositary State shall promptly communicate the receipt of such notification to the other States Parties. Denunciation shall become effective one (1) year after the date of receipt of such notification.

Article 19
Political Offenses and Prejudicial Actions

1. None of the offenses or conduct set forth in Articles 3 and 4 shall be regarded, for the purposes of extradition or mutual legal assistance, as a political offense or as an offense equivalent to a political offense.

2. Nothing in this Convention shall be interpreted as imposing an obligation to extradite or to afford mutual legal assistance, if the requested State Party has substantial grounds for believing that the request for extradition for offenses set forth in Articles 3 and 4 or for mutual legal assistance with respect to such offenses has been made for the purpose of prosecuting or punishing a person on account of that person's race, religion, nationality, ethnic origin, or political belief.

Article 20
State Conduct

This Convention shall not apply to any state conduct undertaken for a public, noncommercial purpose, including activities undertaken by military forces of a State Party, or to a State Party's activities related to an ongoing armed conflict.

Article 21
Dispute Resolution

1. States Parties shall attempt to resolve all disputes that arise under this Convention through negotiation and mediation, with the assistance of the AIIP Secretariat.

2. Any State Party may give notice to another that it intends to seek arbitration of a specified dispute, to commence no sooner than ninety (90) days after such notice is received by the Party to whom it is sent. If the Parties are unable to agree on an arbitral tribunal or on any other necessary aspect of the requested arbitration, the matter will be referred by the requesting Party for decision under the auspices of _____ [ADD ARBITRATION MECHANISM].

3. The AIIP Council shall as soon as practicable develop and propose to the Assembly a dispute resolution mechanism that is informal, speedy, and based on appropriate expert involvement.

Article 22
Languages and Depositary

The original of this Convention, of which the English, French, and Russian texts are equally authentic, shall be deposited with the Depositary State, which shall send certified copies thereof to all States Parties.

IN WITNESS WHEREOF, the undersigned, being duly authorized thereto by their respective Governments, have signed this Convention, opened for signature at _____ [PLACE IN DEPOSITARY STATE] on _____ [DATE].

Conference Agenda

INTERNATIONAL COOPERATION TO COMBAT CYBER CRIME AND TERRORISM

A National Security Forum Sponsored by

| The Consortium for Research on Information Security and Policy (CRISP) | Hoover Institution | The Center for International Security and Cooperation (CISAC) |

Stauffer Auditorium, Hoover Institution
Stanford University, Stanford, California

December 6–7, 1999

MONDAY, DECEMBER 6, 1999

1:00 PM   *Welcome and Introduction*
John Raisian, *Hoover Institution*

1:15 PM   *Session One: Dimensions of the Problem.* (Evaluation of the nature of cyber crimes, including terrorist acts, their costs, and how they threaten cyber commerce and critical national and international infrastructure.)
Moderator: Michael M. May, *CISAC*
Speaker: Peter G. Neumann, *SRI:* Dimensions of the Problem
Panelists: Richard Power, *Computer Security Institute:* Estimating the Cost of Cyber Crime
Alan B. Carroll, *National Infrastructure Protection Center, FBI:* Cyber Terrorism

2:15 PM   *Session Two: International Response to Cyber Crime.* (Outline
of legal initiatives around the world to combat cyber crime
and consideration of the extent of consensus reflected by
those initiatives, including prohibited categories of acts that
are candidates for an international agreement.)
Moderator: David D. Elliott, *CRISP*
Speakers: Marc D. Goodman, *Hoover/CISAC:* The Emerging
Consensus on Criminal Conduct in Cyberspace
Dietrich Neumann, *EU:* European Perspective
George C. C. Chen, *Tsai, Lee & Chen, Taiwan:* Asian
Perspective
Susan Brenner, *University of Dayton School of Law:* U.S. Survey
Drew C. Arena, *U.S. Dept. of Justice:* Multilateral Initiatives

3:45 PM   BREAK

4:15 PM   *Session Three: Threatened Infrastructure—Civil Aviation as an
Example.* (Civil air travel is a major world infrastructure,
increasingly dependent on information technologies. The
universal desire for safe air travel has enabled a worldwide
consensus to prohibit acts endangering civilian aircraft in
international treaties. This Session will examine the potential
contribution of treaties in combating threats to essential
aviation information systems.)
Moderator: Seymour E. Goodman, *CRISP*
Speaker: Hal Whiteman, *Transport Canada:* The Seriousness of
the Cyber Threat to Airline Security and the Importance of
International Cooperation
Panelists: Vidyut Patel, *U.S. FAA:* The Civil Aviation
Information System Infrastructure and International
Interdependence
Peter G. Neumann, *SRI:* Civil Aviation IS at Risk
Mariano-Florentino Cuéllar, *Stanford:* International Aviation
Agreements on Terrorism as Precedents

5:30 PM   BREAK

6:30 PM   RECEPTION at the Stanford Faculty Club

7:15 PM   DINNER in the Main Dining Room, Stanford Faculty Club
(seating for dinner may be limited)

8:15 PM   Keynote Speaker: William J. Perry, *Hoover Institution/CISAC*
          Introduced by: John Raisian, *Hoover Institution*

TUESDAY, DECEMBER 7, 1999

8:30 AM   CONTINENTAL BREAKFAST

9:00 AM   *Session Four: The Technology of Cooperation.* (General
          discussion of existing and potential uses of technologies
          through international cooperation to deter, prevent, identify,
          investigate, and prosecute consensus cyber crimes.)
          Moderator: John Markoff, *New York Times*
          Speakers: Robert E. Kahn, *Corporation for National Research
          Initiatives:* The Role of Technology
          Steven D. Rizzi, *Science Applications International Corp.:* The
          Limits of Technology
          Thomas A. Longstaff, *Carnegie Mellon University:* Trends in
          Network Attacks
          Raymond C. Parks, *Sandia National Laboratories:* Cyber
          Terrorism Modeling
          Joseph Betser, *The Aerospace Corp.:* Tracking Cyber Attacks
          William R. Cheswick, *Lucent Technologies:* Forensic
          Challenges

10:15 AM BREAK

10:45 AM *Session Five: Proposed Technological Measures.* (Description
          and discussion of specific measures to achieve security
          objectives through international technological cooperation.)
          Moderator: Stephen J. Lukasik, *CRISP*
          Speakers: K. C. Claffy, *San Diego SuperComputer Center,
          UCSD:* Understanding Internet Traffic
          Barry Raveendran Greene, *Cisco Systems:* Role of Router
          Hardware and Software
          Randall E. Smith, *Boeing:* Network Intrusion Detection
          Michael Erlinger, *Harvey Mudd College/Internet Engineering
          Task Force:* Internet Protocols
          Clifford Neuman, *USC/Information Sciences Institute:*
          Distributed Authentication Mechanism

12:00 PM LUNCH outside Stauffer Auditorium

1:00 PM   Keynote Speaker: Raisuke Miyawaki, *Ochanomizu Associates,*
           Tokyo
           Introduced by: Seymour E. Goodman, *CRISP*

1:45 PM   *Session Six: Constraints on Cooperation.* (Consideration of
           constitutional, legal, economic, and ethical constraints on use
           of technology to control cyber crime. Focus on the
           application of concepts such as privacy, probable cause, etc.
           to the realities of modern information systems and the
           proposals made in Session Five.)
           Moderator: George L. Fisher, *Stanford Law School*
           Speakers: Barry Steinhardt, *ACLU*
             Dorothy E. Denning, *Georgetown University*
             Caspar Bowden, *Foundation for Information Policy Research,*
             London
             David J. Thelander, *Charles Schwab & Co., Inc.*
             Whitfield Diffie, *Sun Microsystems*
             Boaz Gutman, *Israeli National Police*

3:15 PM   BREAK

3:45 PM   *Session Seven:Legal Mechanisms for International Cooperation.*
           (Discussion of mechanisms for cooperation in draft
           international convention, including provisions related to
           jurisdiction, evidentiary cooperation, extradition, assistance
           to cooperating states, sanctions for noncooperation.)
           Moderator: Abraham D. Sofaer, *Hoover Institution*
           Speaker: Ariel T. Sobelman, *Jaffee Center, Tel Aviv University:*
             The Case for an International Treaty on Cyber Crime
           Panelists: Gregory D. Grove, *CRISP:* Defining Consensus
             Crimes
             Jack L. Goldsmith, *University of Chicago School of Law:*
             Resolving Jurisdictional Conflicts
             Stein Schjolberg, *Chief Judge, Moss City, Norway:* Protecting
             Privacy and Other Rights

5:15 PM   *Session Eight: Wrap-Up Presentation by Conference Co-Chairs.*

5:30 PM   CONFERENCE ENDS

December 1999
Conference Participants

DREW C. ARENA   Former Senior Counsel to the Assistant Attorney General, U.S. Department of Justice; former Counselor for Criminal Justice Matters at the U.S. Mission to the European Union (EU) in Brussels, Belgium. Now retired from over twenty years of federal government service, he has served as the Attorney General's senior representative in Europe for multilateral affairs and has been responsible for Justice Department relations with the EU, the Council of Europe, the United Nations Commission on Criminal Justice, and the G-8's Senior Experts Group on Organized Crime. He has worked extensively with all these organizations on issues relating to cyber crime.

JOSEPH BETSER   Project Leader, Business Development and Program Management, Aerospace Corporation, El Segundo, California. He has served as a Defense Advanced Research Projects Agency (DARPA) Principal Investigator for a number of network management and information assurance projects and led activities in the growing commercial satellite network business, as well as in Department of Defense space architecture planning, and Battle Awareness and Data Dissemination (BADD). He also led the CalREN (California Research and Education Network) ATM Research Consortium (ARC), among the first ATM networks in Southern California, consisting of eleven premier university and research organizations.

CASPAR BOWDEN   Director, Foundation for Information Policy Research (FIPR), London, United Kingdom (*http://www.fipr.org*), an independent non-profit organization that studies the interaction between information technology and society, identifies technical developments with significant social impact, and commissions research into public policy alternatives. He is the co-organizer of the Scrambling for Safety public conferences on U.K. cryptography policy. He was formerly an e-commerce and Internet security consultant, senior researcher of an option-arbitrage trading firm, a financial strategist with Goldman Sachs, and chief algorithm designer for a virtual reality software house.

SUSAN BRENNER   Associate Dean and Professor, University of Dayton School of Law, Dayton, Ohio. The author of numerous publications, she counts cyber crime among her many and diverse interests. In particular, her "Cybercrimes Seminar," featured in a story broadcast by "NBC Nightly News," is a law school seminar taught entirely online, the output of which includes the "Model State Computer Crimes Code" (*http://www. cybercimes.net*).

ALAN B. CARROLL   Supervisory Special Agent (SSA), National Infrastructure Protection Center (NIPC), U.S. Federal Bureau of Investigation (FBI). During his long career in law enforcement, he has specialized in undercover narcotics investigations, as well as bank robbery, kidnapping, and extortion cases. In addition, he has most recently worked in the areas of violent crimes, white-collar crimes, domestic terrorism, and foreign counterintelligence investigations.

GEORGE C. C. CHEN   Principal, Law Firm of Tsai, Lee & Chen, Taipei, Taiwan; former Director of the Science and Technology Law Center, Institute for Information Industry. He has some twenty years of professional experience, having practiced law at a number of firms in Sydney, Taipei, and Toronto; served as an arbitrator for the Commercial Arbitration Association of Taiwan; and taught computer law and international trade law at Tunghai University. He has published extensively in the field of intellectual property law.

WILLIAM R. CHESWICK   Member, Technical Staff, Lucent Technologies, Murray Hill, New Jersey. He has worked in the area of operating system security for nearly thirty years. His experience includes various positions in system management, consulting, software development, and communications design and installation at Temple University, LaSalle College, the Harvard Business School, Manhattan College, and the New Jersey Institute of Technology. He has specialized in firewalls, network security, PC viruses, mailers, and interactive science exhibits, co-authoring in 1994 the first full book on Internet security in 1994 (with Steven M. Bellovin), *Firewalls and Internet Security: Repelling the Wily Hacker* (Reading, Mass.: Addison-Wesley, 1994).

K. C. CLAFFY   Research Scientist, San Diego Supercomputer Center (SDSC)/

Principal Investigator, Cooperative Association for Internet Data Analysis (CAIDA), University of California, San Diego (UCSD), La Jolla. The recipient of numerous grants and awards, she has extensive publications to her credit in her fields of specialization: symbolic systems, and computer science and engineering. Her professional experience also includes positions at the Sony Computer Science Laboratory in Tokyo, Japan; the U.S. Federal Reserve Board; AT&T Bell Laboratories; and Harry Diamond Laboratories.

MARIANO-FLORENTINO CUÉLLAR Law Clerk to the Honorable Judge Mary M. Schroeder, U.S. Court of Appeals for the Ninth Circuit. A member of the Bar of the State of California, from 1997 to 1999 he served as Senior Adviser to the Under Secretary for Enforcement, U.S. Department of the Treasury. While in Washington, D.C., he co-chaired the Initiatives Subcommittee of the Attorney General's Council on White Collar Crime. He has also worked at the President's Council of Economic Advisers and the American Bar Foundation. He holds a Ph.D. in political science from Stanford University and a J.D. from Yale Law School.

DOROTHY E. DENNING Professor, Department of Computer Science, Georgetown University, Washington, D.C. She has over thirty-two years of professional experience, twenty-four in universities (including Purdue University, the University of Rochester, and the University of Michigan) and eight in industry (including work at the Systems Research Center at Digital Equipment Corporation and the Computer Science Laboratory at SRI International), working mainly in the areas of information warfare and security and the impact of information technology on society. She has written over 100 articles and is the author of such books as: *Information Warfare and Security* (New York: ACM Press; Reading, Mass.: Addison-Wesley, 1999), *Internet Besieged: Countering Cyberspace Scofflaws* (New York: ACM Press; Reading, Mass.: Addison-Wesley, 1998), and *Cryptography and Data Security* (Reading, Mass.: Addison-Wesley, 1982).

WHITFIELD DIFFIE Distinguished Engineer, Sun Microsystems. He is best known for his 1975 discovery of the concept of public key cryptography. He has occupied the position of Distinguished Engineer at Sun since 1991 and, since 1993, has worked largely on public policy aspects of cryptography. His opposition to limitations on the business and personal use of cryptography has been the subject of articles in the *New York Times Magazine*, *Wired*, *Omni*, and *Discover*, and he is the author, with Susan Landau, of *Privacy on the Line: The Politics of Wiretapping and Encryption* (Cambridge, Mass.: MIT Press, 1998).

EKATERINA A. DROZDOVA   Doctoral Candidate, Department of Information Systems, Stern School of Business, New York University; former Researcher, Consortium for Research on Information Security and Policy (CRISP), Stanford University; Center for International Security and Cooperation (CISAC), Stanford University. She holds a master's degree in international policy studies from Stanford and has experience in information technology consulting in the Silicon Valley. She has conducted an in-depth survey and analysis of national laws in fifty countries to determine the extent of international consensus against cyber crime, and has published on the impact of the Internet on human rights.

DAVID D. ELLIOTT   Member, Executive Committee, Consortium for Research on Information Security and Policy (CRISP), Stanford University; Consulting Professor, Center for International Security and Cooperation (CISAC), Stanford University; former senior staff member, U.S. National Security Council. A physicist, he has served in senior positions in government and the defense industry, including supervising the SRI International's Strategic Study Center and, as Senior Vice President, overseeing strategic planning at Science Applications International Corporation (SAIC). He has a Ph.D. in high-energy physics from the California Institute of Technology.

MICHAEL ERLINGER   Co-Chairman, Intrusion Detection Working Group, Internet Engineering Task Force (IETF); Professor of Computer Science, Harvey Mudd College, Claremont, California. He has practical experience in managing industrial computer networks both as an employee and as a consultant to various aerospace firms. At IETF, he is developing protocols for the communication of intrusion information. He was formerly chair of the IETF Remote Network Monitoring Working Group, which developed the SNMP-based RMON MIB (RFC 1271) and the Token Ring extensions to RMON (RFC 1513), both of which have gained wide marketplace acceptance.

GEORGE L. FISHER   Professor, Stanford Law School. An award-winning teacher and acknowledged expert in the fields of evidence and criminal law and procedure, he has been an Assistant Attorney General and Assistant District Attorney in the State of Massachusetts. He has also served as a law clerk on the U.S. Court of Appeals for the First Circuit.

JACK L. GOLDSMITH   Professor, University of Chicago School of Law. Formerly an associate professor of law at the University of Virginia School of Law, he has clerked for the U.S. Court of Appeals for the Fourth Circuit, the United States Supreme Court, and the Iran-U.S. Claims Tribunal. Among his many publications are: "Against Cyberanarchy," *University of Chicago Law Review* 65 (1998): 1199, and "The Internet and the Abiding Significance of Territorial Sovereignty," *Indiana Journal of Global Legal Studies* 5 (1998): 475.

MARC D. GOODMAN   Former Officer-in-Charge of the Los Angeles Police Department's (LAPD's) Internet and New Media Unit, LAPD*Online*; Master's Degree Candidate in Management of Information Systems, International Computer Crime and Security Research Centre, London School of Economics; Visiting Fellow, Hoover Institution; Visiting Fellow, Center for International Security and Cooperation, Stanford University. A veteran police officer, Mr. Goodman has had myriad experiences throughout his career, including working as a high-technology crime investigator, a police manager and supervisor, an internal affairs investigator, police watch commander, undercover vice investigator, patrol officer, and police academy instructor. He is the author of "Why the Police Don't Care About Computer Crime," *Harvard Journal of Law and Technology* 10 (Summer 1997): 465.

SEYMOUR E. GOODMAN   (*Conference Co-Chair*)   Professor of International Affairs and Computing, Georgia Institute of Technology, Atlanta; Director, Consortium for Research on Information Security and Policy (CRISP), Stanford University; Visiting Professor, Institute for International Studies (IIS), Stanford University. Professor Goodman studies international developments in the information technologies and related public policy issues. In this capacity, he has served on many government and industry advisory study committees. He has been the International Perspectives Contributing Editor for the Communications of the ACM for the past ten years. He earned his Ph.D. from the California Institute of Technology.

BARRY RAVEENDRAN GREENE   Senior Consultant, Corporate Consulting, Office of the Chief Technology Officer (CTO), Cisco Systems, Inc. Mr. Greene is responsible for business development, network design, and scaling issues for strategic Telecommunications, Internet, Multimedia, System Security, and On-Line service providers, specializing in ISP design, architecture, business planning, and service provisioning; Content Routing, WWW Caching, and Content Replication Technology Development; System and Network Security; Campus Level Systems Integration; and Broadband Network Integration with the Internet. He was formerly Deputy Director of Planning and Operations, SingNet and the Singapore Telecom Internet Exchange. His papers (along with those of others in the CTO Group) are available: *http:// www.cisco.com/public/cons/isp/docuements.*

GREGORY D. GROVE   Visiting Scholar, Consortium for Research on Information Security and Policy (CRISP), Stanford University; Visiting Scholar, Center for International Security and Cooperation (CISAC), Stanford University. A member of the Bar of the State of California, he has served as a criminal prosecutor, studied military law, and has practiced intellectual property and high-technology venture-capital law. His recent publications include a study of legal restrictions upon, and resulting discretion in, the use of military personnel to protect critical infrastructures and an analysis of international legal implications of active defense responses to computer attack. Mr. Grove received an S.B. in electrical engineering from the Massachusetts Institute of Technology and a J.D. from Harvard Law School.

BOAZ GUTMAN   Advocate, Computer Law Lecturer, Ruppin Institute Academic Center; former Chief Superintendent, Computer Crime Division, National Anti-Fraud Investigation Unit "B," Israeli National Police, Tel Aviv, Israel. As lawyer and legal educator, as well as a veteran policeman, in recent years he has been involved in major investigations of cyber crimes in Israel, including cooperative investigations with other countries. In March 1998, he led, together with the FBI, the "Solar Sunrise" (Pentagon hackers) investigation in Israel.

ROBERT E. KAHN   Former senior member, Advanced Research Projects Agency (ARPA), subsequently Defense Advanced Research Projects Agency (DARPA); Chairman, CEO, and President, Corporation for National Research Initiatives (CNRI), Reston, Virginia. An author with extensive publications, and a recipient of numerous awards and honors, he has over thirty-five years of experience, at—among other places—Bell Laboratories and the Massachusetts Institute of Technology. He is one of the founders of Arpanet, the first packet-switched network, and he conceived the idea of open-architecture networking. He has served as Defense Advanced Research Projects Agency's (DARPA's) Director, Information Processing Techniques Office (IPTO), and is a co-inventor of the Transmission Control Protocol/Internet Protocol (TCP/IP) structure. He also coined the term "National Information Infrastructure" (NII) in the mid-1980s, which later became more widely known as the "Information Super Highway."

THOMAS A. LONGSTAFF Manager of Research and Development, Computer Emergency Response Team (CERT)/Coordination Center (CC), Software Engineering Institute (SEI), Carnegie-Mellon University, Pittsburgh, Pennsylvania. He currently manages research and development (R&D) in Survivable Network Technology (SNT) for the Networked Systems Survivability Program at the SEI. His activities include analysis of vulnerability and security incidents and methods for assessing survivability. Prior to joining SEI, he was the technical director for Computer Incident Advisory Capability (CIAC) at Lawrence Livermore National Laboratories (LLNL), Livermore, California.

STEPHEN J. LUKASIK Visiting Scholar, Consortium for Research on Information Security and Policy (CRISP), Stanford University; Visiting Professor, Georgia Institute of Technology; Director Emeritus, Advanced Research Projects Agency (ARPA, now Defense Advanced Research Projects Agency (DARPA)); former chief scientist, Federal Communications Commission (FCC). In addition to long government service involving various leadership and advisory roles with the National Research Council (NRC) and Office of Technology Assessment (OTA), among others, he has held senior positions in industry, including vice president of TRW, Inc., the Xerox Corp., the Northrop Corp., and RAND Corporation. He has lectured at Pepperdine University, and has served on the Board of Trustees of Stevens Institute of Technology and Harvey Mudd College, and on the Engineering Advisory Council for the University of California, Berkeley.

JOHN MARKOFF West Coast Correspondent, *New York Times*, covering the Silicon Valley, computers, and information technologies. He and Lenny Siegel co-authored *The High Cost of High Tech: The Dark Side of the Chip* (New York: Harper & Row, 1985). Also, with Katie Hafner he co-authored *Cyberpunk: Outlaws and Hackers on the Computer Frontier* (New York: Simon & Schuster, 1991). In addition, he co-authored with Tsutomu Shimomura *Takedown: The Pursuit and Capture of Kevin Mitnick, America's Most Wanted Computer Outlaw—by the Man Who Did It* (New York: Hyperion, 1996).

MICHAEL M. MAY Former Co-Director, Center for International Security and Cooperation (CISAC), Stanford University; Professor, Department of Engineering-Economic Systems and Operations Research, Stanford University; Director Emeritus of Lawrence Livermore National Laboratories (LLNL). He worked at LLNL from 1952 to 1988, holding a variety of research and development positions and serving as director from 1965 to 1971. He was technical adviser to the Threshold Test Ban Treaty negotiating team; a member of the U.S. delegation to the Strategic Arms Limitation Talks; and at various times has been a member of the Defense Science Board, the General Advisory Committee to the AEC, the Secretary of Energy Advisory Board, the RAND Corporation Board of Trustees, and the Committee on International Security and Arms Control of the National Academy of Sciences.

RAISUKE MIYAWAKI   Chairman, Ochanomizu Associates, Tokyo, Japan; Senior Adviser, Commission on Critical Infrastructure Protection, Tokyo, Japan. Having joined Japan's National Police Agency (NPA) in 1956, he ultimately served as director of the NPA's criminal investigation division, where he headed the NPA's anti-underworld campaign. From 1986 until 1988, he served in the Senior Cabinet Secretariat of the Prime Minister of Japan, as Adviser for Public Affairs to Prime Minister Yasuhiro Nakasone. Since then, he has been Chairman of Ochanomizu Associates, a Tokyo-based think tank, and an adviser on crime, cyber terrorism, politics, public affairs, and other issues to the top leaders of a number of Japan's largest companies, among them Nippon Telegraph & Telephone (NTT), Dentsu, Inc., and ITO-CHU, Inc. He is the author of *Gullible Japanese: The Structure of Crises In Japan* (Shincho-sha, 1999).

CLIFFORD NEUMAN   Professor, Computer Science Department, University of Southern California (USC); Senior Research Scientist, Information Sciences Institute, USC; Chief Scientist, CyberSafe Corporation. An expert on security and electronic commerce, he is the principal designer of the Kerberos system, a widely used technology for user authentication in Microsoft's Windows 2000, and he recently led development of Defense Advanced Research Projects Agency- (DARPA-) funded extensions to Kerberos, supporting authorization integration with the Public Key infrastructure. He is also the designer of the NetCheque system, a system for electronic micro-payments, and he has served as program chair for both the Internet Society's Symposium on Network and Distributed System Security and the Association for Computing's (ACM's) Conference on Computer and Communications Security.

DIETRICH NEUMANN   Detached National Expert, Justice and Home Affairs, General Secretariat of the Council of the European Union (EU), Brussels, Belgium. A lawyer and former senior police officer in the Federal Bureau of

Investigation in Wiesbaden, Germany (Bundeskriminalamt Wiesbaden), he advises the Secretariat and the Presidency of the EU on questions related to organized crime and to the implementation of the EU's 1997 Action Plan to Fight Organized Crime. He also deals with questions regarding the EU's strategy for combating cyber crime, especially the question of how to integrate the work of the other international fora into the EU's efforts.

PETER G. NEUMANN   Principal Scientist, Computer Science Laboratory, SRI International, Menlo Park, California. With over forty years in various capacities as a computer professional, including twenty-eight at SRI (formerly called the "Stanford Research Institute"), he has long been concerned with security, reliability, human safety, system survivability, and privacy in computer-communication systems and networks, and with how to develop systems that can dependably do what is expected of them. He is the author of *Computer-Related Risks* (Reading, Mass.: Addison-Wesley, 1994) and of "Computer Security in Aviation: Vulnerabilities, Threats, and Risks" (1997), prepared for the White House Commission on Aviation Safety and Security headed by Vice President Al Gore (see *http://www.csl.sri.com/neumann/ air.html*). He is chairman of the Association for Computing (ACM) Committee on Computers and Public Policy, and Moderator of its widely read Internet newsgroup "Risks Forum."

DONN B. PARKER   Senior Management Systems Consultant, Advanced Information Technology, Atomic Tangerine (formerly SRI Consulting (SRIC)), Menlo Park, California. An award-winning, world-renowned consultant, lecturer, writer, and researcher on computer crime and security who is frequently quoted in the news, he has spent thirty of his forty-seven years in the computer field at SRI working in information security and against computer crime and abuse. He is the founder at SRIC of the International Information Integrity Institute (I-4), continuously serving more than seventy-five of the largest multinational corporations in the world for over thirteen years in the protection of their information assets. He has written six books on computer crime, ethics, and information security management, including *Fighting Computer Crime: A New Framework for Protecting Information* (New York: John Wiley & Sons, 1998).

RAYMOND C. PARKS   Principal Member of Technical Staff, Information Design Assurance Red Team and Secure Networks and Information Systems Department, Sandia National Laboratories, Albuquerque, New Mexico. A former U.S. Air Force officer, he is an expert in "red-team" system-intrusion assessment efforts. His research at Sandia has included work on browser-based CORBA clients for remote monitoring of nuclear materials, multiple hypothesis tree tracking of vehicles with unattended ground sensors, UNIX system internals, nuclear weapons component surety and safety analysis, synthetic aperture radar data warehousing, and satellite sensor testing.

VIDYUT PATEL   Program Director, Information Systems Security Infrastructure, U.S. Federal Aviation Administration (FAA).

WILLIAM J. PERRY   Former U.S. Secretary of Defense; Senior Fellow, Hoover Institution; Michael and Barbara Berberian Professor at Stanford University, with a joint appointment in the Department of Engineering–Economic Systems and Operations Research and the Institute for International Studies. He was the nineteenth U.S. Secretary of Defense, serving from February 1994 to January 1997, and his previous government experience included the posts of Deputy Secretary of Defense (1993–94) and Under Secretary of Defense for Research and Engineering (1977–81). His business experience includes positions as laboratory director for General Telephone and Electronics (1954–64); founder and president of ESL (1964–77); executive vice president of Hambrecht & Quist (1981–85); and founder and chairman of Technology Strategies and Alliances (1985–93).

RICHARD POWER   Editorial Director, Computer Security Institute (CSI), San Francisco, California. He is the author of *Current and Future Danger: A CSI Primer on Computer Crime and Information Warfare* (3d ed., San Francisco: CSI, 1999) and *Tangled Web: Tales of Digital Crime from the Shadows of Cyberspace* (New York: Que/Macmillan Publishing, 2000). Recognized as a leading voice on information security, computer crime, industrial espionage, and related subjects, he directs the annual CSI/FBI Computer Crime and Security Survey, and also writes and edits numerous other prominent industry publications, such as *Computer Security Alert*, the *Computer Security Journal*, and *Frontline*.

TONYA L. PUTNAM   Doctoral Candidate, Department of Political Science, Stanford University; J.D. Candidate, Harvard Law School. From 1998 to 1999 she served as a member of counsel on the international legal team of the Republic of Namibia in litigation before the International Court of Justice. Her primary research concerns the extraterritorial jurisdictional reach of U.S. federal courts and its implications for the development of de facto international regulatory frameworks.

JOHN RAISIAN   Director and Senior Fellow, Hoover Institution, Stanford University. An economist with numerous publications to his credit, he has specialized in national and international labor markets and in human resource issues. His professional career has included positions at the RAND Corporation, the University of Washington, the University of Houston, the U.S. Bureau of Labor Statistics, and the U.S. Department of Labor. He was president of Unicon Research Corporation, an economic consulting firm in Los Angeles, after leaving the Labor Department, working there until joining the Hoover Institution in 1986.

STEVEN D. RIZZI   Vice President at Science Applications International Corporation (SAIC) for Advanced Information Technology, Annapolis, Maryland; Appointee of the Governor to the Maryland High Speed Network Development Task Force; Co-chair, Maryland Information Technology Board subcommittee on Internet User Privacy; Member, University of Maryland University College Technical Advisory Group (TAG); Co-chair, SAIC Information Security Subcommittee. He leads a laboratory of computer scientists and engineers who are involved in a range of information technology projects for both government and commercial clients. These projects include basic research in advanced information technology (such as reasoning systems, artificial life, collaborative tools), electronic commerce, information security and protection, intelligent city development, and networked multimedia systems.

STEIN SCHJOLBERG   Chief Judge, Moss Byrett, Norway. In his thirty-year career he has served not only as a judge but also as the Assistant Commissioner of Police and as a Police Attorney in Oslo, Norway. He has published extensively on computer-assisted crime and computers and penal legislation and is a member of an international think tank on global court technology, recently organized by the National Center for State Courts in Williamsburg, Virginia. He has consulted widely on computer crime, including at Interpol, the Organization for Economic Cooperation and Development (OECD), and the Norwegian Ministry of Justice. His authoritative website is located at: *http://mossbyrett.of.no/info/legal.html.*

RANDALL E. SMITH   Principal Engineer, Multilevel Secure Systems, Boeing Phantom Works, Seattle, Washington. His recent research activities include Principal Investigator for the Defense Advanced Research Projects Agency (DARPA) Strategic Intrusion Assessment Multi-Community Cyber Defense contract, where he is investigating issues involved in scaling an intrusion detection and response framework to a cyber defense system spanning multiple administrative domains. He is a member of the DARPA ISO Information Assurance (IA) Experiment Working Group, and has extensive experience developing high-assurance MLS software, specializing in A1 security kernel development, device driver software, and embedded software development, including work on the design, analysis, development, and testing of Boeing's A1 MLS LAN product.

ARIEL T. SOBELMAN Design-Labs, Herzellia, Israel. Former Senior Research Associate and Director of the Information Warfare Project, Jaffee Center for Strategic Studies, Tel Aviv University, Tel Aviv, Israel. A veteran of the Israeli Air Force, his Ph.D. dissertation concerned adaptive network routing algorithms under severe real-time constraints. His experience includes having held the position of U.S.A. Post-Doctoral Project Development Officer at the Trans-European Research and Education Networking Association, Amsterdam, the Netherlands, where he focused on starting a Trans-European Computer Emergency Response Team (CERT).

ABRAHAM D. SOFAER (*Conference Co-Chair*) George P. Shultz Senior Fellow, Hoover Institution; Professor of Law, by Courtesy, Stanford Law School. He served as Legal Adviser to the U.S. Department of State from 1985 to 1990, negotiating several treaties, including extradition and mutual legal assistance agreements, and led the U.S. delegation in negotiations on the International Maritime Organization Convention for the Suppression of Unlawful Acts Against the Safety of Maritime Navigation (the "Maritime Terrorism Convention"). He was a federal district judge in New York City from 1979 to 1985; a Professor of Law at Columbia University School of Law from 1969 to 1979; and a federal prosecutor from 1967 to 1969. He has written extensively on international legal subjects, and currently teaches a course on Transnational Law and Institutions at Stanford Law School.

BARRY STEINHARDT Associate Director, American Civil Liberties Union (ACLU), New York, New York; former President, Electronic Frontier Foundation. He is chair of the ACLU Cyber-liberties Task Force, which coordinates the ACLU's extensive program of information technology issues. He was a co-founder of the Global Internet Liberty Campaign (GILC), the world's first international coalition of Non-Governmental Organizations (NGOs) concerned with the rights of Internet users and one of the originators of the Internet Free Expression Alliance (IFEA), which was formed to monitor issues related to Internet content rating and filtering.

DAVID J. THELANDER   Senior Vice President and Chief Counsel, International Division, Charles Schwab & Co., Inc., San Francisco, California. His distinguished business and legal experience includes significant posts in investment/financial services/banking groups and private law firms. He also served with the U.S. Securities and Exchange Commission in Washington, D.C., initially as Attorney Adviser with the Division of Corporation Finance, and subsequently as Senior Counsel in the Enforcement Division, specializing in complex financial fraud matters.

H. H. WHITEMAN   Director General, Security and Emergency Preparedness, Transport Canada, Ottawa, Canada. In federal government service with Transport Canada since joining the Canadian Coast Guard in 1973, he has held a number of increasingly senior positions, including Director of Security Policy Planning and Legislative Programs, responsible for the development of security policies, regulations, and measures for air, marine, and rail transportation. In August 1995 he assumed, as Acting Director General, Security and Emergency Planning, responsibility for all aspects of departmental and transportation security and emergency preparedness, and in August 1997 he was appointed Director General. He has overseen a major revision of civil aviation security requirements, managing the transfer of responsibility for aviation security screening equipment from the federal government to the air carrier industry, as well as the implementation of new arrangements for protective policing at airports.

GEORGE D. WILSON   Research Fellow, Hoover Institution, Stanford University. Admitted to practice law in California, Colorado, the District of Columbia, and Maryland, as well as various federal courts, he was in private practice in Washington, D.C., and San Francisco from 1987 to 1993, working in the areas of domestic transactional business, legislative, and regulatory law. In 1994 he joined the Hoover Institution as a research assistant, and in 1998 he was appointed a research fellow. At Hoover he focuses on research and writing related to diplomacy, national security, terrorism, and transnational law.

Index